BUILDING INTRANETS WITH LOTUS NOTES & DOMINO 5.0

Third Edition

Other Titles of Interest From Maximum Press

Marketing on the Internet, Fourth Edition: Zimmerman,
  1-885068-36-0

101 Ways to Promote Your Website: Sweeney, 1-885068-37-9

Business-to-Business Internet Marketing, Second Edition:
Silverstein, 1-885068-37-8

Marketing With E-Mail: Kinnard, 1-885068-40-9

Exploring IBM Technology & Products, Second Edition: edited by
Hoskins, 1-885068-31-X

*Exploring IBM Personal Computers, Tenth Edition: Hoskins,
  Wilson, 1-885068-25-5*

Exploring IBM RS/6000 Computers, Ninth Edition:
  Hoskins, Davies, 1-885068-27-1

Exploring IBM AS/400 Computers, Ninth Edition: Hoskins,
  Dimmick, 1-885068-34-4

Exploring IBM S/390 Computers, Sixth Edition:
  Hoskins, Coleman, 1-885068-30-1

Exploring IBM Network Stations: Ho, Lloyd, and Heracleous,
  1-885068-32-8

For more information, visit our Web site at
www.maxpress.com
or e-mail us at *moreinfo@maxpress.com*

BUILDING INTRANETS WITH LOTUS NOTES & DOMINO 5.0

Third Edition

Steve Krantz

MAXIMUM PRESS
605 Silverthorn Road
Gulf Breeze, FL 32561
(850) 934-0819
www.maxpress.com

Publisher: Jim Hoskins

Manager of Finance/Administration: Donna Tryon

Production Manager: ReNae Grant

Cover Design: Lauren Smith Designs

Compositor: PageCrafters Inc.

Copyeditor: Andrew Potter

Proofreader: Kim Steffansson

Indexer: Susan Olason

Printer: P.A. Hutchison

Library of Congress Cataloging-in-Publication Data

Krantz, Steve, 1947-
Building intranets with Lotus Notes and Domino 5.0 / Steve Krantz.—
3rd ed.
p. cm.
Includes bibliographical references and index.
ISBN 1-885068-41-7
1. Intranets (Computer networks)—Computer programs. 2. Lotus Notes.
3. Lotus Domino. I. Title.
TK5105.875.I6 K73 2000
004.6—dc21
00-008043

To my wife Joan (still beautiful, warm, and caring),
To my son Jeffrey (still the computer genius),
To my son Paul (soon off to college),
Thanks for putting up with me!

Acknowledgments

My manager and friend, Albert Schneider, has been a great source of inspiration and support for this book. Peggy Bovaird helped me accurately capture IBM's Global Notes Architecture in Chapter 3. Finally, I want to thank my publisher, editor, and friend Jim Hoskins for his patience, support, and advice.

Disclaimer

The purchase of computer software or hardware is an important and costly business decision. Although the authors and publisher of this book have made reasonable efforts to ensure the accuracy and timeliness of the information contained herein, the authors and publisher assume no liability with respect to loss or damage caused or alleged to be caused by reliance on any information contained herein and disclaim any and all warranties, expressed or implied, as to the accuracy or reliability of said information.

This book is not intended to replace the manufacturer's product documentation or personnel in determining the specifications and capabilities of the products mentioned in this book. The manufacturer's product documentation should always be consulted, as the specifications and capabilities of computer hardware and software products are subject to frequent modification. The reader is solely responsible for the choice of computer hardware and software. All configurations and applications of computer hardware and software should be reviewed with the manufacturer's representatives prior to choosing or using any computer hardware and software.

Trademarks

The words contained in this text that are believed to be trademarked, service marked, or otherwise to hold proprietary rights have been designated as such by use of initial capitalization. No attempt has been made to designate as trademarked or service marked any personal computer words or terms in which proprietary rights might exist. Inclusion, ex-

Foreword

What every company knows—and how it leverages that knowledge—has never been more essential for success than it is today. I have spent the better part of eight years explaining how Lotus Domino and Notes help companies leverage their corporate assets of business knowledge and expertise. An intranet built with the innovative features pioneered by Lotus—rich text messaging, a document database, information sharing, workflow, inter-enterprise and virtual team collaboration, distance learning, integration with. ERP (Enterprise Resource Planning) systems—provides an essential competitive advantage.

Today, people know that they want shared access to information via the Internet, the Web, and intranets. That's a given. Technologists, business managers, and end users understand that sharing information is critical. What is exciting for Lotus—and especially for anyone whose job it is to explain Notes and Domino—is that the vocabulary of collaboration, messaging, and knowledge management is now on everyone's tongue. Now, it seems, virtually everyone is looking for the benefits of these Notes and Domino capabilities, which makes my job a lot easier—and more fun.

Frequently I hear the plea from an IS decision maker: "How can I send job postings through a review and approval cycle before posting them?" or "How can I allow visitors to the Web site to submit resumes, and how can I then review those candidates—all on my intranet?" To anyone at Lotus, of course, this is music to our ears, because what they need is exactly what Notes and Domino can supply.

For anyone who is exploring how to be more competitive in the age of intranets and the Internet, this book is a great place to start. Steve Krantz has captured the breadth of the Notes client and Domino server and delivered it in a concise and easy- to-understand manner, with plenty of supporting detail. Now that Notes and Domino are a big part of many companies' Internet plans, I'm sure the effort has been a lot more fun for Steve, too.

Eileen Rudden
Senior Vice President, Communications Products Division
Lotus Development Corporation

Table of Contents

Chapter 3:
The Domino Server   51

Chapter 4:
Your Intranet Application Programs   95

Chapter 5:
Building Domino Applications   130

Chapter 6:
Rolling Out Your Intranet   168

Introduction

To the Reader

Headlines are blaring everywhere you look with unmistakable messages, "Run your business on the Internet" and "Build an intranet for your business now!" As you dig deeper, the choices are not so clear. A swarm of products, some just invented, others in use, are vying for your attention.

Most of us have used the Internet for garden-variety Web browsing. We either type in a Universal Resource Locator (URL) to get to a special place or find a search site, such as Yahoo!, to help guide us to the information we seek. For example, most of us have sampled Internet shopping (the author is a regular book shopper with *www.Amazon.com*). We realize that the hawks are circling--more and more businesses are establishing presence and enticing us with commercials. Some of us have used our company's intranet site(s). Mostly they are document repositories with access simplified through a point-and-click interface.

A new wave is sensed, however, when our sons or daughters send real-time video of their college dorm room over the Internet or, perhaps more exciting, we see a Domino demo showing a true business workflow application supporting a complex business process directly from a Web browser.

It is clear that traditional intranet technology is evolving rapidly. Many companies are jumping in to provide new products and services. Most companies feel compelled to invest in a Web presence for their very survival. Basic Web technology can provide both the intranet publishing/communication features and the Web presence--an inside and outside presence.

As we know, before Web technology reached its current adolescent period, Notes was developing and intruding on the consciousness of many corporate information technologists. Notes bridged the investment in PCs and PC-based software and the onrush of internetworking and communications technology. It offered the "glue" layer that made the investments worthwhile. It contained a platform for creating group applications rapidly and easily. It offered a stark contrast to cryptic mainframe software technology, isolated PC-based software, and the relatively spare local area network (LAN) operating system extensions. Today Notes/Domino offers a more richly functional base than traditional intranet technology--it includes all of the capabilities of Web-based intranets plus the added benefits of Domino databases. Figure I.1 provides a summary comparison of Notes/Domino versus the traditional intranet updated from *Fortune* magazine to underpin this observation. With Domino, we see a confluence of these two rushing streams of software creativity (Figure I.2). The power of Notes is adapted to enrich the maturing Web environment.

Capability	Domino Intranet	Traditional Intranet
Replication – maintain identical data on multiple systems	A	C
Security – avoid unauthorized access	A	C
Mobile Use – get to your data while traveling	A	D
Publishing – making documents available to all users	B	A
Application Development – build new software to extend the system	B	A
Discussion Tracking – multi-threaded discussion among a large set of users	A	C
Document Management – store data from different applications in a database	C	D
Workflow – support a complete business process through document routing and tracking	B	D
Integration – work with legacy data and software (mainframes)	B	B
Average	B+	C+

Source: Meta Group [Kirkpatrick, 1996]

Figure I.1. Domino vs. traditional intranet.

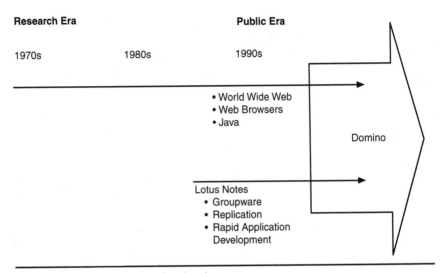

Figure I.2.   Confluence of technology.

About This Book

This book looks from the top down at the subject of intranets, emerging Internet technologies, and groupware technology (an intranet is a new term for the internal network of a business). It is for those of you who are contemplating an investment in an intranet or seek to expand an existing network for your company. It is for information technology managers, department heads, and communicators. It is for members of reengineering teams.

The book intentionally leaves off where the user's guides and administrator's guides begin. From a product perspective, it focuses primarily on the Lotus Development Company's Notes and Domino offerings. If you have never seen Lotus Notes or Domino, this book will provide a good overview. However, you will get more out of the book if you can take advantage of the free trial copies available for download from the Lotus Notes Web site at URL *http://www. lotus.com/notes*. Be warned--the download will take several hours with a 56 Kbps modem and require a considerable amount of free disk space.

If you are familiar with earlier versions of Domino, such as Release 4.x, and have been turned off by administrative or development difficulties, check out the book anyway, because the current version of Domino (Release 5.0) offers major improvements in user interface, system administration, and application development. Here's what's inside.

Chapter 1: Intranet Basics. This chapter starts with a glance back at computer and networking history to set the stage for the present day. It then describes the Internet, intranets, and their tremendous impact on business. It winds up with an assessment of the future of this burgeoning set of technologies.

Chapter 2: The Domino Clients. Over the past decade, the Domino application platform has caught the imagination of thousands of companies and millions of users with its ability to enable information sharing and rapid application development. With the Domino server (covered in Chapter 3), both Lotus Notes and Web browser clients can be effectively supported. This chapter provides an overview of the Lotus Notes client--how the Notes client or a Web browser accesses, creates, and replicates Domino data. Notes security is described next. Domino mail, calendar, and directory functions are reviewed.

Chapter 3: The Domino Server. This chapter is about the Lotus server technology, which is a powerful Web and Notes intranet platform. First, the Domino architecture and how it fits into the Notes and Web environment are defined. Large-enterprise administration is illustrated through examples from IBM's major Notes/Domino migration from 1995 through 1997. Domino administration tools and current competition are described. Finally, Domino futures are discussed.

Chapter 4: Your Intranet Application Programs. An intranet fits in your business with its application programs, defined as end-user software tools that solve business problems, and links to information such as legacy databases. The application programs are of paramount importance in your intranet because they *are* the intranet as far as the users are concerned. For this reason, the selection and development of reliable, effective, and easy-to-use application programs are vital to any computing solution (intranet or not). This chapter assesses the broad spectrum of business applications in terms of personal and team use, and provides concrete examples of how Domino applications fit these needs and can improve productivity and information sharing in your company. Examples of how Notes solutions are being applied within the IBM company are described, development and support issues are discussed, and applications are assessed with regard to their organizational impact, their operating environment, and their relationship to legacy systems. Some real-world examples are described, and a methodology for application development and deployment is discussed. The chapter winds up with a recommendation for ongoing application management.

Chapter 5: Building Domino Applications. After investigating and determining your application program requirements, as described in Chapter 4, you might have decided to build some of them yourself or with the help of a development team. First, this chapter will walk you through an overview of software development in general, relating your requirements to software configurations, considering Notes/ Domino functionality, and providing a few real-world examples. Next, Domino Designer is introduced along with the components of its toolkit for application creation and a little how-to. Finally, a recommended development and management program is provided as you embark on perhaps a new investment in software creativity.

Chapter 6: Rolling Out Your Intranet. This is the "how to do it" chapter from an intranet deployment perspective. The majority of the chapter describes a phased methodology to transform a business from midrange or mainframe-centric computing to a Notes/Domino intranet infrastructure. The chapter ends with a perspective on overall project management and how to evolve to ongoing information technology management.

Finally, a nearly 500-term **glossary** and an **appendix** providing a brief guide to Lotus Development Company resources are included.

Your "Members Only" Web Site

The world of intranets changes every day. That's why there is a companion Web site associated with this book. On this site, you will find updates to the book and other intranets, Notes, and Domino-related resources of interest. However, you have to be a member of the "Building Intranets Insiders Club" to gain access to this site. When you purchased this book, you automatically became a member, so right now you have full privileges.

To get into the "Members Only" section of the companion "Building Intranets" Web site, go to the Maximum Press Web site located at *http://www.maxpress.com* and follow the links to the Building

Intranets area. From there you will see a link to the "Building Intranets Club" section. When you try to enter, you will be asked for a User ID and Password. Type in the following:

- For User ID enter: *notes3e*

- For Password enter: *knee*

You will then be granted full access to the "Members Only" area. Visit the site often and enjoy the updates and resources with our compliments. We ask that you not share the User ID and Password for the site with anyone else.

Thanks again for buying the book!

1

Intranet Basics

This chapter starts with a glance back at computer and networking history to set the stage for the present day. It then describes the Internet, intranets, and their tremendous impact on business. It winds up with an assessment of the future of this burgeoning set of technologies.

A Brief History of Computer Systems and Networks

Figure 1.1 provides a snapshot of the past three decades of computer system and network evolution, leading up the development of today's networked world. Mainframe-centric and minicomputer- centric networks dominated the 1970s. In this environment, users employed dumb terminals to instruct these host systems over the network. A **network** is a data communications system that interconnects computer systems for the purpose of exchanging information. During the 1970s, it became common to interconnect mainframes and minicomputers to create large-scale distributed systems over computer networks we now call **WANs** (Wide Area Networks).

The 1980s brought PCs, workstations, and other types of networks, including LANs and MANs. Figure 1.2 shows a **LAN** (Local Area Network), which is the interconnection of several personal com-

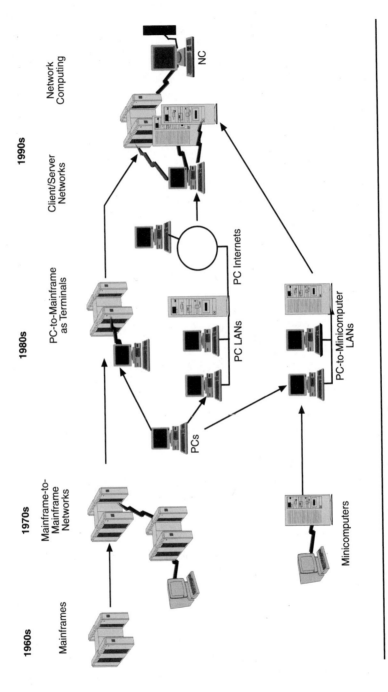

Figure 1.1. Evolution of computer networks.

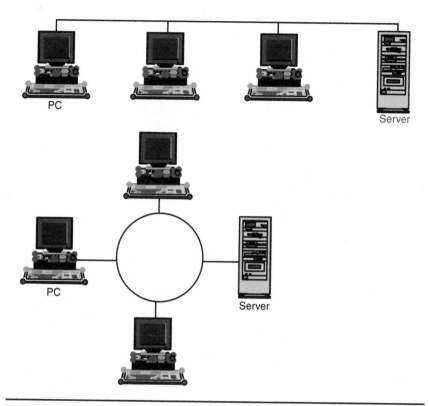

Figure 1.2. Local area network examples.

puters and other hardware such as printers within a small local area
(a room or the floor of a building). Designed originally as a means of
sharing hardware and software among PCs, LANs are used as a general means of communications among PCs. A **MAN** (Metropolitan
Area Network) is similar to a LAN but covers larger geographic distances (up to 50 kilometers). WANs continued to be used for connections that span long geographic distances, typically city to city and
often around the globe.

PCs were quickly linked to the large-scale distributed systems,
but primarily to emulate the dumb terminal, where the local PC computing capability was not exploited. From their beginning, powerful
workstations running engineering/scientific applications used LANs
to share data among users. Little by little, users began installing LANs
to interconnect a few PCs so that they could share printers and ex-

change data files and messages. PC LAN programs and entirely new LAN operating systems were developed. They made the resources of one computer in the network (a **server**) available to other computers in that network (**clients**). These resources (which included disk storage and printers) appeared as if they were attached directly to the client's PC. This was the birth of **client/server** computing.

The breakthrough in technology that made client/server computing practical was the introduction of very-high-speed LANs in the 1980s. Very-high-speed is a relative term. Early token-ring LANs operating at 4 Mbps (million bits per second) were dramatically faster than traditional networks communicating at up to 56 Kbps (thousand bits per second). Such speeds as 56 Kbps are still common in WANs. Advances in communication technology for LANs and WANs have allowed connectivity among users and departments. This has led to increasing demands for better access to information stored on mainframe computers. Add to this the significant advances in operating system software and application programs with greater ease of use, and you have employees achieving higher levels of productivity without having to become computer experts.

Continuing developments through the early 1990s have accelerated the trend to complex client/server networks, now called **network-centric** computing or more simply **network computing**. Hierarchical, host-centric networks are giving way to heterogeneous, flat networks in which clients select the resources they need from a variety of server systems—from floor-standing PC servers to water-cooled mainframes. These "multiple intranet servers interconnected over local and wide area networks constitute the foundation of a distributed intranet." [Cunningham 1999] A distributed intranet is now a fundamental component of a company's business strategy.

The Internet—A Worldwide Revolution

In parallel with all of this activity in mainstream business computing, there was a powerful yet substantially ignored force developing the Internet. Beginning in 1966, almost unnoticed, the Internet grew under the care and guidance of the Department of Defense and U.S. universities. The original goal was to develop a distributed computer network for national defense--a distributed network supported noncentralized data, making it less vulnerable to a disaster. Some key milestones include:

- First **ARPAnet** nodes operational: 1969

- E-mail invented: 1972

- First non-U.S. computer linked: 1973

- New host computer added every 20 days: 1981

- TCP/IP becomes the standard protocol: 1983

- World Wide Web invented: 1991

- Internet backbone privatized: 1995

[Meleis, 1996]

The Internet is a worldwide computer network of over 40 million computers connected together over both public and private networks via TCP/IP (Transmission Control Protocol/Internet Protocol). In the spring of 1994, the federal government decided to commercialize the Internet, leading to its current explosive growth. The Internet also has been described as "the first truly large-scale experiment in creating a global public network devoted to exchanging data." [Bernard, 1996].

Four major applications are used on the Internet: e-mail, news groups, simple file transfer (**FTP**), and hypertext file transfer (World Wide Web). E-mail over the Internet is widely used, employing the Simple Mail Transport Protocol (**SMTP**). Graphics data and file attachments are transported using **MIME** (**Multipurpose Internet Mail Extensions**) encoding. Data is converted (i.e., encoded) using the MIME protocol into an **ASCII** (American Standard Code for Information Interchange) string format, suitable for data transmission with e-mail messages.

News groups are virtual discussion groups that "correspond" on a topic of special interest over the Internet using the Network News Transport Protocol (**NNTP**). This electronic correspondence is collected into files that contain all correspondents' comments. NNTP has tended to be used only by techies because the user interfaces available tend to be unfriendly. It is difficult to administer, especially for security and creation of new groups. More user-friendly groupware packages, such as AltaVista Forum and WebShare, are just appearing on the scene. They are Web browser–based, support multiuser, linked (threaded) discussions, and create easy-to-search databases. Because these are stand-alone products from different vendors, they may not integrate well with your overall environment. For example, security practices may be inconsistent.

Simple file transfer among client and server systems over the Internet is performed using FTP. To the end user, FTP is implemented as a simple command-line program that is used first to gain access to a server and then to send or receive files.

Hypertext file transfer, or the transference of linked files over the Internet embodied in the World Wide Web (WWW, or the Web), has now eclipsed its predecessors as the single most important Internet application. The Web provides the ability to put out on the Internet compound documents (text, graphics, video/audio clips, etc.), which can have hypertext links to other documents on an Internet server, or even to other documents on other computers across the world. Web users are unaware of the locations of documents. They simply click on an object that they might be interested in (which could be a text headline or a graphic) and are presented with the associated information (which could have come from halfway across the world). This is accomplished via the **HTTP (HyperText Transport Protocol)**.

You can think of the Internet as a global network for data, logically equivalent to the global telephone network. Instead of telephones, people have PCs and Web browsers. Instead of telephone numbers, people "dial" **URLs** (Universal Resource Locators). Instead of receiving voices, people receive data files, including text, graphics, sound, and video. Because of the common adherence to data and communications standards, millions of people and businesses are using the Internet for information sharing today. It is predicted that secure commerce over the Internet will soon follow. The major limitation to Internet expansion is speed of data transmission to each user's PC.

The information technology that underlies this process is fairly straightforward. The average user sees the Internet as a vast sea of information that is easily accessed with simple commands from the **GUI** (Graphic User Interface) of his or her personal Web browser. A **Web browser** is a software application that upon user request transmits URLs to Web servers over the network. A URL is the "address" of an **HTML** file on a **Web server**. HTML is the file format standard for the World Wide Web. The Web server is a specialized server that services the user request by transmitting the desired HTML file back to the user's PC, where the Web browser displays it. Figure 1.3 depicts this interaction.

More recently emerging is the Extensible Markup Language standard, or **XML**. XML is a markup language, like HTML, that provides a format for describing structured data. Where HTML provides formatting instructions for on-screen display of data in a general way, XML allows application developers to describe data in a general and structured way. This will permit applications on different computing platforms to transfer and process this data easily. In this sense, XML is a "meta-markup" or higher-level language in the network computing world.

An escalating trend is the introduction of **network computers** (**NCs**) into the marketplace. Oracle, IBM, Sun Microsystems, Apple, and Netscape have formed an alliance to define an NC's standard configuration, called the NC **Reference Profile** (available on the World

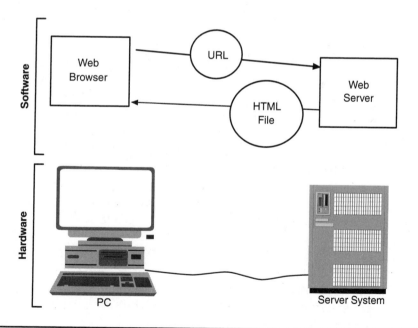

Figure 1.3. Web technology basics.

Wide Web at URL *http://192.86.154.91/nc_ref_profile.html*). An NC includes a 640 by 480 display, a pointing device, a keyboard for text entry, audio output capability (speakers), and a network connection (modem or LAN adapter). Recording and storage media, such as a hard drive or diskette drive, are optional. NC software must use standard IP protocols, such as **TCP**, **DHCP** (Dynamic Host Configuration Protocol), and **SNMP** (Simple Network Management Protocol). It must support and run a Web browser handling **HTML** and **Java**. No operating system or graphic user interface is specified.

Although a standard PC could be configured to meet the NC standard, the NC attraction is that it is a low-cost, storageless, self-booting device that costs around $500. The programs and data used by NCs are delivered by servers on the network. With Web browsing and e-mail as standard capabilities, many types of users could have all of their computing requirements satisfied with an NC at significantly reduced support costs. The IBM Network Station is an example of such a low-cost NC (around $700). It can perform terminal emulation, Web browsing, or even Windows applications in association with an appropriately configured network server.

Recently, Gartner Group, IDC, and Jupiter Communications stated that the NC has great potential based on IBM's leadership. [Anonymous, 1998c]. Predictions that 40% of all enterprises will use NCs by 1999 have been made. On the other hand, a recent *Wall Street Journal* article cites the burgeoning success of low-priced (sub-$1000) Windows 95 PCs as reason to doubt the NC's potential. Clearly, the battle for the desktop is alive and well, and the diversity of product offerings will provide more customer choice. Shaping up is a stratification of workstation products, with the dumb terminal at the low end, the NC at the next higher stratum (today), the low-cost PC next, and full-function PCs and workstations at the high end. "Web Clients" later in this chapter sheds more light on this analysis.

Java is another important development in the network computing world. This new programming language and compiler generates **byte code**, rather than executable machine code as do standard programming languages (see Figure 1.4). Java byte code can then be delivered to and executed on any client system, as long as the Web browser software being used by the client supports the Java language. A Java applet is a program that is transmitted over a network to perform limited-function, useful work on a client system. It remains to be seen if Java applet performance will be acceptable for anything

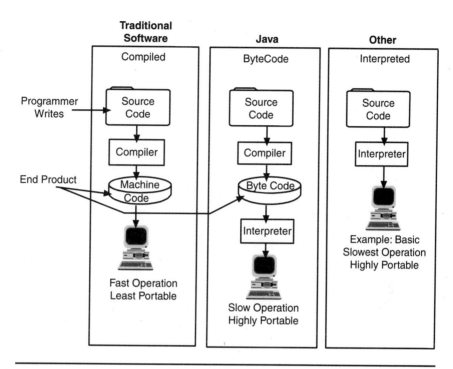

Figure 1.4. Java explained.

other than very simple applications in the near future and if this approach can compete with traditional, high-function compiled software. However, according to Ed Yourdon, the world-famous software development practices expert, Java and the Web "mark the death of fatware and the birth of dynamic computing built on rented components." [Yourdon, 1996].

What Is an Intranet?

An **intranet** (see Figure 1.5) is a new term for the private computer network of a business. This term developed because the **protocol** or language employed on an intranet is the same as that used on the **Internet**. Intranets can be built using any combination of traditional LANs, MANs, and WANs, and equipping the computers on the intranet with the software necessary to communicate using Internet

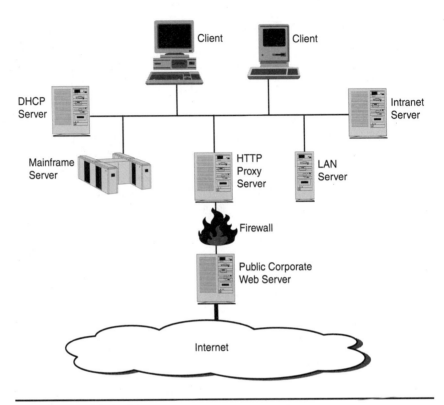

Figure 1.5. Typical intranet.

standards. Typical applications found on intranets include e-mail, browsing Web pages, and providing access to the public Internet.

So what makes an intranet an intranet is the protocol used on the network to exchange information. As on the public Internet, intranets use the **TCP/IP** (Transmission Control Protocol/Internet Protocol), developed by the Department of Defense in the 1970s. The strength of TCP/IP lies in its ability to isolate problem areas and hence improve network management. This makes TCP/IP a natural for complex, multisite networks.

The Difference Between Intranets and the Internet

The difference between an intranet and the Internet lies largely in application, not structure. An intranet typically contains all the networking hardware and software of the Internet, albeit on a much smaller scale. However, an intranet will have boundaries, called **firewalls,** that keep private communications internal and prevent intruders from intranet access. A firewall is a computer system (typically a system called a **router**) that filters unwelcome data traffic and correctly routes the rest. You can think of the firewalls as providing semipermeable barriers, much like the cell wall in biology, around a company's intranet. A firewall lets good stuff come in and keeps out the bad stuff. Figure 1.6 illustrates this relationship between intranet and Internet.

There is no strict definition of an intranet. Intranets can be completely private with no Internet connection. A common feature is to exchange e-mail between the intranet and the Internet community. Some companies extend their intranet for use by select groups outside of the company such as vendors or large customers, a network called an **extranet** (see Figure 1.7). Further, many companies elect to

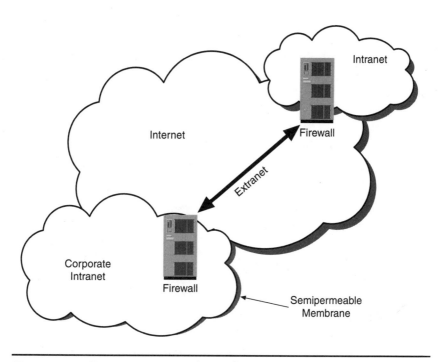

Figure 1.6. Intranet, Internet relationship.

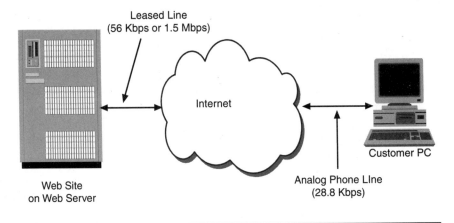

Figure 1.7. Typical extranet.

make portions of their intranet available to anyone on the Internet (called a **Web site**), forming a showcase for products or corporate accomplishments or conduct online business transactions, for example. Some companies even actively push information from their intranet to customers on the Internet.

Businesses can connect to the Internet in one of two ways:

1. A leased line, typically a T1 line operating at 1.5 Mbps, connects directly to the Internet from the company's internal network.

2. Individuals inside the company dial in over the public telephone network to a service provider and establish a virtual connection to the Internet. In this case, the service provider has a leased line to the Internet, and the dialed in user appears as a remote node on the service provider's TCP/IP LAN.

The Business Impact of the Internet, Intranets, and Extranets

The business impact of the Internet is pervasive. Companies are transforming portions of their internal and external operations to take advantage of this technology at an ever-increasing rate. Businesses are interested in intranets because they enable, enhance, and extend communications among their employees, their suppliers, their business partners, and their customers. This is seen as a mutual benefit for all the parties involved. Some companies believe that Internet technologies can be the base for them to reinvent their entire operation.

One key benefit of an intranet for a business is accessibility of information by employees. Another benefit that businesses are leaping on is the opportunity to connect their intranets to the Internet for sales, marketing, customer service, and other activities--all electronically. Electronic commerce, or e-business, on the Internet has been exceeding the most optimistic projections year by year as its truly revolutionary potential is being realized.

An intranet is relatively inexpensive compared to other forms of network systems. Web browsers run on any type of computer. This means that the same electronic information can be viewed by any user. Many different documents can easily be converted for publication on an intranet (using the HTML format). By presenting information in the same way to every computer, a common network that interconnects all computers enables users to find information wherever it resides. Because the same basic programming can be used on almost any type or brand of computer system, businesses will need fewer programmers to write and maintain software.

With an intranet, many organizations have found that information publishing is most straightforward. Corporate intranets typically support the dissemination of policies and procedures documents, customer profiles, and other corporate information to employees throughout the enterprise at a relatively low cost.

Applications on intranets grow in a natural progression from simple document publishing to applications that support business processes. Information technology planners see in the intranet the potential to simplify many different systems with a unified approach that supports the full breadth of business applications.

A Closer Look at Web Technology

The most common form of publishing in intranets (and the Internet) is based on the World Wide Web model used on the Internet. Business on the Internet is targeting the Web world because of its easy to use graphical environment. Because of its popularity, the technology behind the Web deserves a closer look. Web technology is based on the concept of hypertext--files with links to other files--which lets you follow related items from one place to another. Files can be spread across computers at any location in an intranet or the Internet. These files are typically called **Web pages**.

To develop information for display on your intranet, you create Web pages containing HyperText Markup Language (HTML). When you write HTML, you intersperse tags among your text. These tags are commands to the Web browser software being run by the client computer system. Figure 1.8 shows the raw ingredients of an HTML page (a birthday card) containing some text and graphics and the HTML code that stitches the elements together. Figure 1.9 shows how it would be displayed by a Web browser.

A user employs a browser to view Web pages, regardless of where the Web pages are located or what type of computer system you have. Each link in a Web page, or "hotspot," knows the name of its associated file and on which Web server that file is stored. When we select the hotspot, we see that there is an interaction between the Web

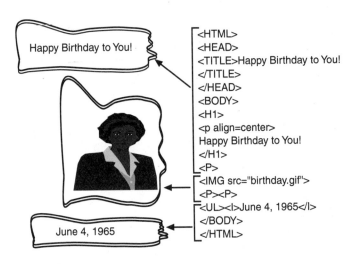

Figure 1.8.   An HTML birthday card.

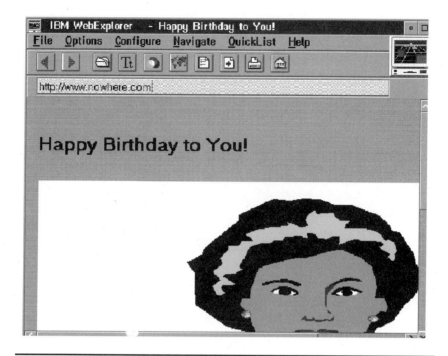

Figure 1.9. Birthday card in Web browser.

browser and the system that is responding to its requests for new HTML files, the Web server. The name of the Web server and the file are combined into a Universal Resource Locator, or **URL**. For example, *http://.netscape.com/home/internet-search.html* is a URL that is interpreted as an address of the file *internet-search.html,* on the server *www.netscape.com,* in the *home* directory, to be retrieved using the HTTP protocol.

Web Browsers

Web browsers are programs used by clients on an intranet or the Internet to view information stored on Web servers. Web browser programs are readily available (usually for free) for almost any type of computer or operating system such as Windows, OS/2, Macintosh, or UNIX. They operate in a common manner on common data, interacting with Web servers to retrieve requested information or to initiate actions. Because of this capability, a company does not have to migrate all users to a common operating system for the sake of a common information access tool. Figure 1.10 is a screen shot of the most popular Web browser today, Netscape Navigator.

Like the rest of the Web infrastructure, Web browsers have improved dramatically over the past two years. Early Web browsers, such as Mosaic, only supported HTML, but newer browsers, such as Netscape Navigator, can handle other forms of data, such as Adobe Acrobat. In addition, they are being augmented to include interpreters for Java programs contained in Web pages. Specialized in-line viewers have been "plugged" into browsers to support such new data types as audio, video, and animation. "Interface publishing," in which text, graphics, and little applications (applets) are sent to the Web browser, has emerged (see the Java discussions in this chapter). Soon to emerge is general support for XML, the data language standard with its companion **XSL**, or XML Style Language. As previously

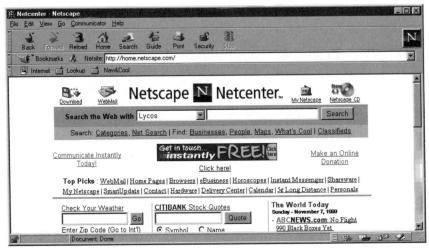

Figure 1.10. Netscape Navigator home page.

mentioned, XML will enhance data interchange at the application level. XSL will provide definition capability for specifying how XML is to be displayed in a general way for cross-application data presentation.

Creating Web Pages

The earliest tools used to create Web pages containing HTML for an intranet were specialized HTML editors. These were typically used by persons responsible for creating Web content or modifying content created by others with different authoring tools.

In addition to creating original HTML documents, many companies have found it useful to convert existing corporate data so that it can be retrieved and displayed on the company's intranet and the World Wide Web. Corporate data exists in many forms: word processing documents, spreadsheets, graphic presentations, tables of relational data, e-mail messages, image files, and video. Each has its own software application for processing or editing. To access this varied data via an intranet, it needs to be converted to the common data formats of HTML. Initially, text was manually converted by adding HTML tags with a text editor. Graphics files were converted to the acceptable formats (e.g., GIF format) by a specialized graphics conversion program.

With the increasing popularity of HTML, many major word processors and other productivity applications have incorporated HTML file import/export, display, and direct Internet-connect features as part of the base application. In this way, all users can continue to use their software applications of choice, each with its own proprietary data format and HTML input/output option, for Web publishing. Lotus Word Pro is an example of a word processor with these features.

Web Clients

The typical Web client is a PC running an operating system, such as Windows 95, and a Web browser. Keep in mind, however, that any type of computer can act as a Web client as long as it has a Web browser program. In the computer industry, there are four major types, or models, of clients, as illustrated in Figure 1.11.

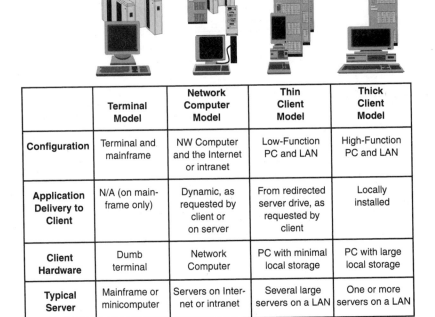

	Terminal Model	Network Computer Model	Thin Client Model	Thick Client Model
Configuration	Terminal and mainframe	NW Computer and the Internet or intranet	Low-Function PC and LAN	High-Function PC and LAN
Application Delivery to Client	N/A (on main-frame only)	Dynamic, as requested by client or on server	From redirected server drive, as requested by client	Locally installed
Client Hardware	Dumb terminal	Network Computer	PC with minimal local storage	PC with large local storage
Typical Server	Mainframe or minicomputer	Servers on Inter-net or intranet	Several large servers on a LAN	One or more servers on a LAN

Figure 1.11. Client models.

The terminal model is represented by a terminal connected to a mainframe, now commonly referred to as a server. The entire application operates on the server while the client sends mouse clicks and keystrokes and receives screens in return. In this case the server is called an **application server**. The most successful use of this approach to supporting Internet clients is through the MetaFrame application from Citrix Systems Corporation. Essentially, Citrix supports Windows applications running over the Internet or intranet, with the user sending keystrokes and mouse clicks and receiving Windows screens on a MetaFrame-enabled PC while the actual application is running on the Metaframe server. The approach is successful because it requires the least network bandwidth and least-capable client PC system. Note that server resources must be beefed up to provide the computing power necessary to run applications for multiple clients simultaneously, a trick perfected by mainframe systems over the past three decades. Two advantages of this approach are the ability to continue to use older PCs (a money saver) and minimizing the installation impact of new or updated applications.

The **thin client** approach is to install only an application stub on the user's system and transmit the complete application image over the network when the user selects it. Behind the scenes, the PC is given access to a network disk as if it were on the user's own system by using the facilities of a network operating system, such as IBM's OS/2 LAN Server program. This facility, called **redirection**, saves hard disk storage at the user's system and minimizes installation impact as in the application server alternative, but it requires higher network bandwidth, making it generally unusable over today's Internet (but highly practical over a company's intranet).

The most common alternative is the "install it all" approach, called **thick client**. This approach requires a full-function client system and impacts users if software upgrades are required, but network traffic is limited to data transmissions. Most of us are familiar with thick clients for both Internet and intranet applications.

The **Network Computer** (**NC**), described at the beginning of this chapter, is the newest of the client approaches. Its low-cost version consists of a high-speed central processor, at least 32 MB of memory, a Web browser, and support for Java. All information requests are fulfilled over the intranet or Internet by server systems. It can be used to surf the Internet or an enterprise's intranet and handle World Wide Web information, including Java applets.

Web Servers

Web servers most simply interact with Web browsers by resolving the supplied Universal Resource Locators (URLs) and sending the requested Web page back. The interaction between Web browser and Web server is not limited to simple file requests, however. HTML commands can initiate actions such as querying a database or sending e-mail to the author of the Web page. These actions are handled by programs on the Web server, called **Common Gateway Interface** (**CGI**) **scripts**--a standard means to link Web servers with outside applications. A CGI program can enable a Web user to fill in a form and receive in response information from a database. CGI programs are typically written in PERL (**Practical Extraction and Support Language**), Java, or C. More advanced features, such as **forms**, which incorporate a dialogue box for user selections that provides specific information back to the server for special processing, are available.

As additional advanced features are enabled, your intranet is being extended from a two-tier model (i.e., Web browser to Web server) to a three-tier model, as in Figure 1.12. The Web server provides the basic services and the other server, the third tier, provides the requested application-specific processing. An example of a third-tier server is a large relational database system that would satisfy a user's query. Three-tier technology is increasingly being used for e-business, the use of the Internet to conduct complete sales transactions between buyers and sellers.

Selecting an appropriate Web server depends on client usage patterns, data storage requirements, and the network capacity. If your users demand more than just simple Web page retrieval in requesting services, a higher-performance processor is indicated. Additional disk storage will be required if large files are stored. If users are connected to the server via a LAN connection, multiple LAN adapters may be needed in the server to provide adequate communication performance.

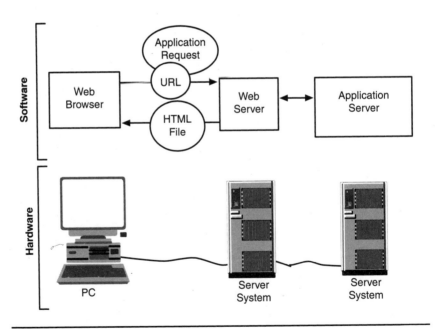

Figure 1.12. Three-tier interaction.

Intranet Security

Right now, most intranets are used for distributing information as documents, such as corporate procedures, descriptions of products and services, and so on. As companies increasingly seek to transact real business over an intranet or the Internet, they will demand higher levels of security. According to Stallings [1995], there are four major threats to an intranet:

1. Unauthorized alteration of data

2. Impersonating another intranet user

3. Eavesdropping on messages passed between a server and a browser

4. Unauthorized access to the Web server and its operating system

To avoid unauthorized data alteration and impersonation, both the Web server and client must support data encryption. The most common approach is to use a public key/private key method. For data protection, the public key is used to encrypt the data by the sender and the private key, known only to the receiver, is used to decrypt the data. To prevent impersonation, the sender uses his or her private key for encryption and the receiver uses the sender's public key for decryption and validation of the user's identity. The **SSL** (Secure Sockets Layer) protocol is the de facto standard method that intranet programmers can employ to secure all transmissions between client and server via encryption. The use of this protocol is increasingly common--as Web browser-user options when completing a sales transaction, for example.

Securing the Web server itself requires, at a minimum, limitations and controls on administrator access. Next, security fixes should be applied to the underlying operating system, if available. These come from various sources: the operating system vendor, CIAC (the Department of Energy's Computer Incident Advisory Capability), and CERT (the Computer Emergency Response Team sponsored by DARPA - Defense Advanced Research Projects Agency). [Stallings, 1995].

Finally, securing the network itself through firewalls, systems that review and filter all transmissions from external sources, prevents external tampering.

Intranet Futures

With all the attention being focused on the Internet, corporate intranets, and new applications, the future looks very bright for network computing. General trends are:

- Increasing demand from users for higher-speed networks. Figure 1.13 shows the trends leading from a demand for 56 thousand bits per second (Kbps) to 100 million bits per second (Mbps) for virtual reality data transmission.

- A corresponding response from network service providers to provide higher network bandwidth.

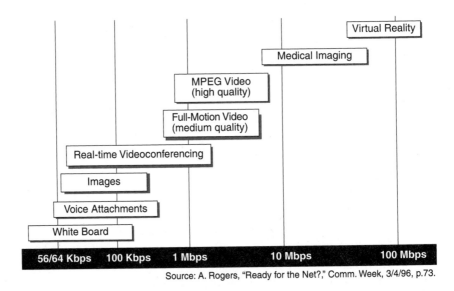

Source: A. Rogers, "Ready for the Net?," Comm. Week, 3/4/96, p.73.

Figure 1.13. Demand for network bandwidth.

- Corresponding responses from Web content providers by scaling up server functionality and/or duplicating information at several locations to improve data delivery time to requesters.

- Software developers taking advantage of these trends by creating increasingly dynamic, complex, and data-hungry applications.

Providers of information technology must keep the current environment functioning and satisfy new user requirements, all within an environment of strict cost control. The current environment is arguably the easiest part of the job. As new information technologies explode in today's dynamic environment, aggressive technology users naturally seek the leverage points within these technologies. The Internet erupts, greatly expanding everyone's ability to communicate and access information, and access is granted. Figure 1.14 reflects a perspective on the evolving use of the Internet over time. [Marshak, 1996] The initial Web experience for most businesses was access,

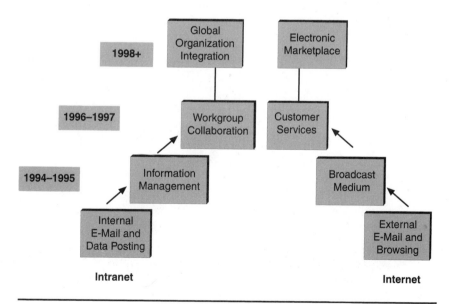

Figure 1.14. Evolution of the World Wide Web.

followed by creating a Web site to reach out to customers and enabling information sharing. We are now in a period of intense Internet investment, forming a true worldwide electronic marketplace.

It is likely that the typical user's desktop will include a variety of intranet-based applications of various types: browser-based, browser plug-ins, and standalone. Browser-based applications use the native facilities within your Web browser to deliver data and applications to your PC. In the future, browser applications will start to employ XML and XSL as the base Web data content formats in this category to deliver new and more powerful end-user applications.

Browser plug-ins are applications that can be selected from within a browser interface and support alternate data file formats for advanced function. Interesting examples are plug-ins for Adobe Photoshop graphics, Shockwave for streaming audio and video, and VRML for 3D graphics. **VRML** stands for Virtual Reality Markup Language, which provides three-dimensional, virtual reality interaction for the client user with a remote server.

Standalone applications will increasingly include new forms of dynamic Web content delivery. A sample of today's Web applications, such as PointCast, Internet Phone, Winamp, and Sametime instant messaging, gives an indication of where we are going in the future. The PointCast application is a personalized news retrieval service that delivers an on-screen window of ever-changing information to connected Web browser users. The Internet Phone application converts your voice to a digital signal and sends it over the Internet, enabling you to have a voice conversation with any Internet user. The Winamp application plays digital audio in the form of MP3 files--both the application and thousands of digital MP3 "songs" are readily downloadable from the Web. Instant messaging—the ability to determine if your colleague or neighbor is actively online and send a message is—becoming the "microwave oven" of new Internet applications (i.e., once you use it, it becomes indispensable). It is not only fun for the recreational online user but can be very, very useful for intranet-based users. The Lotus Sametime product includes this capability plus others, like Chat. These products are great add-ons to enrich an intranet.

Standard applications are increasingly taking advantage of Internet and intranet connections by adding network-based functionality. For example, a user of Freelance Graphics can easily access a page on

Lotus's Web site that makes available any new SmartMasters for use with Freelance. A SmartMaster file provides a useful background for new presentations. Quicken 2000, a traditional PC-based financial management application, provides an array of online features for its users, including the ability to send online payments, receive online bills, and receive credit card charges over the Internet. New applications will be self-maintaining in the future as they assume an Internet connection, detect it, and upgrade themselves after user confirmation.

We can see that as the Internet erupts, it is greatly expanding everyone's ability to communicate and access information. Intranets intrude on our consciousness, borrowing from the Internet eruption, and information technologists must respond. Aggressive users request, and information technology organizations invest. Change occurs in the form of new products, new services, and new terminology, trumpeted in today's diverse media. This change occurs very rapidly, given the highly independent nature of the swarm of product developers in the information technology industry.

Despite the swarm, some trends are emerging. The Internet is evolving into a worldwide, public communications network that is transforming how information is exchanged among businesses and individuals. It is easy and inexpensive for businesses to establish a presence on the Internet. This can mean as small a presence as a company brochure or as large a one as an entire Internet-based enterprise. It is easy and inexpensive for individuals to access information on the Internet--all they need is a PC, a modem, Web browser software, and Internet access from a service provider. These are the computing equivalent of the telephone. Open information technology standards such as TCP/IP, HTTP, and XML are emerging as universal standards for computing and information exchange. Network capacity and transmission speeds are increasing for business and individuals alike, and there is every reason to expect this to continue based on related technological advances (e.g., computer processor speeds and the availability of cable modems and Asymmetric Digital Subscriber Line (**ADSL**) services to the home).

In the face of these trends, the impact on service providers is very large. Achieving economies of scale in order to achieve low support cost per user has long been the service provider's goal. Figure 1.15 shows the past three computing "eras" characterized by typical clients, relative network bandwidth, typical servers, and relative cost.

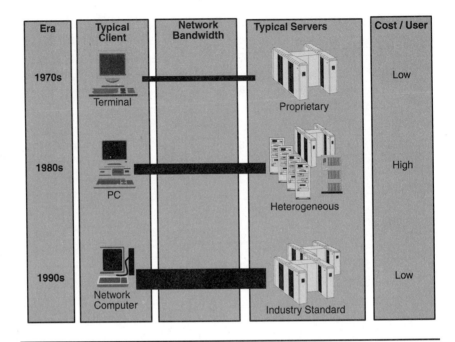

Era	Typical Client	Network Bandwidth	Typical Servers	Cost / User
1970s	Terminal		Proprietary	Low
1980s	PC		Heterogeneous	High
1990s	Network Computer		Industry Standard	Low

Figure 1.15. Cost/user trends.

The 1970s were dominated by large mainframes running interactive and batch applications while interacting thinly with dumb terminal clients. Essentially, keystrokes were sent from PC to mainframe and screens were sent in the opposite direction. Network speeds of 300 to 9600 bps (bits per second) were adequate. This was a "low" cost per user era because terminals were standard and inexpensive, networks were simple, and economies of scale were easily reached with lights-out mainframe management (i.e., the glass house).

The 1980s through the middle of the 1990s has been the decade of the PC, the LAN, and client/server computing. Typical LANs operated (and continue to operate) at 10 to 16 Mbps (million bits per second). The additional speed facilitated large file transfers to feed the PC-based applications or submit large files to print. A diversity of PC server systems emerged, with prior-era minicomputers and mainframes recasting themselves in this vein. With a lack of standards and users clamoring for new client/server applications, cost per user figures skyrocketed. It was justified in terms of increased user flexibility and productivity over prior applications.

It appears that we are embarking on the era of "network computing" at the end of this decade based on dramatic increases in network bandwidth and the trend to the universal Web client or browser. Ubiquity of client software (the browser) has led to immense investment in software applications to exploit it. This leads to homogenization of server requirements, in turn leading to a convenient and cost-effective consolidation of diverse, smaller servers into larger, more powerful systems. Economies of scale in terms of support cost per user lost in the previous era can now be regained--the mainframe is back!

Accompanying these trends is Sun Microsystems' investment in the Java compiler technology to create processor-neutral program code, transportable over a network and executable on *any* receiving computer properly equipped with a Java interpreter. The availability of increasingly fast, inexpensive processors in PCs makes interpreting processor-neutral code, such as Java, viable—and potentially competitive with processor-specific compiled code. A viable Java piggybacks on the trends to a universal client and faster networks to possibly solve the very costly and difficult problem of code delivery to the client system.

To go one step farther, if code can be dynamically delivered to a universal client upon request, why not eliminate all code and data storage at the client? This observation has led to the development of the network computer, or NC, by several major corporations. Substituting NCs for PCs further reduces cost per user, potentially returning information technology budgets back to the terminal-mainframe era of the 1970s! Estimates of cost reduction are in the range of three-to-one to five-to-one.

Clearly, PCs are not going to disappear overnight for many classes of users in a business when NCs arrive. Specialist users with large complex applications, such as CAD (Computer-Aided Design), will still require a locally resident, compiled version of the software. However, the NC appears to be a great near-term solution for users with only occasional or "low-compute" needs. Administrators, managers, security personnel, maintenance staff, and visitors should be the first targets for NC delivery. Over time, as more complex applications become "Java"-ized, NCs could replace PCs for increasing numbers of users. To underscore this point, Sun Microsystems and Microsoft have recently announced plans to "rent" usage of their office productivity applications with a Web browser as hosting "platform." It remains to be seen if large applications, such as Word, could be delivered via a Web browser with acceptable performance and human factors.

Summary

We have taken a quick look at the present and future of intranets for business. It is clear that many businesses today are aggressively making this investment to improve communication for all employees. Further, it is clear that the information technology industry has discovered the value of a standard infrastructure and communications platform (i.e., the intranet technologies) and is building on them as rapidly as possible. The goal is to achieve an intranet that is secure, flexible, transparent, and scalable, and that can reach employees, business partners, and customers alike. As we shall see in the coming chapters, the key to a successful intranet lies in its consistency and the software maturity of its products.

2

The Domino Clients

Over the past decade, the Domino application platform has caught the imagination of thousands of companies and millions of users with its ability to enable information sharing and rapid application development. With the Domino server (covered in Chapter 3), both Lotus Notes and Web browser clients can be effectively supported. This chapter provides an overview of the Lotus Notes client and how the Notes client or a Web browser accesses, creates, and replicates Domino data. Domino security is described next. Domino mail, calendar, and directory functions are reviewed.

What Is Groupware?

Groupware remains one of the hottest buzzwords in network computing jargon today. The objective of groupware is to improve the sharing of information among members of a group or team. A simple example is a database on a server containing articles to be published as a newsletter by a team of writers. Each writer can add his or her own article and create comments about the articles of others. These comments are stored in the database associated with the article, and, again, all writers can "share" the comments. Adding an approval form to be used by the authors and editors to approve an article (which also resides in the Domino database), can make everyone aware of the progress of any article in the newsletter. This is an example of the workgroup collaboration environment offered by groupware. A recent Gartner Group study, investigating the profiles of 338 enterprises using groupware, determined four main uses: e-mail and calendaring; collaborative file sharing, discussion databases, and project coordination; Web-based collaboration; and electronic publishing. [Anonymous, 1998a]

Groupware applications can also be used to support workflow—-generally described as a business process in which a sequence of activities by a team results in a useful work. In a workflow groupware application, for example, a document is updated based upon the value of a field of information or the state of the business process.

Spectacular benefits can be achieved if business processes are reengineered and groupware applications are developed to support them. In effect, the groupware application is the embodiment of the process. In this way organizations can gain a competitive advantage with improved coordination of effort and collaboration between members of local or widely dispersed teams. This, in turn, improves their responsiveness to the marketplace.

Many groupware products on the market today use network computing elements to create groupware applications. They incorporate a shared, distributed, document database that resides on a server, an easy-to-use GUI on the client, a wide area e-mail function, and built-in security to allow access control for critical information. One notable feature, called **rapid application development,** makes it possible to change a groupware application as rapidly as required to meet business needs. Finally, many groupware products support documents that contain **rich text.** Rich text describes a document that can contain text, graphics, scanned images, audio, and full-motion video data. Sometimes such documents are called **compound documents.** This feature alone can improve the communication quality of shared information.

Introduction to the Lotus Notes Client

Lotus Notes, the best-known groupware product, incorporates information sharing and workflow features in providing a platform for the creation of groupware applications. Figure 2.1 illustrates this notion of Notes as a platform from an extension of the formal definition of the **OSI** (Opens Systems Interconnect) communications protocol stack. Each layer of the stack refers to a software layer (usually implemented as a service program) that adds protocol information to the actual data as it is being transmitted over a network and removes protocol information from the data as it is received.

One can think of a data being handed from one layer to another as it is moved up or down the stack, with each layer providing its own unique contribution. Notes and Domino reside at the top of the stack, the application layer. They "split" the application layer: The Notes client and Domino server software are the bottom layer or platform for the Domino applications that form the end-user-customizable top layer. People familiar with Domino will sometimes call a Domino application a Domino database because a Domino application is a combination of a customized application with application software (code, logic, etc.) and data.

Throughout this book, the terms "Domino application" and "Domino database" are used interchangeably.

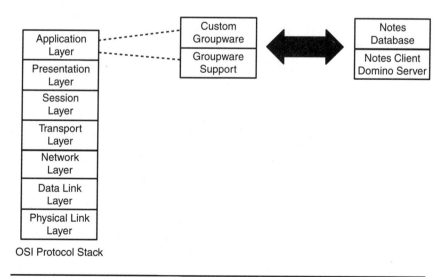

OSI Protocol Stack

Figure 2.1. Expanding the stack.

The Notes Client User Interface

The Notes client is the software that is installed on the end user's PC. Prior Notes user interfaces utilized a notebook metaphor, with the main body of the screen or workspace sectioned into notebook tabs. Each tab of the notebook graphically contained one or more icons, each of which represented a Domino database. The Notes User Interface (UI) is undergoing a major revision with version 5.0. The concept of portfolios, which integrates Domino databases with Web or intranet content cohesively, is being introduced. Figure 2.2 illustrates the migration process that current Notes 4.x users will experience. When the Notes 5.0 client is started for the first time, a conversion process is begun that converts each Notes 4.x notebook "tab" to a separate portfolio.

The menu items across the top of the screen are standard for the whole application, but (and this is important) they offer different

This is an example of the database icons on the first tab of a typical Notes 4.x desktop.

This is an example of the database icons on the first tab of a typical Notes 5.x desktop converted to a portfolio.

Here is an example of the remaining "tabs" being converted to portfolios.

2000 Lotus Development Corporation. Used with permission of Lotus Development Corporation.

Figure 2.2. Notes 4.x to 5.0 desktop conversion.

choices depending upon which Domino database in the portfolio is currently selected by the user. For example, if the selected database is the Mail database, then by selecting "Create," the user will be creating a mail memo. If the selected database is some other application, selecting "Create" will produce some other fill-in form. This approach is consistently applied throughout the application in a most elegant fashion. In addition, top-of-screen menu items dynamically appear based on their availability. Beneath the command set is the SmartIcon bar. SmartIcons provide shortcuts to many user actions and are customizable. They can be created to link to external applications or perform multistep operations for one or more Domino applications. An unlimited number of Domino applications or Web links can be windowed on the desktop for additional flexibility. Previously, users were limited to nine simultaneous windows.

With Notes 5.0, the ability to provide support for a customized client look and feel is available through a "headlines" database, which defines the content of a "knowledge navigator" or customized "home page." The headlines database can draw upon content from one or more Domino database or Web pages and present a unique opening screen (i.e., customized home page) as shown in Figure 2.3. Figure 2.4 illustrates the data transfer. Knowledge navigators can be created to provide both real-time updates and static content to your end users. The implications of this topic for knowledge management are discussed in more detail in Chapter 4.

One of the most powerful Notes client features is the ability to operate in either connected or disconnected mode. Connected mode means that your Notes client is interacting over a network in real time with one or more Domino databases residing on a Domino server. Disconnected mode means that your Notes client is interacting with one or more Domino databases residing as replica copies on your personal workstation. Notes offers a great deal of flexibility in connected mode, allowing you to communicate over an office network or remotely via a modem. Disconnected mode is ideal for the traveler who needs to continue Notes-related work, but cannot get connected to the office or home network. Prior to travel, you set up your "Replicate" notebook tab, as in Figure 2.5, selecting one or more databases to be localized to your PC, and then click on "Start" to update local replicas of these databases. During travel, on a plane for example, you do your e-mail or other Domino database interactions. When you arrive at your destination, you simply get connected to

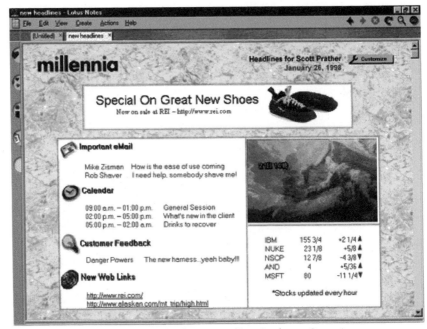

Figure 2.3. Headlines customized home page.

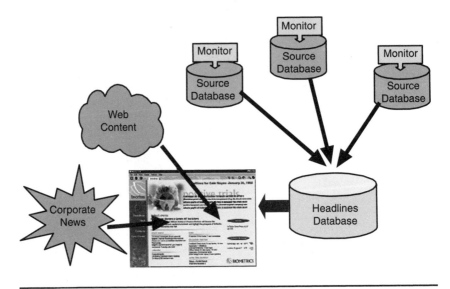

Figure 2.4. Headlines data transfer.

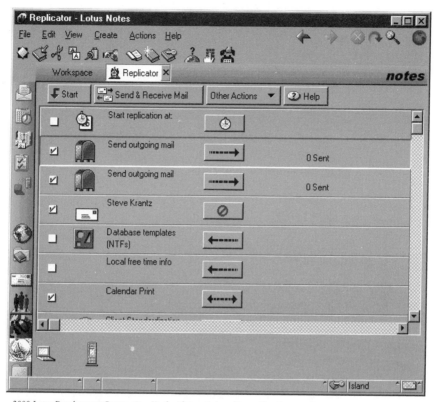

2000 Lotus Development Corporation. Used with permission of Lotus Development Corporation.

Figure 2.5. Lotus Notes replicator page.

your home network to replicate your disconnected work items back to their respective servers. See "Getting It From Here to There: Replication and Routing for a discussion of how Domino supports this capability through **replication.**

Notes 5.0 client supports the following operating systems:

- Windows 95

- Windows 98

- Windows NT

- Macintosh PowerPC

The following operating systems will be supported by Web browser clients only:

- OS/2

- UNIX

- HP-UX

- Sun Solaris (SPARC and X86)

- IBM AIX

Figure 2.6 shows the communications protocols supported by the Notes 5.0 client. Figure 2.7 shows the other, higher-level client/server protocols support by the Notes 5.0 client—mail, security, directory, and application protocols.

	AppleTalk	Banyan Vines	NetBIOS	NetBEUI	SPX	TCP/IP
OS/2 V3.0		✓	✓	✓	✓	✓
Windows NT		✓	✓	✓	✓	✓
Windows 95		✓	✓	✓	✓	✓
Windows 3.1		✓	✓	✓	✓	✓
UNIX					✓	✓
Macintosh	✓					✓

Figure 2.6. Protocols supported by Notes 5.0 client.

Mail and Other	Notes 5.0 Client	Domino 5.0 Server
POP3	Yes (native)	Yes
IMAP4	Yes (native)	Yes
MIME	Yes (native)	Yes
NNTP	Yes (native)	Yes
HTML	Yes (native)	Yes
SMTP	Yes	Yes
FTP	No	No
Application		
Frames	Native	Native
HTTP	HTTP 1.1	HTTP 1.1
JAVA	Notes Object Int. + Java Classes	Notes Object Int. + Java Classes
JavaScript	Yes	Yes
CORBA / IIOP	Yes. Java-based Client classes	Yes-C++ CB-based server classes
CGI	NA	Yes
Security		
SSL	SSL3 (128 Bit)	SSL 3 (128 Bit)
X.509v3 Certificates	Combine Notes-based RSA and X.509	Combine Notes-based RSA and X.509
S/MIME	Yes	Yes
Directory	LDAP v 3	LDAP v 3
	Read/Write	Read/Write
	Authentication	Authentication
Management	No	SNMP

Figure 2.7. Notes and Domino 5.0 higher-level protocols.

Serving Clients with Domino

A **server** system is a system on a network that provides services to requesting clients. The Domino server is the focal point for service for tens to thousands of Notes and Web browser clients. Database operation, replication, and routing are conducted on the Domino server. The software is implemented for use on most industry-standard computer systems, both singleprocessor and multiprocessor. It operates on most popular operating systems, including Windows NT, several flavors of UNIX, and OS/2. In turn, these operating systems work on a broad range of powerful server systems, including ones based on RISC, Intel, and IBM S/390 processors, so Domino is scalable to operate effectively for small, medium, and large enterprises.

Operating systems supported by the Domino server include

- OS/2

- Windows NT/Intel, NT/Alpha

- Windows 95, Windows 98

- Sun Solaris (SPARC and Intel)

- AIX

- HP-UX

- LINUX

- AS/400

- OS/390

Figure 2.8 shows the communications protocols supported by the Domino server. Domino is described in more detail in Chapter 3.

The Domino Database

Most user interaction with the Notes client is with a Domino database. The database is a single file (**xxxxxxxx.NSF**) containing one or more documents (records). A document can be a single data item, a simple text file, a form with one or more data fields, a graphics file, or a combination of these and other data objects (e.g., sound, video).

	AppleTalk	Banyan Vines	NetBIOS	NetBEUI	SPX and SPXII	TCP/IP
OS/2 V3.0	Lotus	✓	✓	✓	Novell Netware SPX	✓
Windows NT	✓	✓	✓	✓	✓	✓
UNIX					✓	✓

Figure 2.8. Protocols supported by Domino 5.0 Server.

The document format and views of a document in a database are easily specified (programmed) through the Notes GUI interface. Multiple forms can be defined for a database. A critical feature is the ability to route e-mail to and from a Domino database (the mail message can be one of the forms). This provides the basis for workflow applications. Through simple commands, access to the database can be granted to one or more users. Domino databases can reside remotely on a Domino server or locally on your PC, as Figure 2.9 illustrates.

You can track multiple changes to a document with version control. Documents can be identified with an expiration date for automated removal, if needed. Current and prior versions, created by one or more group members, can be easily saved and viewed, based on how the Domino database is designed. You can link one document to another with a simple point-and-click method, creating a document hierarchy as is done on the World Wide Web. In fact, Notes documents can be linked directly to Web documents!

As Notes and Domino have evolved, so has Domino database capacity. See Figure 2.10 for a comparison from Notes Release 3 to Notes/Domino Release 4 to Notes/Domino Release 5. There is no inherent size limit in this new version. The database size has been tested to 64 GB and certified to 32 GB. Other improvements to the "On-Disk Structure" (ODS) of the Domino database include the ability to compact a database in place without use of additional storage, plus the database can be read/write accessed during the compaction.

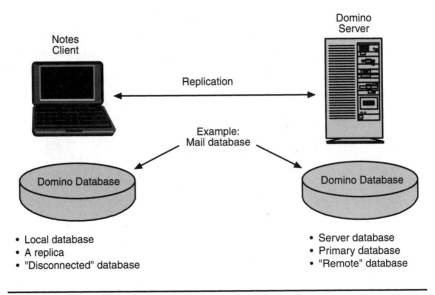

Figure 2.9. Local and remote Domino databases.

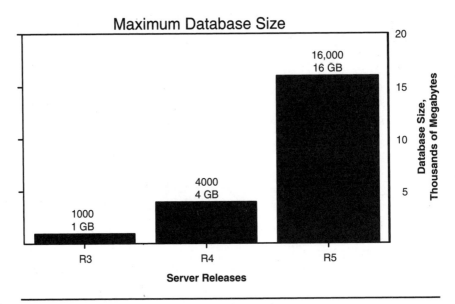

Figure 2.10. Domino database capacity evolution.

Viewing Data in Domino Databases

The current Notes user interface includes simultaneous, multiple window panes that simplify examining database documents. The panes include a folder or navigator window, a document list window, and a document viewing window. This reduces the amount of effort required to browse through a Domino database for a specific document. For an example, refer to Figure 2.11, which shows the Notes e-mail interface.

The document folder window is how Domino allows the user to organize documents in the Domino database. Documents can be dragged and dropped into a folder as they arrive (as in e-mail) or as they are created (as in end-user editing). The document folder window can list standard and customized folders and views as in Figure 2.12, or it can be replaced with a graphic **navigator** (with a

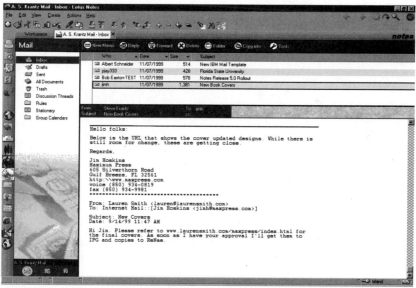

2000 Lotus Development Corporation. Used with permission of Lotus Development Corporation.

Figure 2.11. Notes e-mail interface.

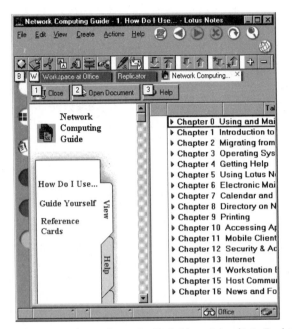

2000 Lotus Development Corporation. Used with permission of Lotus Development Corporation.

Figure 2.12. Example of a Domino database navigator.

little custom programming). A navigator is a graphical image with hotspots for user selection. A simple example is a map of the United States with a selectable hotspot on each state for a geographical database.

The document list window, also called a view window, provides a traditional way of viewing multiple documents by their titles and other fields contained in the documents. Highlighting an item in this window brings it up in the third window, the document viewing window. Double-clicking on an item in this window typically brings up (or maximizes) the document on the Notes desktop. These views or lists are customizable both by the Domino application developer as standard features of the application and by the end user. Because traditional relational databases offer views of data based on selected fields of information in tabular form, Domino supports this with an easy-to-use form fill-in method. Custom views of data can be created literally in minutes. Figure 2.11 illustrates a view inside a Mail database.

When you view a set of documents, selected field names appear as columns and the documents are capsulized in sort order as single lines, as in Figure 2.13. Domino views employ an expand-and-collapse approach, with associated documents of different types within a database. For example, if a parent document has one or more child documents, you can view just the parent or the parent and all its children (documents, that is). Searching for data within or attached to a document is also easy. A full-text search capability with point-and-click human factors is available. Data can be sorted in a user-requested sequence.

File attachments to documents can be viewed directly by one of the over 150 file viewing programs included. This avoids unnecessarily detaching the file (copying it to your local disk) or launching the program that natively supports the file type (e.g., launching Freelance to view a .PRZ file).

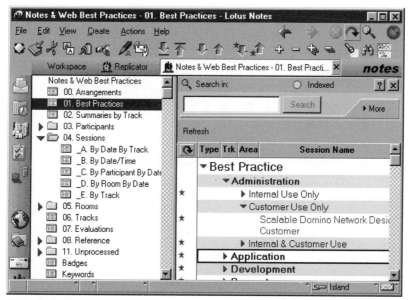

2000 Lotus Development Corporation. Used with permission of Lotus Development Corporation.

Figure 2.13. Domino database view example.

Data Replication for Notes Clients

A key Domino database feature is replication. According to Vaskevitch [1993], replication provides "automatic tiered storage" for Domino users, which keeps geographically dispersed Domino databases in line automatically through the routine transmission of changes. This differs from the traditional, central database in which only a single copy is maintained and all users must log in to the central repository for update and/or access. The advantages are that geographically dispersed users can have copies of a Domino database on each of their PCs for convenient independent access and consistent performance. The disadvantage is that the data may be backlevel and that periodically the users must connect to the network for replication of changes to occur. This is a two-way process in which users' changes propagate to the server and vice versa. Eventually, all users are at the latest level. Vaskevitch calls this, appropriately, "sophisticated self-adaptive storage migration." Note that updates to a document by two independent users must be manually resolved (they are noted as conflicts in the database, however). Clearly, this approach is not appropriate for online transaction-oriented databases and their applications, but for today's team-oriented, data-sharing environment, replication is perfect.

Domino replication operates either between servers or between client and server. Server-to-server replication propagates Domino data across a network for access by groups of users to optimize their on-line performance. Server-to-client replication supports the needs of the mobile user who selectively needs Domino data in a disconnected mode (when traveling on an airplane or working at home). Client-to-server replication selectively updates Domino data for other members of the team to access. The replicating client user can perform these operations with great specificity—for example, with documents changed in a specific time period or only for modified fields—and in the background while the user does other tasks. See Figure 2.9 for an illustration.

Data Linkages

Getting your data to you does not only apply to newly created Domino data, it also applies to mainframe data from legacy databases, from relational databases on mainframes and other servers, and from the Internet. Domino can act as a front end to traditional systems by creating advanced applications with Domino programming tools such as the LotusScript Data Object (called the LS:DO for short). For batch-type data transfers, the Lotus Enterprise Integrator (formerly Notes Pump) application allows administrators to schedule data import or export to Domino databases from most major legacy and relational databases. Figure 2.14 illustrates the Domino server software architecture, which combines support for both Domino databases and **API**s (Application Program Interfaces) with support for HTML documents, the basic file type of the World Wide Web. Chapter 4 provides more details on linking to external data with Domino.

With the integration of Notes and the Internet in Release 4.x, the strengths of Notes, supporting user collaboration and simplifying specification of automated tasks, combine to improve your access to

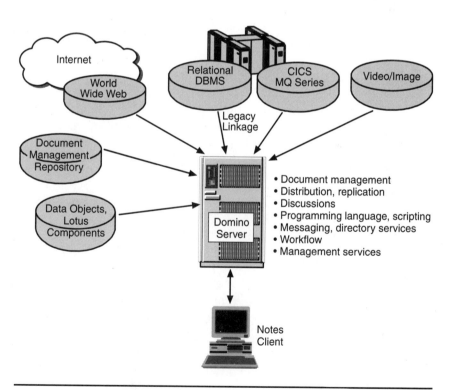

Figure 2.14. The Domino environment.

data on the Internet. Lotus Personal Web Navigator is a Web browser that can be added to any Notes desktop. When installed, Notes becomes "aware" of any URLs in Domino database documents—when you click on them, the Web page they reference is automatically retrieved from the Internet or your intranet. Alternatively, other Web browsers, such as Netscape Navigator, may be selected to perform this function if they are installed on your PC. In addition, a Domino agent can easily be created to automatically scan one or more Web sites, identify new or changed pages, and inform your staff by posting the Web links in a Domino database.

Creating and Changing Domino Data

Included as a base capability is a document editor with many of the same features offered in full-function word processors. This is available for use in any document with a **rich text** field. Rich text is a term describing the capability of a document or a part of a document to contain text, graphics, scanned images, audio, and full-motion video data.

A very useful feature for team collaboration in editing is the Permanent Pen feature. When you initiate it, you can establish a "permanent" color or font that is used for any changes to a document throughout your editing process. This simplifies the editing process. With a convention for each editor, multiple contributions can be easily recognized.

Client Security

Domino provides comprehensive security features to prevent data loss and ensure private communications. Enforced authentication methods are employed during communication between client systems and server systems running Domino (essentially, the user's certificate, contained in the user's Notes ID file, is validated). Access Control Lists (ACLs), the next level of security, can be specified with any Domino database to itemize the allowable roles or actions by users. Roles include depositor, reader, author, editor, designer, and manager. Encryption can be used to protect individual messages, data fields, and entire databases to prevent unauthorized interpretation. Finally, digital signatures can secure user-to-user communication so that the receiving user knows that no tampering or forgery occurred in transit.

Because Domino has very strong security features, which sometimes run afoul of national laws, there is more then one type of Notes license, depending on whether the product will be exported or used exclusively in North America. The significant difference between these licenses is the method of encryption used when securing data in Notes. The North American version now uses a full 128-bit encryption key. The International version uses a 64-bit encryption key with a "workfactor reduction field" of 24 bits. These 24 bits are encrypted using the U.S. government's (National Security Agency) public key, thus giving the U.S. government the ability to decrypt the international transmissions if necessary, while continuing to provide 64-bit strong encryption to everyone else. The versions are completely interoperable when communicating.

Security is almost as robust for Web browser clients as for Notes clients. Figure 2.15 summarizes the differences between Notes client and Web browser client security handling.

An additional security concern that is sometimes overlooked is **execution control** security, the ability to allow only code that is trusted to run (execute) on a person's workstation. With application environments like Notes, users can receive links for Notes applications

Types/Levels of Security	Notes Clients	Web Browser Clients
Access Control	Replicated ACL, roles, groups for databases, documents, fields in documents, and server access lists.	Access right via operating system and server index (document based only).
Authentication	Secure interchange with X.509 v3 digital certificates and Notes certificates (pre-5.0 clients).	Secure interchange with X.509 v3 digital certificates.
Encryption	Local database encryption mail encryption, document encryption, 64-bit network transaction encryption using SSL and RSA.	SSL-encrypted transactions only.

Figure 2.15. Notes client vs. Web security.

without any control on the source of the applications. Notes provides the ability to prevent the execution of such code on the Notes client through the use of Execution Control Lists (ECLs). Notes application developers can "sign" their applications, indicating their Notes ID or that of their organization. Notes clients can be set up, through ECL user preferences, to accept these trusted signers in advance. Any other Notes applications to be run will cause a prompt to the user to accept or reject the signer. Users should be educated to only accept known signers and reject all others (especially unsigned executables).

E-Mail and Messaging

Notes e-mail user interface is consistent with cc:Mail's user interface. It includes a three-pane window--one for navigation, one for document selection, and one for document viewing, as shown in Figure 2.11. Mail messages can be "mood stamped" (you can select an appropriate graphical icon to indicate message priority to your recipient). A key security feature can be employed to prevent the recipient from forwarding or copying a message's content.

Server storage space is minimized with a "single-copy object store." This means that only a single copy of a message is maintained on the server. For example, if you send a message to your department and their e-mail databases reside on a single server, only one copy of the message is physically stored on the server.

Calendaring and Scheduling

The Domino Mail database has the ability to maintain personal and group calendars. Inside the calendar view of your mail database, you can create personal or public calendar events. You can determine free time availability for invitees from other Domino or non-Domino domains, such as OfficeVision running on an IBM mainframe, in order to create meetings. You receive all meeting invitations, delegations, proposed reschedules, and accept/decline notices directly in your Domino mail inbox. Your conference rooms can be treated as resources to determine their availability for your meetings. There is a rich set of controls to create a personalized calendar profile. Figure 2.16 shows the new Domino 5.0 group calendar interface. It provides an overview of a group's time schedule and lets you display the individual calendars for each member. The mobile advantages of Domino are available to calendar users. Scheduling a meeting off-line, for example, is no more complicated than creating a mail message off-line (see the discussions of disconnected mode earlier in this chapter, in "The Notes Client User Interface"). Users will have the option to play a sound, launch an application, or send an e-mail message as the alarm notification.

Notes 5.0 adds the concept of place of user, helping the traveling user to be more efficient. This will add travel information to the calendar that may change the information read by the application, so if someone is going to be located in some other place when a Calendar free-time search is requested, there will be information there to account for changes in location.

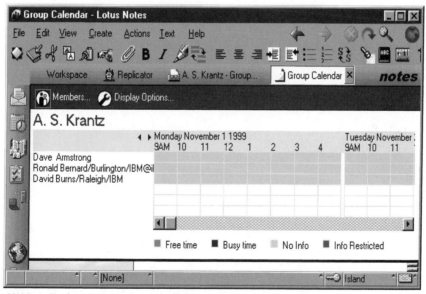

Figure 2.16. Domino 5.0. group calendar interface.

Summary

Over the past decade, Domino has been evolving to become the standard for groupware around the world. It incorporates ease of use, flexibility, and powerful scalability of operation to support highly diverse user requirements--a major accomplishment in a highly competitive environment. The majority of businesses that have invested in Domino treat it as the basis for their computing infrastructure. Its top benefits are communication and knowledge sharing improvements. By improving business processes for its customers, Domino has been estimated to provide a return on investment exceeding 150%.

3

The Domino Server

This chapter is about the Lotus server technology, which is a powerful Web and Notes intranet platform. First, we define the Domino architecture and how it fits into the Notes and Web environment. Large-enterprise administration is illustrated through examples from IBM's major Notes/Domino migration from 1995 through 1997. Domino administration tools and current competition are described. Finally, the future prospects for Domino are discussed.

What Is Domino?

Chapter 2 focused on the Lotus Notes and Web browser clients in combination with a Domino server. With Release 5.0, both clients offer broad and deep functionality to their users. Domino supports this rich client functionality as illustrated in Figure 3.1.

Domino's Rich Functionality

Under the covers, Domino consists of various server tasks or independent programs supporting clients, database access, data conver-

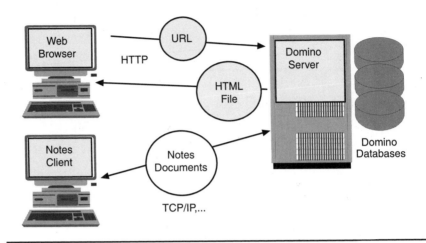

Figure 3.1.   Domino technology basics.

sion (e.g., Domino document to HTML format), linkage with other servers, and other activities. Administrators can extend Domino's capabilities by running programs called server agents and servlets to do perform unique activities in association with Domino databases. For example, a server agent can be scheduled to run on Domino to automatically screen and classify mail as it is received in a user's Domino mail database.

How Does Domino Work for Web Browser Clients?

One Domino server task, called the HTTP (HyperText Transport Protocol) "server," supports the Web browser clients accessing Domino data. This task uses the Domino API (Application Program Interface) to integrate itself with the rest of the Domino server in the same way that all other server tasks do. The Domino HTTP server is a TCP/IP (Transmission Control Protocol/Internet Protocol) application that implements the HyperText Transfer Protocol. It answers URL (Universal Resource Locator) requests from Web browsers by sending back pages of data encoded in HyperText Markup Language (HTML). It also handles URL requests and HTML forms that trigger executable programs as per the Common Gateway Interface (CGI) specification.

As we discussed in Chapter 1, the Web browser requests a specific Web page from a Web server by passing a URL (Uniform Resource Locator) to the Web server. The Domino server examines the URL in the incoming request and quickly decides if the request is for an item in a Domino database or an HTML file (which also may be stored on a Domino server). If it is a request for an HTML file, Domino treats it just as any other Web server would and returns the HTML file to the client using the industry-standard HTTP protocol. However, if the request is for a document in a Domino database, Domino accesses it directly, converts it to HTML format on the fly, and passes it back to the client.

Figure 3.2 illustrates the underlying software architecture. In programming terms, when a Web browser client interacts with the Domino server, the Domino engine works with the Domino server component to automatically translate the information in Domino databases into the HTML format. Once the conversion is performed, the HTTP server component transmits the information to the Web

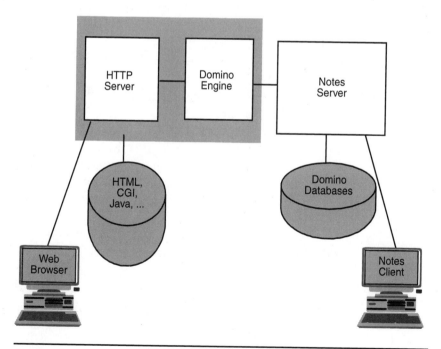

Figure 3.2. Domino architecture.

browser client. This component also can run CGI programs, reference Java files, and so on. On the other hand, transactions from Notes clients interact directly with the Notes server component.

Through Domino, Web clients are connected to the server in a way that provides access to all the information in Domino databases. This includes opening Domino databases not only to view documents but also to create, edit, and delete documents. This was a challenge, because the native Domino and Web environments use different protocols, different data models, and different approaches to security. To remedy this, Lotus first added support for HTTP—the communications protocol used on the Web. They then devised a URL interface that communicates with **Domino objects**. Domino objects include databases, views, forms, navigators, and operations such as Open, Edit, Create, and Delete. The connection between URLs and Notes objects make it possible for the Web browser to access a document in a Domino database or an HTML-formatted document with equal facility and without the user being aware. Essentially, all the things that you click in the Notes client to make something happen, such as document links and buttons, become URLs in the Web client. When translating Domino constructs to HTML for the Web client, Domino automatically creates URLs where needed. Figure 3.3 compares the Notes client to the Web client.

In addition to supporting a standard URL interface, Domino supports a set of extensions to the URL interface that enable URLs to further expose the advanced functionality of Notes to the Web client. For example, a URL can be extended (i.e., instructions added at the end) to request opening a Domino database (e.g., *http://domino.lotus.com/domino.nsf?OpenDatabase*). Figure 3.4 illustrates the extension to Web clients that Domino brings to the Notes environment in the context of an intranet. Figure 2.8 identifies the industry-standard protocols supported by Domino.

E-Mail and Calendar with Domino

E-mail is quickly becoming a standard for Internet end users, as it has been for users of competing, proprietary LAN-based and host-based e-mail systems. Major examples are Microsoft Mail, cc:Mail, and IBM's OfficeVision/VM mail. The major online services, such as America Online, and the major Web browsers have incorporated

	Notes Client	Web Browser Client
Hardware	PC	NC or PC
Software	Operating System, Notes Client with Web Navigator, Word Processor, Spreadsheet, Business Graphics	Web Browser
Web Surfing?	Yes	Yes
Groupware (Notes Applications)?	Yes	Yes
Productivity Applications?	Yes	Yes, eSuite

Figure 3.3. Client comparison.

e-mail features into their products, based on the Internet standard Simple Mail Transport Protocol (SMTP).

Domino supports Internet or intranet e-mail from any Web browser. If the mail server is "Domino-ized," the user can read and send mail by entering the URL for his or her mail database, name, and password. Behind the scenes, the Web browser user is employing a Domino mail database, which provides much of the function of a native Domino Mail user. Standard functions, such as Read, Reply, and Delete, are available, but a few, such as Forward, are not. With native SMTP support, e-mail service is fully interoperable within your intranet and the Internet (see "Intranet Gateways" later in this chapter).

An "anti-spam" feature is available with Domino to keep unwanted mail from wasting valuable resources. Unwanted mail can be filtered from your intranet's users by identifying sending user, send-

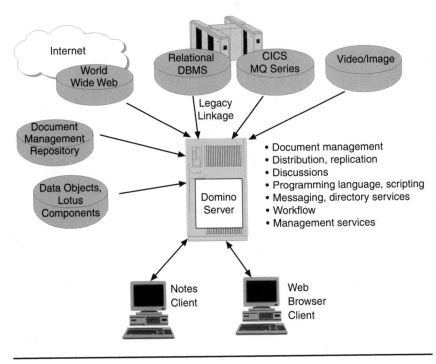

Figure 3.4. Domino intranet.

ing host, and sending domain. In addition, mail can be denied/allowed based upon recipient's address inside the intranet.

Personal and group calendaring and scheduling, although commonly available in proprietary products, are not yet common offerings as Web browser features. As discussed in Chapter 2, Domino Mail includes a full-function personal and group calendar capability. This, too, is available to the Web browser user via Domino. Figure 3.5 is a sample of how the Domino Calendar appears as rendered by Domino.

Directory Services

A directory is typically a table providing e-mail address information for the users of a messaging system. A special Domino database, called the Directory, serves this purpose and also provides a central reposi-

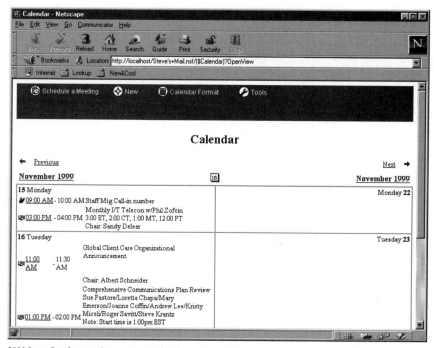

Figure 3.5. The Domino calendar.

tory for data routing and replication among a set of Domino servers or other network destinations, such as a fax machine.

You can store distribution lists, called groups, in the Directory to simplify mail routing to well-defined business units, such as individual departments. You can customize mail routing information based upon unique requirements. Addresses for foreign e-mail systems, such as Internet e-mail, can be stored. Figure 3.6 illustrates a typical Domino group.

In large Domino installations there are often multiple Domino domains. This is done either to avoid one overly large directory or because of the company's organizational or political structure. There are two methods available to accomplish this: daisy-chaining (the traditional method) and Directory Assistance (formerly called Master Address Book).

Domino supports "daisy-chaining" your Domain Directories on each server. This allows Domino to route within the current domain

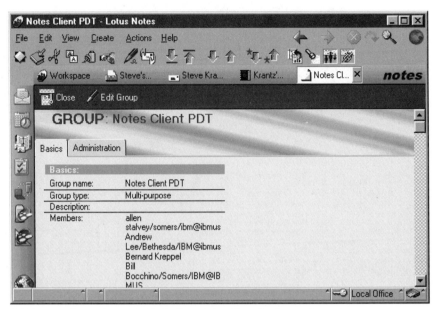

Figure 3.6. A typical Domino group.

and to any others in your enterprise. The first directory in the list should be that of the current domain. The order of the succeeding directories in the list should reflect the communication pattern of the e-mail users of the current domain. For example, the second directory in the list should be that containing addresses most frequently used by the current domain's users. Depending on your use of a prior e-mail system, the last directory in the chain of directories should contain names and mail addresses for all individuals who have yet to move to Domino. This directory, in conjunction with the other directories in the daisy chain, will give Domino mail senders the ability to use Domino native addressing regardless of the recipient's domain, location, or e-mail platform. Daisy-chaining is limited to seven directories.

Directory Assistance, a more flexible approach for the large enterprise, supports an unlimited number of directories. A key feature of Directory Assistance is support for directory access across dissimilar mail systems on your intranet and extranets with the Lightweight Directory Access Protocol (LDAP). This is an emerging industry standard for e-mail address directories. For example, you can address mail to somebody whose name is in an Exchange directory or an X.500 mail directory.

If a mail user does a search for the name Steve Krantz using the DAP protocol, the DAP server not only looks for all Steve Krantzes locally, it also checks other servers it knows about. With LDAP version 3 in Domino 5.0, the server performs both local and "chained" searches to these other servers, simplifying directory lookup in a heterogeneous environment. An additional feature with LDAP version 3 support that applies to the client is the ability to add, delete, or modify a directory entry.

A new feature, the Directory Catalog, is a highly compact lookup directory for the users of large enterprises. Today's directory averages 9000 bytes per entry. The Directory Catalog will have only 110 bytes per entry, reducing directory size by a factor of 80 or more. This makes it possible for the mobile users in a large enterprise to carry the entire company's directory on their notebook PC! Figure 3.7 illustrates how the Directory Catalog operates.

Domino Administration

As with any other intranet capability, the establishment of your Internet presence, the care of Notes clients and Web browser clients, and the care and feeding of your Domino servers must be addressed in a comprehensive manner. Following is an overview of the systems administrator's role in building an intranet's Domino server structure and managing it.

With Domino 5.0 comes an improved administrator's tool, called the Domino Administrator. It offers a comprehensive interface for administration of people, groups, files, servers, messaging, database replication, and configuration. See Administrative Tools section for more details. Figure 3.8 illustrates the Domino Administrator's welcome screen.

As you establish your Domino infrastructure, you need to take into account your planned number of users and their expected usage of Domino. Both the number of registered users and the number of concurrently active users influence a server's capacity. The number of registered users on a mail server, for example, impacts the amount of

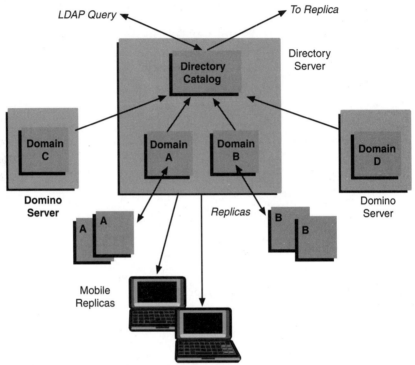

2000 Lotus Development Corporation. Used with permission of Lotus Development Corporation.

Figure 3.7. Enterprise directory.

server storage required. The number of observed active users will impact server response time. If multimedia data is heavily used in a database, that database will consume both more storage and processor cycles than one with just text data.

In general, multiple servers usually will be dedicated to certain tasks in order to balance load and to simplify administration. Mail servers will store mail databases and perform mail routing tasks. Dedicating a server to mail can reduce network traffic, as mail sent between users whose mail files are on the same server does not need to be routed through the network. Database servers are used to store application databases. Grouping applications together correctly will ease their administration and will reduce replication workload. A passthru server can be set up to allow a user to connect to multiple servers with a single connection. You can dedicate a server to be a

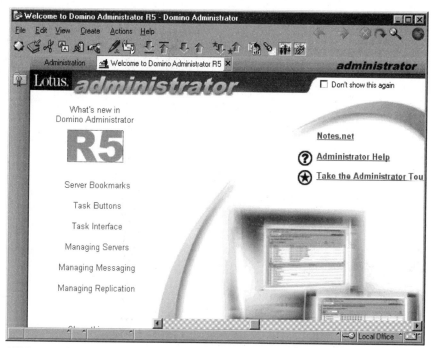

2000 Lotus Development Corporation. Used with permission of Lotus Development Corporation.

Figure 3.8. Domino Administrator's welcome screen.

remote server, providing connectivity for external users or external servers together with a secure, single point of entry. Gateway servers connect Domino to non-Domino systems.

Some administrators also dedicate one or more servers as hot backup servers, storing copies of critical databases. A hot backup server can be put into production if a database server goes down. More advanced servers, such as the IBM RS/6000, can be configured with a high-availability operating system that links two servers redundantly to provide dynamic backup and recovery of operation should one server fail. With Domino 5.0, features have been built in to the Domino database to improve backup and recovery. First, transaction logging can be enabled to allow rollback and roll forward of database transactions, facilitating log-based recovery of Domino databases in the event of a crash. Second, a full backup API is provided to vendors of backup/recovery software to support online backup with very fast implementations.

Inside IBM, the RS/6000 Scalable PowerParallel System (SP) is being used as the primary server platform for its Notes/Domino deployment, running on the AIX 4.21 operating system. The SP can be configured for from 2 to 512 nodes, or processors, in a single configuration. A high-speed switch interconnects all nodes, creating a highly powerful and scalable server system. The advantages of this platform include an expected increase in number of enrolled users per node by a factor of 8 versus an Intel platform and the ability to manage all nodes easily from a single console. Total system RAM starts as 128 MB and is expandable to 1 **TB** (1 trillion bytes). Online disk storage can range from 2 **GB** (2 billion bytes) to 9 TB.

For administrative purposes, Domino servers are grouped into **domains,** with each domain defined by a Directory. A domain will have a specific purpose or function. Two principal types are mail domains and database domains.

Production Database Servers

A typical site requires production database services. The database domain that supports this requirement may have users at numerous sites, but the domain itself will typically be housed within a given site. The servers within the production database domain should be segmented by the type of information they hold. A useful segmentation is (1) enterprise-wide servers, (2) business unit servers, and (3) Rapid Application Development (RAD) servers. The enterprise-wide servers should contain production databases for all company employees. The business unit servers should contain databases for a specific business unit. The RAD servers would contain "focused workgroup" databases for short-term or informal business processes. Note that some enterprise-wide and business unit servers may need to be deemed mission critical because of the nature of the databases they support. This implies that they will receive the highest level of protection (e.g., hardware redundancy, backup power, etc.) in the production environment. Chapter 4 discusses this application segmentation in more detail.

There may be other specialized servers in the domain. For example, you might set up a template server to contain all approved application templates for your Domino databases (a Domino template contains the design of a Domino database from which other instances, or replicas, can be created), or you might set up a production control server, used for running production jobs (API or otherwise) for applications within the site.

Database replication, an important service in the production database domain, is discussed in more detail later in this chapter. In addition, database documents are routed for mail-enabled work flow applications. Essentially, the workflow application database may be the target for mail or may send mail to other databases or users. This, too, is important and is considered later as part of mail message routing.

Production Mail Servers

Your sites' e-mail is handled by one or more Domino mail domains. A given mail domain may service clients across several sites. Unlike database domains, the servers that compose the domain itself may also be housed cross-site. This capability is important to support distributed work groups that have high-end communication needs. Domino mail routing can be provided at three service levels, as Figure 3.9 illustrates.

Each mail server in the domain should have the primary Directory replicated to it for high-performance routing lookup. If a secondary Directory (i.e., one linked to the primary) lookup is required, a redirected lookup to that domain's hub server can be set up. This avoids replication of the secondary Directory to each and every server,

Service Level	Service Description
High	Routes mail at once to next hop
Medium	Routes mail at next connection interval (the default)
Low	Routes mail overnight (12 a.m. – 6 a.m.)

Figure 3.9. Mail routing service levels.

thereby saving disk space. These secondary lookups occur when mail is routed across domains. If this additional load impacts hub server performance, a dedicated "lookup" server could be added to the infrastructure to perform this function. Directory redirection should not be used with mail domains that span multiple sites due to negative network performance impact. In these situations, Public Directories should be replicated to the various spoke servers.

Domino has the enhanced capability of single message storage, called shared mail. Your administrators can conserve server disk space by storing a single copy of a message sent to multiple individuals on the same server with this feature. The users' mail databases are linked with the shared mail file, which allows them to access the shared mail transparently. It is estimated that this architecture will result in a 30% savings of disk space on mail servers. It does add some additional administrative overhead (e.g., it is more difficult to backup user mail files), so only use it if your mail users employ multiple addresses or courtesy copying frequently.

Supporting Web Clients

With Domino, you have the option of making your Domino servers available to users with Web browsers. For inter-enterprise and external customer communications (e.g., an extranet), enabling Web browser access turning on Domino for those servers outside your firewall is a natural and simple choice. Inside your company, "Domino-ized" servers offering both Notes client and Web browser access may make sense for data requiring general access for all users, those with PCs, and just NC access for truly occasional users, with limited Domino database access needs satisfied by a Web browser rather than a Notes desktop.

What's in a Domain?

The typical corporate intranet places its servers at one or more physical sites. Within a site, the servers will be organized into one or more Domino domains. A mail domain will provide electronic mail services. A database domain is defined to provide support for all other services. Database domains will be used for both production work and nonproduction work such as development testing. The Domino Directory contains a definition of the domain in terms of servers, their mail routing connections, replication schedules, and user names and addresses. Essentially, the Directory defines the domain and is the vehicle for central administration and security (see Figure 3.10).

A small company will usually have a single domain. A larger company might have multiple domains, each with its own Directory. A separate domain might be set up for each country in an international enterprise--this is precisely what the IBM company has done in its corporate-wide Notes/Domino deployment. The Domain Directories are consolidated into four databases, which are mutually replicated among all domains so that all users can address anyone in the enterprise.

As a major example, the Domino domain structure within IBM uses the concept of domains organized by function. The two primary functions supported are mail and database. A key observation is that documents are typically routed from mail database to mail database,

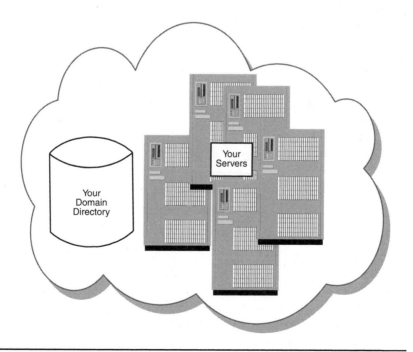

Figure 3.10. Your Domino domain.

whereas general database documents typically are replicated from database to database. Figure 3.11 illustrates the site concept for domain organization for a typical IBM site. Segregating mail and database domains yields the following benefits:

- Domain Directories can be optimized for each domain because of different performance and data requirements for mail and database.

- Access control can be standardized for the database domain, with a single entry/exit point for replication.

- Administrative duties can be segregated, and therefore standardized, by domain function.

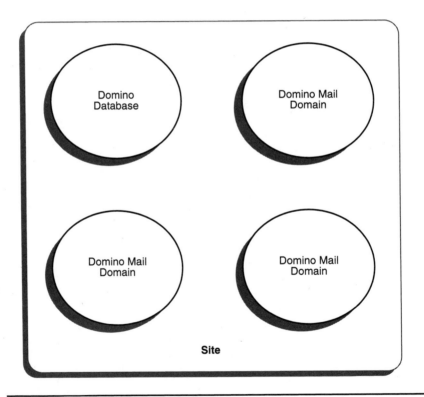

Figure 3.11. Site concept.

The IBM Mail domain strategy defines a single mail domain by country. The choice of defining a mail domain by country has the following virtues:

- It is easily understood by users.

- National languages can be considered (e.g., character sets).

- Consistency with IBM's Internet naming convention is maintained.

- Most mail traffic will occur within a country, so most mail will be within the country's domain and, therefore, will be most efficient.

- Administrative activity will be minimized because most user movement tends to be within a given country.

If Directory performance becomes a problem because too many people are in a domain (the U.S. domain comes to mind), a fallback alternative design of more then one domain per country is in place.

More than one mail domain will be supported within an IBM computing site. Support for the Directory (or directories) and other system-related files requiring replication will be provided by a hub/spoke, pull/pull replication architecture (see "Getting It from Here to There" for more details). The mail and database domains are, of course, production domains; that is, real work gets performed on them. In addition, IBM has set up small development domains for their programmers.

The applications development domain is a Domino environment in which authorized Domino developers may perform new application development, make enhancements, and fix bugs. This environment mirrors many of the aspects found in production but will be a separate physical and logical environment and will be restricted to developer staff only. The servers that compose this domain span a number of sites and geographic locations. The decision to place a server at a given site depends on the unique development needs of that site and the customers it serves. The application development domain is a closed environment with one external (outside its own domain) connection to the application test domain.

The application test domain is an independent Domino environment in which the administrative staff performs integration testing on applications that have passed through the development process. There are database connection records from the application development domain to the test domain and from the test domain to each site's production database domain. Figure 3.12 shows the relationship of the application development domain and the test domain to the production domains at a site.

Getting It from Here to There: Replication and Routing

Domino uses two approaches to transmit data from place to place over a network: replication and routing. Replication is the process by which information is distributed among servers or between servers and clients. Routing is the process by which mail is passed among servers or between servers and clients.

How the servers are organized within a domain determines the efficiency of replication and routing. There are four primary types of server organizations to consider in your routing and replication infrastructure, as illustrated in Figure 3.13:

1. **Hub and Spoke.** One or more hub servers replicate or route to spoke servers. The hub connects to each spoke server to perform scheduled replication/routing. A hub can be used to

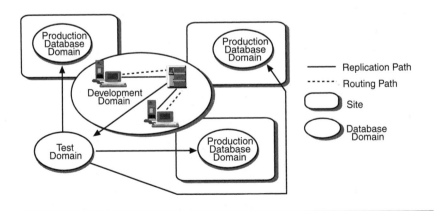

Figure 3.12. Development and test domains.

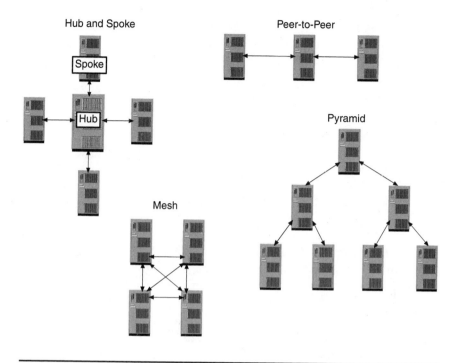

Figure 3.13. Server organization examples.

bridge between two networks running different network protocols if the hub server runs both protocols.

2. **Pyramid.** Servers are arranged in a pyramid configuration. One server replicates with two servers on the next level down and so on. This is less efficient than the hub-and-spoke configuration because of the time elapsed before the information reaches to lowest level of the pyramid. However, this approach works well in international organizations in which slower long-distance network connections must be negotiated and time zone differences obviate the need for more frequent communication.

3. **Peer-to-Peer.** Replication or routing is scheduled between adjacent servers in a domain. This works best for small sites with few servers.

4. **Mesh.** Replication or routing is scheduled among a set of servers, and each server communicates with every other as shown. This approach is typically employed among a set of hub servers to minimize the number of routing hubs in a chain of communication.

Most Domino server installations are organized in a hub-and-spoke topology, with all hubs arranged in a mesh. This approach minimizes the number of hops for replication and routing, where a hop is defined as a direct data transmission from server to server. It also offers the benefit of simpler administration because fewer connection records in the Directory need to be maintained. A good rule of thumb for a large, possibly international, network is to design it such that there are a maximum of three hops for replication and maximum of five hops for mail routing. Figure 3.14 summarizes a "time-to-traverse" replication strategy.

A typical replication strategy in a hub-and-spoke topology is to have the hubs initiate the replication to the spokes and with other hubs. A typical mail routing strategy is to initiate server-to-server routing based on a preset schedule, such as every 15 minutes. However, thresholds can be set up so that mail routing is initiated when a

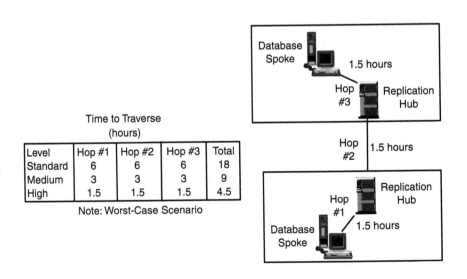

Time to Traverse (hours)

Level	Hop #1	Hop #2	Hop #3	Total
Standard	6	6	6	18
Medium	3	3	3	9
High	1.5	1.5	1.5	4.5

Note: Worst-Case Scenario

Figure 3.14. Intersite replication service levels.

specified number of messages are pending to be routed. Your mail routing strategy can be combined with your replication strategy, because servers can replicate and route mail during the same connection. Similarly, you need to establish a well-defined set of replication service levels to meet the needs of your database owners. It is useful to set up three or four main levels of service.

1. **Standard Service.** Once per day, 7 days per week.

2. **Medium Service.** Every 8 hours, 24 hours per day, 7 days per week.

3. **High Service.** Every 4 hours, 24 hours per day, 7 days per week.

4. **Priority Service.** Hourly, 24 hours per day, 7 days per week.

IBM has consolidated its computing resources into several large, centralized computing sites for operational and cost efficiency. These sites supply enterprise computing services to many other IBM locations around the world. The IBM database domains, supported at these sites, are built based on a hub-and-spoke architecture using the traditional pull/pull replication method. This means that hub servers initiate replication with each of the spoke servers. There is a hub server dedicated to each of the replication priority service levels (high, medium, and standard) within a domain. Domino 5.0 introduces a new multithreaded replicator technology that greatly enhances a hub's ability to service outlying spoke servers. Connectivity for inter-enterprise replication and mail-enabled database applications is supported. Database connectivity among the sites is achieved with a hierarchical design, with hubs connected peer to peer between sites (see Figure 3.15). This was selected because of the limited number of sites and the need for quick intersite replication.

Intrasite routing (i.e., connectivity to other mail domains within the site) is handled with a hierarchical design. Minor domain hub servers route to the major domain's routing hub server on the site, which in turn routes mail to the target domain's routing hub server. Figure 3.16 illustrates this approach. The major domains' routing hub servers on each site are connected in a worldwide mesh to provide intersite mail routing.

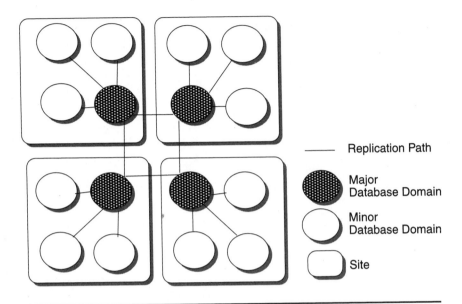

Figure 3.15. Intersite mail routing.

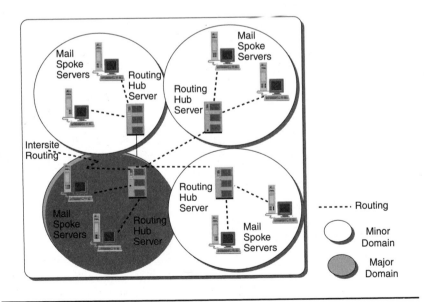

Figure 3.16. Intrasite routing.

Within a domain on a typical network, Domino mail routing service should be nearly instantaneous from the user's perception, with no more than a 1- to 2-minute delay during peak periods of the working day. When routing across domains or from site to site, a reasonable goal is 10-minute routing service times, with no more than a 30-minute delay during peak periods. In the unlikely event of a system or network link failure, Domino servers should be configured for a 24-hour mail store-and-forward period. This feature allows Domino to periodically retry linking to a server and routing messages for up to a day.

Intranet Gateways

So far we have discussed the simple cases of Domino-to-Domino mail routing. The complexity comes in supporting mail transfer between different systems in your enterprise and between your enterprise and individuals outside the company. This means that you need gateways (systems designed to translate a received file into another format and pass it on to its intended destination on the network). Your gateway and interconnect strategy should provide a tiered service approach as illustrated in Figure 3.17. The bottom tier is the Domino servers, the second tier is comprised of the hub servers, and the top tier is occupied by the gateway servers with their specific functionality. Each gateway requirement will vary depending on its user population and communication needs.

For e-mail interoperability with the Internet, you could use a Domino server as an Internet gateway because it includes native SMTP support. The Directory records should be created to specify e-mail transport via SMTP both to and from your Internet gateway. The same service levels provided for internal e-mail routing should apply to Internet e-mail up to the point of transfer to the SMTP gateway.

Sometimes gateway systems are required temporarily (during a migration period) or for relatively light loads. For example, if two e-mail systems are needed during a short migration period, then a simple system-to-system gateway should be fine. However, if the co-existence period is expected to be long, multiple systems are involved, message contents include rich text and attachments, and message traffic is heavy at times (requiring management), then installation of a **backbone switch** may be appropriate. A backbone switch, or mail switch, is a

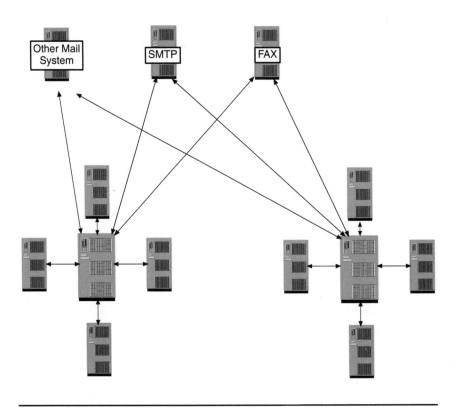

Figure 3.17. Gateway interconnect strategy.

gateway system that supports multiple mail protocols, including industry standards such as **X.400**, and is designed for high levels of traffic. The Lotus Message Switch (LMS), is an example of a backbone switch. The LMS was chosen by IBM as its backbone switch for coexistence between Lotus Domino Mail and OfficeVision/VM during its large-scale migration to Notes. In addition to support for multiple mail protocols (e.g., SMTP, OfficeVision), the LMS provides directory synchronization, cross-directory maintenance, and integrated management features. Directory synchronization means that the e-mail addressing directories for different e-mail systems are maintained in synch to ensure accurate communications.

Domino-to-Domino data exchange between your company and a business partner is a common strategy if both parties have Domino

infrastructures. This is a likely requirement if rich text is an important component, a workflow application is needed, or highly secure
or encrypted communications are needed. This extranet, as initially
discussed in Chapter 1, can be established over the Internet or a private WAN link, as shown in Figure 3.18. The intranet users, your
employees, deposit/access data from the Domino server on the intranet.
Internal server–to–external server replication occurs through your
firewall, making the Domino data available to your business partner.
Note that this method doesn't work for mail routing over IP (Internet
Protocol).

As your intranet matures, a major opportunity for cost reduction
that should be considered is utilizing a fax gateway for softcopy fax
support. Small to medium-sized companies should consider the
Domino Fax Server product as a solution. Large companies should
consider installing the Lotus mailFax product in conjunction with
the Lotus Mail Switch, as illustrated in Figure 3.19. As described in
Chapter 2, faxes can be originated from Notes e-mail and will be
received there as well by your users. Similarly, the Lotus Pager Gateway product can be established on your intranet to route pages to
and from users' Domino mail. This gateway will be welcomed by
your administrators, too, for handling their communications and
alerts.

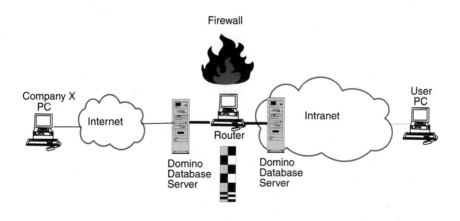

Figure 3.18. Inter-enterprise Domino data exchange.

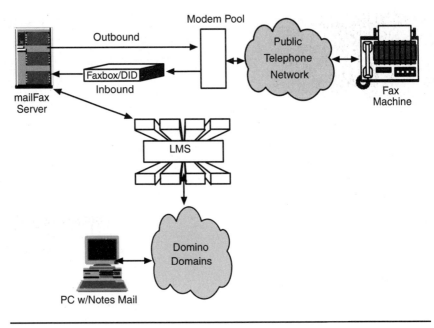

Figure 3.19. mailFax infrastructure.

Server Performance Considerations

As we have seen, a typical Domino infrastructure at a large company will contain a suite of specialized servers serving different application and data distribution (routing, replications) requirements. Earlier in this section, we discussed server selection based on availability, processing power, and replication requirements in a very general context. It is a good idea to zero in on specific categories of Domino servers and their unique application demands to avoid performance bottlenecks. Figure 3.20 looks at mail servers, database servers, mail routing hubs, and database replication hubs separately. [Mullen, 1996]. Of the four, the database replication hub will benefit most from multiple CPUs or processors due to its intensive logical processing. Domino is very sensitive to available system memory (RAM) in general--all servers, except the mail routing and replication hubs, will benefit from increasing RAM. For example, IBM has standardized on 1 GB of RAM for all Mail servers and 512 MB of RAM for hubs.

	Mail Server	Database Server	Mail Routing Hub	Replication Hub
CPU	Single	Single	Single	Multiple
RAM	Yes	Yes	No	Yes
NSF Buffer	Yes	Yes	No	No

[Mullen, 1996]

Figure 3.20. Domino server performance characteristics.

The NSF buffer is a table kept in RAM by Domino to contain indices to Domino databases that are currently in use. Increasing the size of this buffer will improve Domino's performance when there is a lot of end-user interaction—requesting views and full-text searches. This occurs on mail and database servers.

What's in a Name?

As described in Chapter 2, every Domino user has a unique name to identify him or her to the Domino application. This name is used to grant authority to access Domino applications by specification in an Access Control List (ACL), and it is used to transmit mail and other documents to the user. Your organization's names are placed in the Directory, enabling users to address a Domino mail message to anyone in the enterprise.

Some thought up front is required as you assign names to your users. Basically, you want to avoid name collisions or duplicates, and you want a naming scheme that is easily administered (and remembered). No matter what size your company is, you should implement a hierarchical naming scheme that considers your company's organizational units. Not only will this ensure unique names, administration will be simplified. Figure 3.21 illustrates the naming approach that IBM is using across its large company.

A hierarchical name should always have a common name (e.g., Jane Doe) and an organization name (e.g., YourCo). Optionally, you can include country code and up to four levels of organizational unit

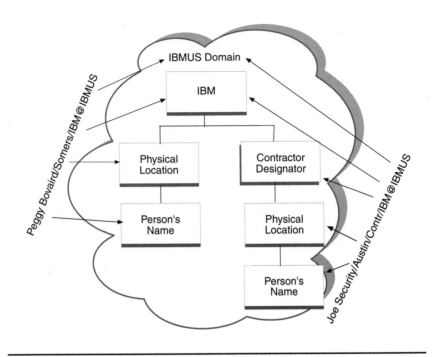

Figure 3.21. IBM naming hierarchy.

names. Within your hierarchy, you should limit the number of organizational units. A good approach is to define the organizational unit around your company's geography. For example, if your company operates in California, Oregon, and Washington, you should define one organizational unit for each state. In addition, you should create an organizational unit for external connections (the YourCo unit). Figure 3.22 provides an example.

The hierarchy you set up for names also is used for managing data access with the Notes certificate administration process. Figure 3.23 illustrates how certificates provide security in a Domino system. When your Notes ID--the personalized file, stored on your PC, that identifies you as a valid Notes licensee--is created, it is stamped with a certificate. Whenever you attempt to connect to a Domino server, your certificate authenticates you to the server, allowing you to use Domino. If your company uses hierarchical certificates, each user will get a company certificate (the highest level) for access to the

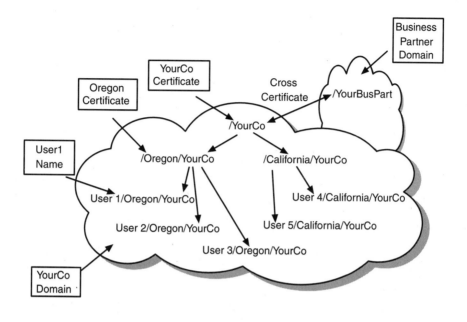

Figure 3.22. Notes naming and certification hierarchy.

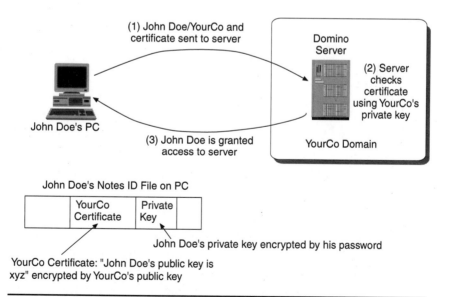

Figure 3.23. Getting certified.

generally accessible Domino servers and Domino databases. Typically, a user will get additional organizational certificates for access to more restricted servers and, hence, databases.

Because all other certificate levels descend from the company certificate, tight control of the certificate file is very important. If security is compromised, this top-level certificate would need to be re-created, as would all of the lower levels, and all user and server IDs would need to be recertified. Tight physical control of this certificate is key! Four levels of password protection held by four different individuals is recommended, with any two of these passwords/individuals needed to allow access to the certificate.

One of the main benefits of using hierarchical certification is apparent when adjusting access controls in Domino databases. For example, you create an ACL entry in a company bulletins database to ***/YourCo** and set its role to be Reader. This entry implies that anyone with a name in the Directory that has a last qualifier of YourCo (i.e., has a YourCo certificate) can read data from the database. The * is a wildcard, which means anything before the **/YourCo** is OK. To block everyone else, just set the default entry in the ACL to No Access—this forces the ACL check for valid names, which will only be YourCo employees.

Many enterprises use Notes-style addressing for purely intranet communication and Internet-style e-mail addressing for extranet or Internet communication. For cxample, my e-mail address is Steve Krantz/Boca Raton/IBM@IBMUS in Notes-style addressing, but krantz@us.ibm.com in Internet-style addressing. With Domino 5.0, you can take advantage of the ability to standardize your employee's e-mail address usage with the Internet style alone while continuing to use the Notes naming hierarchy for certification and authentication. For many people, this improves e-mail usability significantly. The Directory supports this by placing the Internet-style e-mail address in the new Internet address field in each Person document.

Domain Names

Domain names should have their own standard, too, if your company is large and has multiple, international domains. A simple convention using your company's name, followed by a country code, followed by a sequence number can easily be established. Inside IBM, domains are named with IBM as leading characters and the standard

CCITT (International Consultative Committee for Telephony and Telegraphy) country code. For example, IBMGB is the name of the mail domain in IBM United Kingdom, where IBM are the lead characters and GB is the CCITT code.

Network and Connect Record Names

Servers can be associated with each other as members of the same domain by being defined in the Directory of that domain (the Server document). Within a domain, it is useful to group servers as part of the same network within a domain by having the administrator specifying a common Network Name for each server in the group in its respective Server document. A common Network Name will present a set of servers to users in the File>Open Database dialogue box conveniently. Also, no connection records are needed to route mail among servers with the same Network Name. These servers must be physically connected on the network and have a common network protocol (e.g., TCP/IP). On a large network, a naming convention for Network Names is important. An example on IBM's large network is TCPIP0A, where TCPIP is the protocol (TCP/IP), 0 is the port number, and A is the first protocol on this port. Figure 3.24 illustrates the Named Network concept.

User Group Names

Public group names are group names that reside in a Directory. They are used for e-mail distribution lists and are convenient as ACL entries to control access control to databases. Because they are public, it is useful to reserve a few names and have a naming convention for the rest. For example, IBM Domino administration has reserved public group names for administrators, contractors, local domain servers, servers in other domains, and terminated employees (for security purposes). Users need public groups for easy communication with departments or larger organizations, so a naming convention is useful here too. The recommended approach for IBM is to divide up the group name into sections delimited by dashes as follows: **aaaaa-bbbb-cccc-dddd**. The first section would be for a unique description, the second for business organization subgroup, the third for geographic region, and the last for the business organization. Be careful, though, not to use server names as group names!

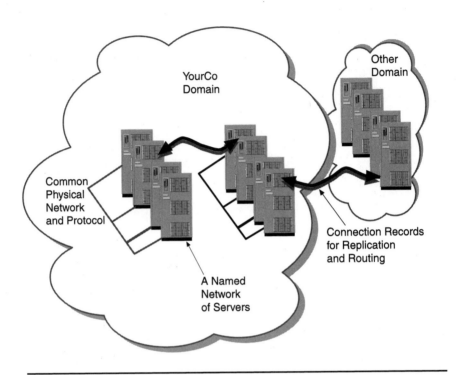

Figure 3.24. Named network illustration.

Server Names

Domino servers need names, too. Server names are used with connection records, server records, access control lists, user groups, and desktop icons, and as components in the hierarchical naming scheme. They should be meaningful and unique so that they are easily recognized (primarily by administrators and secondarily by users). Administrators need to name servers in their daily tasks. Users, on the other hand, can be shielded from server names—by using database catalogs, for example. A simple naming convention with the first two characters reserved for a domain "code" and the remaining unique to the server can be adopted.

Like user names, server names should be hierarchical and have organizational unit and organization elements. An example hierarchy is illustrated in Figure 3.25. The top-level organizational certifier should be the same for both the server and client hierarchy. The

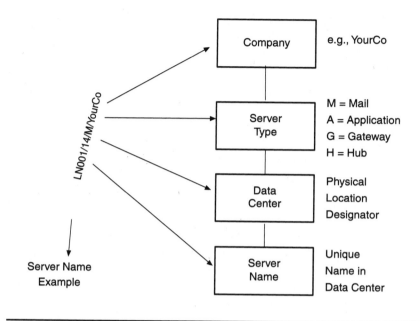

Figure 3.25. Server name hierarchy.

server type code is a single-letter alphabetic character that identifies the purpose of the machine. This type code in the name gives administrators and application developers broader capability for controlling access. For example, */H/YourCo may be listed in the database ACL as Manager instead of a group name or explicit server name(s). This eliminates group security issues or failed replication due to groups being deleted from the Directory. Similarly, */A/YourCo can be listed as Editor in an application's ACL instead of the explicit server name. The Data Center code is useful to control Notes access (e.g., over the WAN) as well as by administrators to quickly identify the server's physical location and support group.

Administrative Tools

The Domino Administrator provides an administrative control panel (see Figure 3.26) that lets administrators manage multiple local and remote Domino servers from their personal PCs. Administrators will

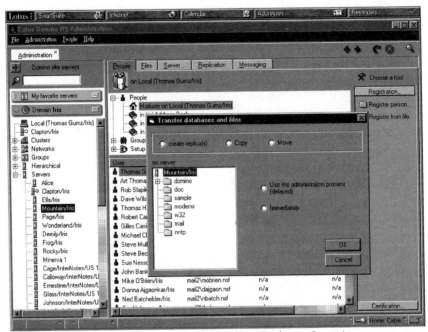

2000 Lotus Development Corporation. Used with permission of Lotus Development Corporation.

Figure 3.26. Domino Administrator.

have high-level, quick, and easy access to replication information. They can drill down to the network, cluster, and server that they are responsible for. They can track, compile, and analyze system usage, and they can monitor trends for more efficient resource planning and deployment. Because there are no Domino maintenance procedures that require taking the server off-line, round-the-clock (i.e., 7 × 24) availability is practical. This enhanced user interface provides drag and drop features to allow administrators to move databases and users from server to server, with accompanying information update such as connection documents, configuration documents, and a client's location document. Administration can also be performed across domains.

Other tools, databases, and files that round out the administrator's kit bag include the following:

- The Directory is the Domino database that contains all the information that defines your Domino system. It contains connection (server-to-server communication), program (server task specification), and group documents (which define sets of users for access control purposes), and other documents for user management.

- Administration databases help analyze and track your Domino system operation. They include a log of server activities, statistics databases (a compilation of events and alarms, and how to respond to them), authorization lists (certificates), and a catalog of all Domino databases.

- Administrator program tools consist of administrator commands to start up, shut down, or otherwise control Domino server functions. There are specialized server programs that perform batch operations for server maintenance (e.g., database space compaction). An Agent Manager is provided to control server-based agent operation. Agents can be event or schedule triggered to run other programs and/or interact with Domino databases. An Administration Process program helps automate user-related administration tasks.

- The **NOTES.INI** file contains configuration details about how Notes is to run.

Domino Security

For most significant end-user applications, such as business commerce transactions, security is a critical issue. Sensitive transactions need secure data transmission between your intranet and the Internet, for example. Remote users from external locations need to be authenticated before being granted access to your key intranet servers.

Domino provides secure data communications and user authentication for Web browser clients. Authentication is enabled by adding an encrypted user password field in the Person record of the Directory. When users try to access restricted information on the server, they are challenged for this password. Note that this password is distinct from the Notes password that is part of the traditional Notes client ID file.

For the garden-variety anonymous Web client there will be no corresponding entry in the Directory. These clients would only be able to access unrestricted information from your Web site. Information that is unrestricted or available for public access by an anonymous user is indicated explicitly by creating an Anonymous entry in the ACL of any Domino database with unrestricted information. Assigning an appropriate role, such as Reader, to Anonymous enables any random browser to read the database's contents. If you do not add an Anonymous entry, the default entry role is used to determine access and can serve a similar purpose. Conversely, to protect databases from anonymous users, simply assign No Access to Anonymous. Domino will then challenge all seeking access for their name and password. After a successful password challenge, the user name must then match the ACL entry, as usual.

On your Web site, you should set the default access to Reader on your home database to allow everyone to access it. If you register users to your site, requesting their name and returning a password, you can add this information to the Directory dynamically. In addition, you can create a group with all user names (Usernames Group) and insert it in databases restricted to registered users. If you have a discussion database, for example, default access can be set to No Access, causing a subsequent password challenge and a lookup in the ACL for the supplied user name. If Usernames Group is in the ACL, the requesting user's name must be present in the group. This allows the user to contribute to the discussion, assuming, of course, that the role assigned to Usernames is Author.

The combination of Notes role-based security and Domino offers very powerful features. For example, a Web browser client can create Web pages when using an application via Domino through an assigned role in the Access Control List. Each time the user retrieves a page that user previously created, he or she is given the option to change or delete it. Another user, with a more restrictive role in the ACL, would not see these options. Similarly, a Domino-based intranet, using Domino's selective replication in combination with its granular security, offers powerful features to communicate with business partners or customers across the Internet. For example, you could create a product information database with both cost and price information that you replicate to your customers through your firewall. However, you selectively protect the cost data through field-level security restriction.

Note that the certificate-based authentication for Notes clients is more secure than the Web client capability, as previously discussed. The Notes client ID file contains an encrypted certificate and through interaction with the server authenticates the user with additional confidence. Figure 2.15 contrasts Notes and Web client security.

Domino includes Secure Sockets Layers (SSL) support to provide secure communications between client and server. This includes server authentication and encryption of data during transmission.

Setting Up a Web Site with Domino

A Domino Web site from a Notes perspective appears as one or more Domino databases. At a minimum, you need one home database. The home page document in the home database with a designated URL becomes your Web site's home page via Domino. By entering the name of your home database as the Home URL setting in the associated server record in the Directory, you direct Domino to open it when a user visits the Web site. Your home page can either be the About page of the database or a navigator. Setting the Launch option of your home database to your home page (i.e., the About document or a selected navigator) establishes the home page to Domino. Hence, it appears automatically for each new visitor. If you want to include more than one Domino database as part of your Web site, add links to these databases on your home page document.

You must create a special Domino users group in the Directory to register Web users. You can then give group members access to databases at a variety of security levels—Depositor, Author, Editor, and so on. Security administration is at the database level, where access control is precise and superior to industry-standard Web server offerings. You can also create an Anonymous entry in an ACL to give access to unregistered users.

A typical site provides a variety of user applications—document repositories, discussions, product order taking, and so on—so it is useful to create multiple Domino databases for your Domino Web site. This will simplify application development and maintenance. Data entry can be readily distributed among multiple authors. In fact, this approach enables both local and remote authorship, because Domino supports local, personal replicas. Creating separate databases makes it possible to treat separately applications that grow arbitrarily large and require more careful management.

As a company-level Web site, the Domino server greatly simplifies the process of managing Web pages. The Domino document database organization creates stable, implied links that facilitate creation of Web applications. When these features are considered from a Web site administration perspective, the value is compelling. A striking contrast is provided by an example in *Computer Reseller News.* [Anonymous, 1996]. If we consider a Web page about a new customer to our Web site, it would be useful to have an indexed listing sorted by categories such as by author, by customer, by industry, or by product ordered. For example, I want to be able to click on the page's author's name to get a list of all of the author's pages or click on the customer's name to get a list of all of the customer's orders, and so on. Links quickly multiply. If I have 1000 pages (customers) and each page has 10 links, there are 10,000 links to maintain manually! On the other hand, Domino document databases are much more sophisticated than Web page file management systems. Every Web page you store in a Domino database can be automatically indexed by a set of predefined views (e.g., author, date, customer, etc.). In addition, the administrator is a point and click away from adding new views—each implying new links for browser clients.

A unique Domino feature is the ability to host multiple, "virtual" Web sites on a single physical server. This capability can be used to have multiple, independent applications within your intranet. In addition, this is especially useful to an Internet Service Provider (**ISP**) that supports more than one customer. Each virtual Web site can be set up with its own unique, permanent IP address, home page, and so on. However, the Domino databases and directories are the same for all virtual sites.

Domino supports up to six servers, which can be clustered for load balancing and redundancy for Notes client activity. This facility is called the Domino Cluster Manager. At an administrator-determined threshold level, if the number of sessions are excessive, they are automatically migrated to another server in the cluster. This capability is supported by Domino's powerful replication feature. By configuring a server cluster to replicate in real time, it appears as a single server to the end user. The servers become mutually redundant and, as a result, fault tolerant.

An Internet Cluster Manager (ICM) has been included with Domino Release 5.0 to provide similar load balancing and redundancy for Web clients. Web clients direct requests for databases to the ICM which then determines the best server to process the request.

Domino vs. the Competition

Figure 3.27 provides a summary comparison of data, database, application development, and user interfaces for Notes, Domino, and traditional intranet environments.

Considering a business' overall requirements in context, an intranet composed of Domino servers with a mix of Notes and Web browser

	Notes/Domino Intranet	Domino Intranet	Traditional Intranet
Client type	Notes client	Web browser client	Web browser client
Database	Documents with rich text, hypertext, forms, tables, multimedia	Documents with text, graphics, multimedia, hypertext	Documents with text, graphics, multimedia, hypertext
Data management	Distributed, field-level data replication	Distributed, field-level data replication	Mirroring
Application development	Database customization with Java, LotusScript, formula language, CGI, C++	Database customization with Java, LotusScript, formula language, CGI, C++	Java , Microsoft's ActiveX emerging (Multiple Development Tools); Server APIs: CGI, industry-standard languages (C, C++, PERL, etc.)
User interface	Mature, windowed, notebook metaphor	Rapidly developing	Rapidly developing

Figure 3.27. Data and application comparison.

clients appears to meet the need for both internal applications and external Internet presence. Figure 3.28 illustrates this in terms of a logical network and provides the notion of segmenting client functionality--knowledge workers with full-function PCs receiving the full Notes client, administrative workers with network computers (NCs) receiving a Web browser. This approach is a cost-effective solution that minimizes client support. At the highest levels of consideration, Figure 3.29 contrasts a combined Notes/Domino environment with the traditional intranet.

It appears that there are three major competitors to Lotus in providing a comprehensive product that attempts to duplicate Domino/Notes functionality: Netscape's SuiteSpot, Microsoft's Exchange, and Novell's GroupWise. Netscape's SuiteSpot originated as what we have been calling a garden-variety traditional intranet product and is broadening its offering to include the Domino groupware features. Microsoft's Exchange is broadening its product to stay competitive with Netscape and at the same time build in competitive groupware features. Novell's GroupWise appears to be following a path similar to Microsoft.

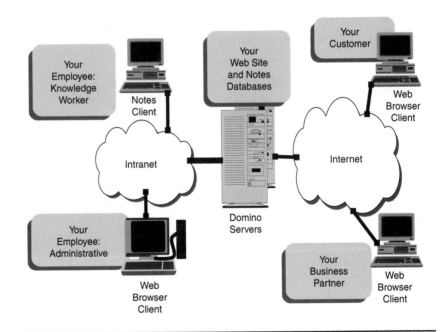

Figure 3.28. The Domino platform.

	Notes/Domino Intranet	Traditional Intranet
Openness, interoperating across heterogeneous domains	Yes	Yes
Scaleability, no loss of function or performance	Yes	Yes
Data integrity, security and auditabliity	Yes, mature	Budding
Interoperability, internal and external	Notes-to-Domino server and browser-to-Domino server intranet with Internet connection through firewall	Browser-to-server intranet with Internet connection through firewall
Strategic application delivery	Mature to known users	Budding - known and unknown users

[Kador, 1996]

Figure 3.29. Notes/Domino vs. traditional intranet.

There are many trade press comparisons and consultant studies of the major groupware product suites. Following are extracts from a few of them:

In an October, 1999 InternetWeek *article, David Drucker wrote that "despite the improvements, it appears that [Microsoft] Exchange 2000 won't be a Lotus Notes killer." Deficits in knowledge management and collaboration tools were cited as reasons for this analysis.*

InternetWeek *has given its groupware Best of Breed award to Lotus. [Rist, 1998]*

The Gartner group has recognized Notes popularity in non-Web" groupware and predicts that over time most Notes/ Domino applications will be Web-based. [Anonymous, 1998a]

A WebWeek *article shows Lotus Notes/Domino 4.6 leading its competitors Microsoft (Exchange 5.5) and Netscape in e-mail users by a large margin. [Roberts, 1998]*

In a satisfaction study comparing Web server software, Domino 4.5 was rated superior to Microsoft's Internet Information Server in 72 of 75 product and vendor attributes. [Anonymous, 1998a, 1998b]

A significant Notes/Domino differentiator is its scalability. Notes/Domino scales to hundreds of thousands of users, far exceeding the capability of competitors such as Microsoft Exchange. The Directory can support one million entries and scale to support tens of thousands of simultaneous user client connections per single server, such as the IBM S/390.

Lower cost is the general perception of most companies when considering a traditional intranet solution versus a Notes/Domino intranet solution. However, prior studies have indicated that Notes/Domino has demonstrated lowest cost of ownership over the long term. Analyzing relative costs of development, deployment, and maintenance revealed that Domino was relatively easier and much quicker to set up and operate than the traditional intranet solutions. Deployment and maintenance hours were reduced as well.

According to a Gartner Group study, most enterprises using Domino are spending a lot more on implementation than those using other products. However, they determined that the Domino "usage profile" was very different from that of its competitors. It is likely that the use of Notes in creating custom groupware, an area not well served by competition, was driving the Domino implementation costs higher. They do concede that "it is possible to do some things inexpensively with Domino," based on details gleaned from their enterprise surveys. Gartner concludes that business requirements are most important for this type of product, and cost is secondary. Cost per user per month varied from $2 to $44 based on unique usage from enterprise to enterprise.

Domino Futures

Lotus's continuing Domino strategy is to extend Domino as a "pure" Internet standards-based offering. With Release 5.0, Notes clients support Java applet execution, and Domino servers will serve pages that include Java applets and scripting languages such as JavaScript. (A scripting language allows a user to create a "script" or a set of interpreted application controls.) This support will enable developers to deliver Java-based solutions to Notes and Web browser users through the Domino platform.

One Lotus goal is to improve the consistency of the user interfaces delivered by Domino to Web browsers and to Notes clients. Java applets will be used to bridge the current gaps. Development tools will be created to foster Java agents and applications to promote cross-platform development. This means a commitment to the JavaBeans specification for Domino and its clients. Current Notes customers have much to gain with very little additional investment to extend Domino support to all intranet users. This will enable them to expand delivery of groupware applications to Web browser clients. This can simplify support for remote users (e.g., travelers or work-at-home folk) and for public intranet access facilities via inexpensive NC devices.

Businesses with an existing traditional intranet seeking to deliver groupware applications to their employees have a different choice. They can supplement their current intranet with Domino servers or rebuild it for long-term ease of management with a comprehensive Domino environment.

Most businesses need to consider their total requirements and invest in a comprehensive product suite for their intranet. In contrast with traditional intranet suites, a pure Domino infrastructure is superior. By combining Domino with Notes, a mix of client capability is available, making an unbeatable, low-cost-of-ownership combination.

Summary

Technically, Domino is a server platform designed to support both Notes and Web browser clients. For the end user, Domino enriches the capability of the Web browser client as well as the functionality of the Notes client. For the administrator/developer, Domino's Notes heritage greatly simplifies application development and Web site management.

Note that three primary configurations of the Domino Server are now being delivered by Lotus to its customers: the Domino Mail Server, the Domino Application Server, and the Domino Enterprise Server. Each includes the base server capabilities plus features/functions to address e-mail, applications, and enterprise requirements, respectively. The Domino Mail Server consists of the base including Notes and Internet messaging support, the Domino Application Server incorporates the Mail Server function plus tools and features to support Notes groupware applications, and the Domino Enterprise Server incorporates the Application Server function plus server clustering.

4

Your Intranet Application Programs

An intranet fits in your business with its application programs, defined as end-user software tools that solve business problems, and links to information such as legacy databases. The application programs are of paramount importance in your intranet because they *are* the intranet as far as the users are concerned. For this reason, the selection and development of reliable, effective, and easy-to-use application programs is vital to any computing solution (intranet or not). This chapter assesses the broad spectrum of business applications in terms of personal and team use, and provides concrete examples showing how Domino applications fit these needs and can improve productivity and information sharing in your company. Examples of how Domino solutions are being applied within the IBM company are described, development and support issues are discussed, and applications are assessed with regard to their organizational impact, their operating environment, and their relationship to legacy systems. Some real-world examples are described, and a methodology for application development and deployment is discussed. The chapter winds up with a recommendation for ongoing application management.

Selecting Applications

You should define a set of basic requirements that all intranet application programs should meet. For the most part, these requirements will be obvious characteristics that all users would recognize and agree upon. Nevertheless, they should be explicitly defined up front so that they are addressed early on in the application selection process. Following are a reasonable requirements starter set:

- **Consistent, User-Friendly Interfaces.** A graphic user interface (GUI) is a highly recommended standard. Consistent, friendly interfaces are easy for users to learn and remember.

- **Solid Performance.** Within a major application area, applications should exhibit acceptable performance on the site's standard operating system and hardware platform. Trivial user interactions, such as menu selections, should be instantaneous. File loading or saving time should be proportional to file size. For example, a small file (a page of text) should load instantaneously. Other interactions will vary by application, but a good rule of thumb is that the delay should not impede the user from completing his or her task.

- **Reliability.** Applications should have a track record of reliability in the user community at large prior to wide deployment. For standard application categories, such as word processors or spreadsheets, many solid candidates meet this criterion. For more specialized or new applications, an internal testing program may be required to assure reliability.

- **Interoperability.** Your applications should exhibit inter-operability. Data files created in one application should be able to be used by a second application. Interoperability with **legacy** applications (i.e., existing mainframe applications) and systems is often mandatory. Applications where this is usually important include electronic mail, calendaring, and file transfer.

- **Low Cost.** Depending upon the size of your user community, there are alternatives to minimize application cost. These include purchase of an enterprise license covering all users or purchase of network licenses, whereby license fees are paid based on the number of simultaneous network users (not individual copies).

Interoperability, user productivity, and low costs are very important to intranet management. A highly effective way to foster all three is to control software application use and development. You can control use by buying, installing, and supporting only standard applications on the enterprise network. With only standard applications available for use (e.g., one word processor, one spreadsheet), interoperability is assured. All users learn one, and only one, tool, resulting in increased knowledge sharing and expertise. Volume purchase discounts for licenses are possible, resulting in lower costs.

Application Categories

Figure 4.1 shows a conceptual view of an enterprise and its application programs. Most application programs can be placed in one of the three categories depicted in the figure. The outer ring corresponds to individual user applications, or personal applications, which aid the users in their daily office activities. The middle ring corresponds to team applications, applications that support teams of users. In an intranet, these applications are sometimes called workflow or groupware applications that run on servers. Team applications facilitate the flow of work among a group or team of users communicating on an intranet.

There is an inner core of applications that support the enterprise. These are a subset of the general team applications category, historically called **decision support** applications, or applications that provide users with access to a database containing enterprise-level business information. Today, this category of applications and associated data is called knowledge management. Enterprise-level and lower-level decision makers use knowledge management applications to make major decisions affecting the company (the really big team).

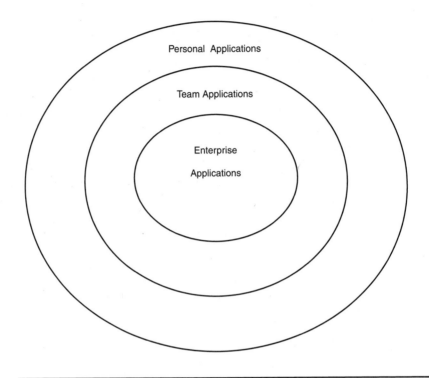

Figure 4.1. Enterprise application model.

Personal Applications Defined

Personal applications include electronic mail (e-mail), calendar, directory, word processing, spreadsheet calculations, business graphics applications, and database. This list represents, at a high level, the vast majority of individual application requirements in an enterprise. They are also "building blocks" for team applications, as we shall see.

Team Applications Defined

Team applications are defined at a high level as applications that are used by two or more individuals to share information. To understand them better, team applications can be categorized as e-mail, meetings, **forms processing** (e.g., surveys, requests for service, and applications), **document management** (e.g., creation, review, and storage of articles, and other publications), knowledge management, and **groupware** (as a general-purpose, catch-all category).

E-mail shows up in both the personal and team categories—it is special. It is used by individuals for simple correspondence, so it fits within the personal category. It is also an important "building block" application for other team applications.

Clearly, personal and team applications are highly interrelated. Personal applications are the building blocks upon which team applications are built. Figure 4.2 shows these relationships. From the individual user perspective (row 1), e-mail is important to communicate with other team members, to inform others of meetings, to transmit a form or document, and to transmit information for knowledge management or group sharing.

Team Applications

	E-Mail	Meet-ings	Forms	Docu-ments	Group-ware	Decision Support	
E-Mail	✓	✓	✓	✓	✓	✓	(1)
Calendar		✓			✓		(2)
Directory	✓	✓	✓	✓	✓	✓	(3)
Word Processing	✓	✓	✓	✓	✓	✓	(4)
Spreadsheet	✓			✓	✓	✓	(5)
Business Graphics	✓			✓	✓	✓	(6)
Database	✓		✓	✓	✓	✓	(7)
	(1)	(2)	(3)	(4)	(5)	(6)	

Personal Applications

Figure 4.2. Application interrelationships.

Correspondingly, from the team perspective (column 1), e-mail draws on most or all of the office applications for information generation and addressing (directory). Aside from keeping an individual's schedule, the calendar application supports the scheduling of team meetings (row 2). From the team perspective (column 2), the calendar application drives meeting scheduling through the use of the directory, supplemented by e-mail for notices and agendas created by the word processor. The directory application, aside from providing phone numbers to the individual, is a resource to workflow applications for e-mail addressing (row 3). The word processor (row 4) is useful to all workflow applications. The spreadsheet and business graphics applications (rows 5 and 6) create information useful for e-mail, documents, knowledge management, and group sharing. Forms processing (column 3) uses the word processor for creation, the directory for addressing, and e-mail for transmission. Document management and groupware applications draw on most of the office applications for creation and distribution of information (columns 4 and 5). The database application stores information for the individual user (row 7) and serves as the repository for all forms of team applications. A general conclusion is that personal applications and team applications are inseparable, because their requirements are inseparable.

Applications: The "Make or Buy" Decision

For all but a very few businesses, off-the-shelf office applications make the most sense. There is a broad selection of maturing client/server application alternatives that satisfy the majority of user requirements. You will see that in the area of team applications, you will need to invest in application building.

Application Program Requirements and Selection

Once you have settled on your basic application requirements, it is time to "peel the onion" and determine your specific requirements by application. Before any application programs are considered, it is imperative to clearly explore and define the actual and detailed needs of the users. The results of this exploration should be clearly documented. Failure to do this results in poor selection and dissatisfied end users. We will look at the two major application categories, personal and team, in turn.

Personal Applications Requirements

Understanding the personal application requirements for a business is a major first step in most organizations. A typical set of requirements, by application, includes:

- **Electronic Mail.** This must provide rapid worldwide transmission, near-instantaneous response time to create and send a message, the ability to categorize and store incoming and outgoing messages, consistent worldwide addressing for individuals and groups, and easy printing. Additional key features include mail reply (pressing a key initiates a new message with the incoming message's sender address filled in) and mail forward (pressing a key initiates a new message with the incoming message attached).

- **Calendar.** Requirements are the ability to specify daily and recurrent meetings and appointments, the ability to view other users' calendars, and the ability to conveniently print calendar information. An individual in a business working with others needs a calendar application to take advantage of associates' schedules to schedule meetings during open time slots. Additional requirements include putting "notes" or memos on the calendar and allowing calendar entries to be large enough to include meeting agendas.

- **Phone and Mail Directory.** An enterprise-wide directory containing your users' names, phone numbers, e-mail addresses, and other pertinent data is necessary. The directory should be searchable with both strict and fuzzy criteria. It should be easy to create a list of e-mail addresses for use and reuse to send mail to the group of users selected.

- **Word Processing.** A WYSIWYG word processor with a graphic user interface (**GUI**) is the requirement. **WYSIWYG** stands for What You See Is What You Get. It means that the on-screen view of the document created by the word processor looks like the printed output. The word processor's native file output format should be interoperable with the standard e-mail application. Print output options should include industry-standard data streams, such as PCL5 or PostScript.

- **Spreadsheet.** Three-dimensional spreadsheet capability with a GUI interface is the requirement (a three-dimensional spreadsheet is one that supports multiple two-dimensional sheets in a single file).

- **Business Graphics.** The ability to create visuals for presentations including text and graphics, and to create charts and graphs from numeric data is the requirement. The application should have a GUI interface. The native file output format should be accepted by the standard e-mail application selected. Print output options should include industry-standard data streams.

Selecting the Personal Applications

Once the requirements are clear, the application selection process can begin. You should gather information about available personal applications that meet your requirements. A good initial technique to employ is a paper comparison based upon vendor-supplied features. Requirements should be rated numerically (a scale from 1 to 10 is fine), with mandatory requirements receiving the highest value. Each application under evaluation should then be numerically rated for each applicable requirement (a scale of 1 to 10 works here, too), with top features receiving the highest rating. Multiplying each requirement rating by the corresponding application rating and then summing all values for an application provides an objective measurement. Figure 4.3 provides a simple example of this method. This measurement can be used to narrow down a field of several competitors to two or three. At this point, installation and application testing

Requirement	Rank	Rating	Application 1 Rank × Rating	Rating	Application 2 Rank × Rating	Rank	Application 3 Rank × Rating
Function 1	9	6	54	8	72	5	45
Function 2	5	5	25	6	30	8	40
Function 3	2	7	14	4	8	9	18
Function 4	8	8	64	3	24	10	80
Total			157		134		183

Selected Application

Figure 4.3. Application comparison.

(benchmarking) should be used to make the final selection. Following is a discussion of how Lotus Notes/Domino and Microsoft Office products meet personal application requirements.

For E-mail, It's Domino Mail

Lotus Domino, as we know, offers a mature, fully integrated e-mail system, as described in Chapter 2. As a Domino database, it shares the same three-pane user interface as other databases: a view pane where you select which messages to view, a pane listing the messages in the current view selection, and a preview pane of the currently selected message. Standard views include inbox, drafts, sent, and to do. You can create new messages and reply or forward old ones, attach files to your mail messages, and add a "mood stamp" to your messages to enliven them and set a priority on delivery. Received mail can be organized into folders for easy retrieval, which can be done with a simple drag and drop from the message list pane to the view pane's folder.

The Promise of Integrated Messaging

Beyond e-mail is the concept of integrated messaging: establishing a common processing platform for different forms of messages, such as e-mail, fax, pages, video, and voice. Each of these forms either originates or can be transformed in its processing into computer-readable form. An e-mail application, such as Lotus Domino, is an example of a primary platform for integrated messaging. Today, a user's Lotus Domino mail database with supporting applications (e.g., Fax for Domino) installed can support receipt, review, and response to e-mail, voice, fax, and page messages. In the future, a voice-mail system could support receipt, review, and response to e-mail, voice, and page messages. Synchronization of a user's voice-mail box and e-mail box using administrator-and user-defined rules are critical to successful development of this technology.

Fax data is transmitted over telephone lines in a compressed digital format (Group IV fax standard), allowing it to be readily supported by your employees' e-mail application. Called softcopy fax, the e-mail application, such as Lotus Domino, can be extended today to transmit faxes to a telephone number and receive/review inbound faxes directly within the Notes client. A Fax for Domino server must be installed on the network to serve as the control and distribution point for both inbound and outbound faxes to provide this functionality. Routing of faxes directly to Domino e-mail is supported in several ways—server administrator intervention and installation of **DID** (Direct Inward Dialing) lines for each incoming fax number are two examples. Optical Character Recognition (**OCR**) software is a common application option available to convert fax softcopy data to text for use in word processing. While viewing a fax, you can copy and paste graphical portions into WYSIWYG word processor documents, such as Microsoft Word, or into a Domino database document.

Pager systems are rapidly evolving from unidirectional, numerical data (telephone number), wireless, communication systems into sophisticated, two-way data transfer systems in which immediate employee contact is critical. As paging is integrated into e-mail and voice-mail platforms, your employees should be able to route incoming pages to e-mail, voice mail, fax, or pager as required. Similarly, more and more employees are using sophisticated cellular phone technology to stay connected with colleagues and the Internet. Mobile

Services for Domino provides a set of capabilities that can easily be enabled on a Domino server to support mobile employees with these wireless devices. Mobile Services for Domino is integrated with Domino's messaging and routing services. It functions as a "foreign" Domino mail domain and routes messages to and from pagers, cellular phones, and other mobile devices that support one-and two-way messaging. When you install Mobile Services for Domino, you can optionally create a Web site that enables your employees and customers to send messages to mobile devices and receive replies from a Web browser.

For Calendaring, It's Domino Calendaring and Scheduling

As described in Chapter 2, the Domino Mail database incorporates a calendar function. Key features such as personal and group scheduling with intersystem free-time search (e.g., with OfficeVision calendars) and the ability to operate in a disconnected mode make this a useful tool for most users.

For the Directory, It's the Domino Directory

The Domino Directory is a central repository for users to find e-mail addresses and for administrators to describe data routing and replication among a set of Domino servers. It can easily be extended to contain user telephone numbers or other related personnel information, making it a critical central repository for your organization. However, larger enterprises use the Directory solely for e-mail routing to maintain routing performance. With Release 5.0, the new Directory Catalog, described in Chapter 3, provides a compact, high-performance tool for end users to do convenient lookups.

For Personal Productivity, It's Microsoft Office

For word processing, spreadsheets, and business graphics, Microsoft Word, Excel, and PowerPoint are good selections (i.e., Microsoft Office). Word is a full-function, WYSIWYG word processor, with features competitive with other leading word processors. Excel meets the requirements for a three-dimensional GUI spreadsheet program. PowerPoint meets the requirements for business graphics and the ability to create high-quality visuals for presentations. The most compelling reason for selecting the Microsoft application suite is its easy integration with Lotus Notes, the centerpiece of the office client.

Team Application Requirements

Understanding the team application requirements for a business is a major second step in most organizations. A general set of requirements, by application, includes:

- **E-mail.** E-mail is considered the oldest and most widely used team application. Immediacy of transmission and receipt, the ability to attach all kinds of data files, and interoperability across diverse e-mail systems are the most important requirements from a team perspective.

- **Meetings.** An application that supports meetings should make it easy to schedule, reschedule, and cancel them over the intranet. It should also support repositories for meeting agendas, minutes, and visuals.

- **Forms.** A forms processing application needs to support easy form creation and modification over the intranet. It should be easy to use across a large number of employees. It must support form routing across the intranet and sometimes over the Internet, and it must support a database in which forms are stored, compiled, and ultimately reported on. In some cases, this database may have to be very large.

- **Document Management.** A document management application must be able to store multiple documents in a central repository for secure, multiuser access over the intranet. Multiple versions of a document for historical and group editing purposes may be required.

- **Groupware.** The term "groupware" is used in this book as a catch-all for general-purpose team applications that do not fit into the other categories and may use elements of each to support team activities. Customized applications should be easy to create, support a wide variety of data types for documents for sharing purposes, support intranet or Internet document routing, and be able to interface with other data repositories including end-user e-mail.

- **Knowledge Management.** A knowledge management application contains or allows the creation of a repository of summarized information to be used by analysts and executives for purposes of strategic decision making. It must link to or incorporate data analysis tools such as spreadsheet programs and must link to a large variety of data formats and databases. In particular, it must have the ability link to operational databases, such as relational databases on mainframe systems. It must be able to display summarized information in a variety of textual or graphic formats.

Selecting Team Applications

Once the requirements are clear, you should gather information about available team applications that meet your requirements. A good initial technique to employ is the same as the one for personal applications. Again, Figure 4.3 provides a simple example of this method. Team applications are generally more expensive than personal applications and require more preparation to support and install, so pilot testing and benchmarking is critical to a successful deployment. Following is a discussion of how Lotus Notes/Domino meets team application requirements.

E-Mail

As described in Chapter 2, Domino Mail meets the needs of large, medium, and small organizations for information sharing via e-mail. It is interoperable with most major e-mail systems and handles Internet e-mail natively. Its interface can be customized to meet enterprise-specific requirements. Important features such as "away-from-the-office" notifications or automated mail forwarding can be employed to keep a business going even during temporary manpower shifts.

Meetings: Face to Face, Telecons, Videocons

For many of us, meetings occupy a major part of our working day. Unfortunately, a common view is that "most meetings are run poorly, take far too long and accomplish far too little." [Williamson, 1996]. Therefore, tools that enhance a meeting's value while it is going on and preserve its results for the future are very valuable. With the right environmental ingredients and Lotus Domino, your company can establish communications grounded on "Domino-based meetings."

Business meetings have evolved over the past decade to incorporate advanced telephony and video tools to save dollars and shrink schedules. This was partially due to the impact of lower profit margins, which shrank travel budgets, and greater worldwide competition. At IBM, this caused the continuous reduction of site-to-site travel, which has led to the increasing use of teleconferences and, to a lesser extent, videoconferences with off-site participants.

Because of the easy availability of telephones with improved conferencing features, more often than not, telecons have become a standard for remote attendees. Coupled with fax or softcopy transmission of visuals for display, telecons have been as effective as face-to-face interactions on many occasions. However, videoconferencing remains impractical for general use because of the lack of easy-to-use public facilities.

Domino-Based Meetings

One of the most compelling uses of Domino is in support of face-to-face meetings, telecons, and videocons. This use requires a well-defined Domino database for meeting information storage (Meeting databases), Domino Calendaring & Scheduling for meeting setup, upgraded conference rooms with network-attached PCs and projection displays, and a change in how meetings are set up and run. This is a paradigm shift in meeting operation that offers immense value in improved information sharing and reduced use of paper-based processes.

As the IBM Boca Raton site started on its journey to a client/server computing environment in mid-1993, a Domino database was set up to capture all tasks by the development and support teams. Initially, these were simple tasks of a week's duration. Each task owner was responsible for keeping his or her tasks current in the database on a weekly basis. At a set time each week, a 2-hour meeting was conducted to review the tasks due during that period. The meeting moderator would sort the database by task, print the set of tasks due, and create overheads, a traditional team status meeting.

This approach was highly successful through the spring of 1995. By then, the network environment had matured and such detailed task-by-task reviews were no longer required. At the same time, the team was requested to provide summary information to management on the ongoing status of the computing environment. At this time, a Domino Status database was created to contain this information. A standard format to represent this status was created as in Figure 4.4. A status document was then created for each major project, and the project owner was responsible for maintaining its currency on a weekly basis. At this time, a set of other critical changes were made in the review meeting's operation:

- A notebook PC was brought into the conference room, connected to the site network, and connected to a projection panel that sat on top of the overhead projector.

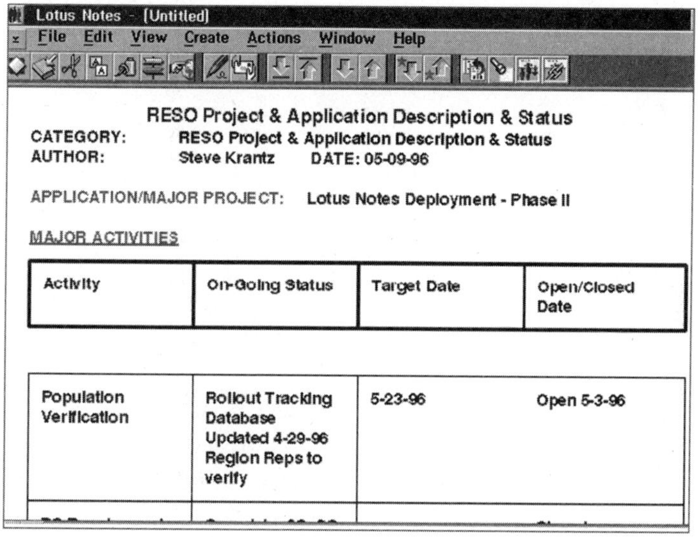

2000 Lotus Development Corporation. Used with permission of Lotus Development Corporation.

Figure 4.4. Status document.

- The moderator booted the PC, brought up Lotus Notes, brought up the database, and ran the meeting online.

- New items, changed items, or new projects were directly entered into the database right in the meeting.

This approach was very successful in running the large-scale network migration and support project, and simultaneously informing management of current status. Anyone on site could access the database to learn status. All team members could create or change their project status documents. No overheads or hardcopy were involved in the meeting at any time.

In August 1994 a major, in-depth review of the network environment was called. This required that each team member prepare a chart presentation and deliver it to the assembled reviewers. Traditionally, a meeting such as this would have required hundreds of visuals, hundreds of pages of copied materials, hours at the copy machine, ultimate distribution of meeting minutes, and so forth. It was decided to run a Domino-based meeting instead.

All presenters were requested to attach or embed softcopy versions of their visuals in the Status database in advance of the meeting. With one exception, everyone complied. The meeting was conducted entirely from the database. Because Lotus Domino supports multiple windows to access individual documents in a database, one window was used for the meeting's agenda, one for the meeting minutes, and one for the current presentation. When the presenter stepped up to speak, the current presentation window was enlarged and the visuals displayed.

The presenters used divergent formats (e.g., Freelance, Ami Pro, ASCII text). However, this presented no problem, because the displaying PC was equipped with viewer programs for each file format in advance. This feature was previously developed as part of an Attachment Viewer SmartIcon created initially for our Domino Mail template. The Attachment Viewer accessed a lookup table (in a user-customizable reference Domino database) based on file extension and invoked an associated command file that called the appropriate viewer program. With Notes Release 5.0, file viewing capability is built into the application, so the Attachment Viewer is no longer required.

A Domino-based meeting (DBM) is a one-time or ongoing meeting in which all presentation visuals, agendas, minutes, and action items are displayed and stored in a Domino database. Meeting rooms must be equipped with network-attached PCs configured with Lotus Notes and connected to a projection panel device to support DBMs. Prior to the DBM, the following occurs:

- The meeting initiator establishes the Meeting database on the Meeting server, which can be any Domino database server. The attendee list can be used as the Access Control List (ACL) for the database, or the default access can be set to Author to give attendees the ability to create their own documents.

- The meeting initiator schedules the meeting with Domino Calendaring & Scheduling, inviting attendees and presenters and informing them of the location of the meeting, and includes a link to the associated Meeting database.

- The meeting initiator places the Meeting Agenda as a document in the Meeting database.

- All presenters gain access to the Meeting database and either import or attach the file containing their visuals to a new database document. They then check to make sure that each visual in the file is effectively viewable when displayed.

- Just prior to the meeting, the meeting initiator goes to the meeting room, boots up the network-attached PC configured with Lotus Notes, accesses the Meeting database, and ensures that it can be projected onto the display screen in the meeting room. Figure 4.5 illustrates a simple Meeting database.

During the DBM, the following occurs:

- The presenters access the documents containing their visuals and proceed to step through them using the PC's controls.

- The meeting initiator keeps meeting minutes in a separate document in the Meeting database (see Figure 4.6). If the meeting room is equipped with more than one network port, this can be done with a separate, Notes-enabled PC while presentations are ongoing.

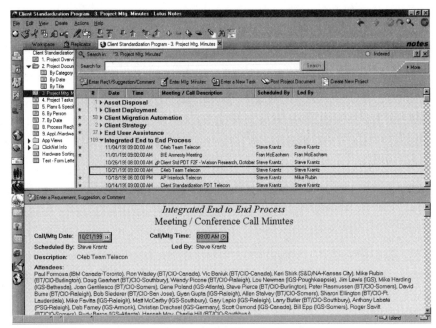

Figure 4.5. Meeting database view.

After the DBM, the following occurs:

- The minutes document is finalized in the Meeting database.

- Presenters and attendees can now independently access all visuals, minutes, agenda, and any other documents in the Meeting database!

Figure 4.7 illustrates the general concept of the Domino-based meeting. Observe that Domino-based meetings easily support remote attendees.

Run Your Own Domino-Based Meetings

To adopt Domino-based meetings in your organization, you need to do the following:

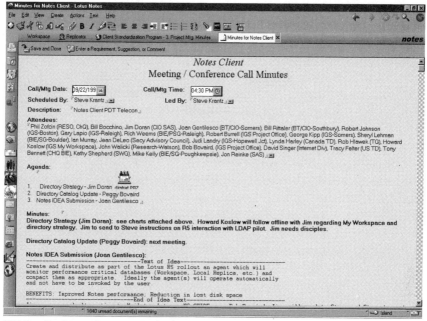

Figure 4.6. Minutes of meeting.

- Install Lotus Notes/Domino and educate all employees in its use.

- Make it easy for any employee, and especially secretaries, to set up Meeting databases. A suggested approach is to set up a special Meetings server that is used just for this purpose. Your Domino administrator should be aware of this process and support it with a phone call or e-mail message. Don't forget to use the attendee list as the database's ACL or set the default access to Author if the meeting is nonconfidential.

- Equip each conference room with a PC with Notes installed, a projection display, a projection screen, and one or more network ports. Don't forget to secure the system if it is placed in a public conference room.

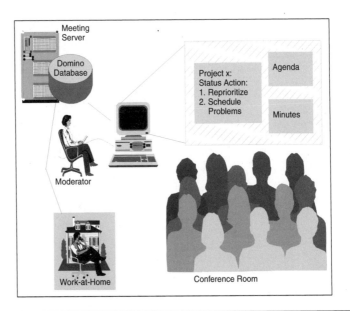

Figure 4.7. Domino-based meetings.

- Finally, educate all employees in the conduct of Domino-based meetings. Make sure they understand the need to attach or embed and then test their visuals files prior to any DBM. Overheads are not allowed. Hardcopies are not allowed!

After face-to-face meetings are conquered, the next step is to address telecon operation. In general, telecon attendees just need simultaneous access to the Meeting database and audio telephone connectivity. Two additional steps may need to be taken to support this requirement. First, remote attendees may need to be certified to the Meeting database in advance. This is a process step that should be included at the meeting setup stage with Domino administration. Second, remote attendees may be in their home or in a hotel room with only a single telephone connection with which to communicate. In this case, they should plan to replicate the Meeting database to their PC in advance of the meeting so that they can see the visuals in disconnected mode and use the telephone for voice connectivity.

A recent enhancement to IBM's internal Calendar and Scheduling makes Domino-based meetings even more convenient for IBM's users. IBM's Research Division has pioneered the ability to automatically schedule a teleconference from the Calendar invitation form. This new feature allows the end user to select a telecon vendor, number of lines, and duration of the telecon. They then click on "Reserve," which contacts the selected telecon vendor in real time over the Internet and sets up the teleconference, and the call-in number and pass code are returned, appearing automatically on the invitation form. After selecting invitees in the standard manner (Notes IDs or groups) and saving the invitation, the telecon is successfully set up.

With the development of TeamRoom, the next generation of the Domino discussion database, Lotus has clearly recognized the value of the Domino-based meeting. TeamRoom was designed for teams that come together for a specific project that has a defined end point. It is a repository to store common information such as plans, reports, procedural information, and meeting minutes. It can also be used for task management, such as assigning action items, tracking issues, and managing joint work on reports or presentations. The TeamRoom application is currently available for download off the Lotus Web site (*www.lotus.com/home.nsf/tabs/institute*).

A version of TeamRoom, called Lotus Instant TeamRoom, is available as a "rented" application from ISPs (Internet Service Providers) offering public Domino servers. As does the regular TeamRoom application, Instant TeamRoom supports threaded discussion and document management—described in *PC Magazine* as having "unmatched depth and sophistication." [Alwang, 1998] To create an account, you connect to the Lotus Web site at *www.lotus.com,* select a service provider, enter your payment information, and provide names and e-mail addresses. The Instant TeamRoom server automatically sends each user an e-mail containing the server's URL, the user name, and a password to log in and get going.

Meetings of the Future

If we peer into the future, we see that Domino-based meetings will be a critical ingredient in meeting operations. Stepping through Figure 4.8, we can contrast the three primary meeting modes—face to face, telecon, and videocon—with regard to their three primary elements—voice, visage, and visuals. Face-to-face meetings will continue to be the best method of communicating among human beings but also will remain the most costly. Telecons lack visage, or faces, but are a low-cost, effective method of communicating. Finally, any-to-any

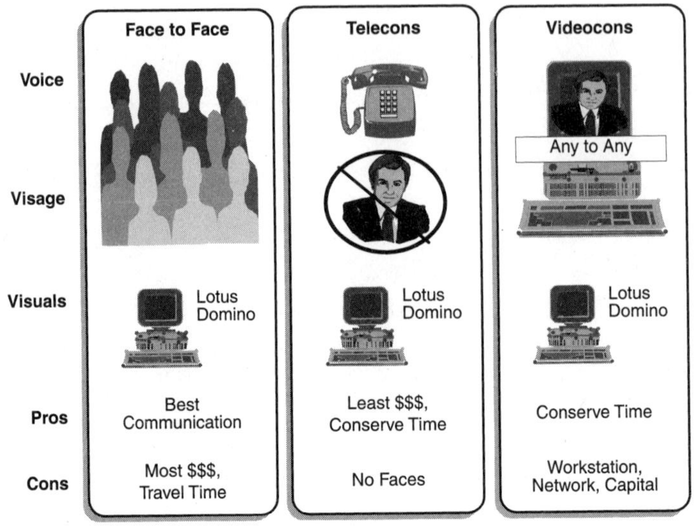

Face to Face	Telecons	Videocons
Voice		Any to Any
Visage		
Visuals Lotus Domino	Lotus Domino	Lotus Domino
Pros Best Communication	Least $$$, Conserve Time	Conserve Time
Cons Most $$$, Travel Time	No Faces	Workstation, Network, Capital

Figure 4.8. 1990s meeting technology.

videocons, facilitated by emerging high-speed telecommunications, will emerge as an alternative when real-time images are important. These images may be talking heads or whiteboard images for brainstorming sessions. In all three cases, Domino Meeting databases can be the visuals repository of choice.

Forms

A document in a Domino database can be readily customized to provide fill-in-the-blank forms. Each data field on the form can be associated with a formula, a key list, or radio buttons to simplify data input and perform input data validation. As multiple users complete them, the forms can be stored in the Domino database on the server or routed based on workflow rules to approvers' or reviewers' e-mail inboxes for action. After review or approval, the response can flow back to the original database for completion of the process. As we will see with respect to knowledge management applications, if a large relational database is needed to store the information for analysis purposes, easy linkage to a such a database is possible from Domino.

Document Management

As a team application, document management is the creation, review, and editing cycle used to produce a finished document, such as a newsletter, magazine article, or book. A document management system should be able to accommodate a complete range of documents, from e-mail messages and discussion databases on up to formal documents, such as legal contracts. In addition, it should be able to make all these documents accessible to Web browsers and be easy to set up and use. Most important, a document management system should establish an environment in which document creation, review, and approval can be done in a collaborative fashion among individuals inside and outside an enterprise.

With Domino.Doc on your intranet, your team can use its document management features to store documents; create document revision histories, comments, and approvals; and ultimately publish either soft-or hardcopy. Domino.Doc provides a platform for managing documents that includes different content types, such as text, flat images, 3D images, audio, and video. Domino.Doc supports the Open Document Management API (ODMA) standard, which defines how desktop applications interact with document management repositories. This enables it to support ODMA applications that are part of Microsoft Office, Lotus SmartSuite, and Corel Office, for example. In particular, you can use your own preferred editing tool, such as Microsoft Word, to retrieve, modify, and store document content.

Documents are saved to a Domino.Doc file cabinet. This allows the author to initiate rules for ownership and storage, and set access permissions for co-authors and readers. An author can also specify a document's "type" and associated attributes. This kind of profile information is used to describe the document and is extremely useful for searching and managing collections of documents. Figure 4.9 illustrates document check-out with Domino.Doc using a Web browser.

Knowledge Management

For many years, IBM has earned a reputation for leadership in database technology. The hierarchical database system IMS has been used for decades on IBM mainframe platforms. Built on solid theoretical

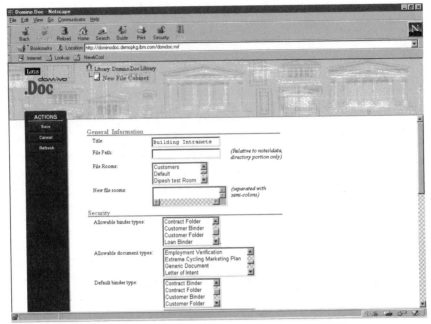

2000 Lotus Development Corporation. Used with permission of Lotus Development Corporation.

Figure 4.9.   Creating a new file cabinet with Domino.Doc.

and practical results, the relational database model, created by IBM's E. F. Codd, is an established industry standard. Most large corporations have built large databases using the DB/2 and SQL/DS relational database products sold by IBM for MVS and VM mainframes, respectively. Moreover, the IBM-defined interface, Structured Query Language (**SQL**), is a widely supported standard for database access on platforms from PCs to workstations to minicomputers from many vendors.

Vaskevitch [1993] draws the distinction between knowledge management databases and operational databases. Operational databases tend to contain real-time information for immediate decision making. Knowledge management databases, also called analytic databases, require summaries of information to provide comparisons over periods of time. Operational databases should feed knowledge management databases at regular time intervals. With a solid design, the knowledge management database can provide consistent and correct views at any level of the business. Both should be available locally to satisfy operational or analytic requirements, but they should be linked such that upper levels in the business hierarchy can perform operational or analytic decisions. Vaskevitch has created the term **federation of databases**, which is a set of internally consistent databases that are tied together by another database that is "designed to meet the needs of senior management," to define this linkage.

An example of a federation of databases was the CIO database project in IBM Boca Raton, a knowledge management database built with Lotus Notes whose purpose was to provide a set of weekly measurements of the network environment. It was fed weekly from two operational databases: initially, the Network Status and Help Desk databases. The Network Status database periodically gathered network performance statistics and client workstation asset data. The Help Desk database contained a record of each user problem encountered by the Help Desk staff. Figure 4.10 illustrates this.

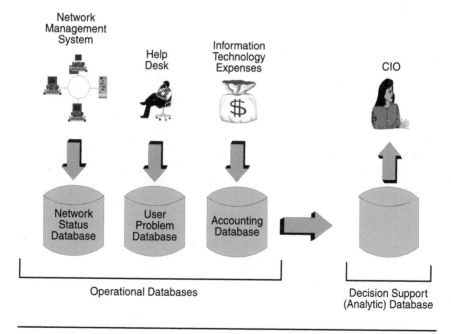

Figure 4.10. Federation of databases example: A CIO database.

Another significant knowledge management project was the construction of a product planning database by the IBM PC Company. Its goals were these:

- Create a central database containing all PC Company product plans.

- Enable distributed input across the PC Company planning community.

- Share plan information in a user-friendly, yet secure, manner for timely decision making.

A DB/2 relational database design was created to describe the PC Company products—desktop systems, mobile systems, servers, displays, monitors, and peripherals. A GUI was created to enter product plan data into the database. A set of batch queries was completed to generate summary reports to be distributed to company-approved recipients in a secure manner. Significantly, a Domino database was created to extract periodic information from the DB/2 repository, called PSPLAN. It gave convenient access to the data to authorized users for analytic purposes. Ultimately, PSPLAN data tables will become part of a PC Company **information warehouse** (a large centralized repository for multiple databases that can be accessed with a common query tool) linking the critical processes of the business to a central repository. In this way, the federation of databases idea will become a reality for critical PC Company knowledge management.

In the future, the business rules that were programmed in mainframe applications in the past will be programmed in server-based workflow (or team) applications. Business processes will define the workflow for these next-generation applications. [Vaskevitch, 1993]

The number of enterprises interested in knowledge management is increasing, causing consultants such as the Delphi Group (Boston) to predict that sales of knowledge management software will be approximately $570 million in 1999. [Anonymous, 1999]. Several major enterprises are making significant investments in their management of knowledge and have chosen Lotus Domino as the primary tool. [Mahon, 1998] With Notes and Domino 5.0, Lotus is significantly extending an enterprise's ability to manage its knowledge and deliver it effectively to your users. For example, Lotus has just announced

Domino Extended Search 2.0 (DES), which combines the ability to seamlessly search across an enterprise's Notes databases, relational databases, and the Web from a Notes client or Web browser. Data search results can be "normalized" from these diverse sources for ready analysis. With one search, users can access a combined results list with a ranked view of internal documents, external research and Internet sources. Searches can be saved for reuse and sharing with colleagues. Figure 4.11 illustrates this.

DES will index all document types and return paged results for display while adhering to your security authorizations. The search is automatically created on either a server or a person's PC. The results can be customized for easy viewing, with features such as categorization and relevance ranking, plus a link to go directly to the indexed document.

The Headlines database, described in Chapter 2 as a customized knowledge navigator, is another example. Lotus customers want a single focal point on the Notes desktop to point to the key repositories of enterprise knowledge. In Domino, this means providing a summarized set of documents based on preselected criteria that trigger retrievals to the Headlines database. Data selected could be from either your intranet or the Internet.

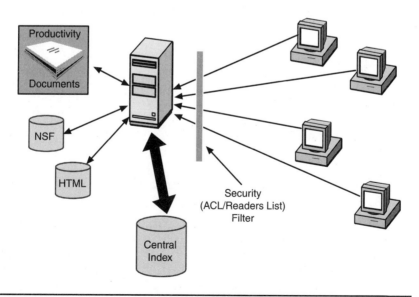

Figure 4.11. Domino knowledge management.

Linking to External Data

As we know, the Domino database is nonrelational, which means it is primarily suitable for storing unstructured business information. Non-Domino, or external, data can take many forms, both industry-standard and proprietary formats. Relational data, for example, is stored in structured data tables. Most medium and large-sized enterprises have a large investment in relational databases. Figure 4.12 provides a comparison between the Domino database and a relational database. Non-Domino data, in several different formats, can be integrated in the Domino environment to yield the best of both of worlds with products that provide the necessary linkage.

There are three types of tools, called access models, which allow movement of data to and from Lotus Domino to the enterprise environment, as follows:

- **Point in Time Data Duplication Model.** The Lotus Enterprise Integrator (formerly NotesPump) application supports this model.

- **Real-Time Data Access Model.** Java Data Object API classes support this model.

- **Extended Transaction Model.** MQSeries tool supports this model.

Each model has unique characteristics and associated tools, which we will discuss in Chapter 5.

Groupware

Groupware is one of the hottest buzzwords in computing jargon. The objective of groupware is, in general, to improve the sharing of information among members of a group or team. A simple example is a database on a server containing articles to be published as a newsletter by a team of writers. Each writer can add his or her own article and create comments about the articles of others. These comments are stored in the database associated with the article, and all writers

Type	Relational Database	Domino Database
Physical Data	Database management system	An NSF file
Designer View	Create one or more tables of data	Create one or more documents and views of document data
User View	Table of data	Document or view of multiple document fields
Data Field	Attribute in a column	Field in a document
Record	Row	Document
Data Access	SQL Query— a logical selection statement	View creation
Combine data from different sources	SQL Query joining related fields in two or more tables to create new table	No join for documents in separate NSF files

Figure 4.12. Relational DBMS vs. Domino database.

can "share" the comments. If an approval form (to be used by the editor to approve an article, which also resides in the database) is added, everyone can be made aware of the progress of the newsletter.

Spectacular benefits can be achieved if business processes are reengineered and groupware applications are developed to support them. Organizations can gain a competitive advantage by improving their responsiveness to the marketplace. They can enjoy improved coordination of effort and collaboration between members of local or widely dispersed teams.

Many groupware products on the market today use network computing elements to create groupware applications. They incorporate a shared, distributed, document database that resides on a server, an easy-to-use GUI on the client, a wide area e-mail function, and built-in security to allow access control for critical information. A notable feature, discussed later in this chapter is **rapid application development,** which means that a groupware application can be changed as rapidly as required to meet business needs. Finally, many groupware products support documents that contain **rich text**. Rich text describes a document that can contain text, graphics, scanned images, audio, and full-motion video data. Sometimes such documents are called **compound documents**. This feature alone can improve the communication quality of shared information.

Based on the IBM Boca Raton experience in 1993 through 1995, groupware applications were being developed as much as 90 percent faster with Notes than with traditional development tools. Using Notes, teams could share, distribute, and build upon existing work, whether they are on-site or traveling. Users could post documents where other users can immediately see them, regardless of the document type: text, graphics, CAD (Computer-Aided Design) drawings, images, spreadsheets, tables, and so on.

It is much more efficient to post files (e.g., accounting ledgers) in a Domino database than to distribute that information through mail. The advantages of groupware databases over mail include the following:

- There is less traffic on the network.

- Domino (groupware) databases enable sharing of information in one repository.

- Domino databases enable different types of applications to be built on top of the basic data store, including workflow, discussion, and broadcast applications.

Real-World Groupware Examples

A few examples of real-world groupware follow, based on the author's experience over the past seven years.

- IBM's Client Standardization Program was established in early 1998 to promote common PC software use worldwide, improve document interchange, standardize support, and reduce cost as a result. To facilitate information sharing among the worldwide teams, a custom database was built to contain meeting agendas and minutes, process documents, policy statements, presentations, requirements documents, and project plans. In this way, we were able to run highly effective Domino-based meetings using international teleconferences (see "Domino-Based Meetings" earlier in this chapter).

- The IBM PC Company migrated their large spreadsheet library of side-by-side, PC-to-PC comparisons to a database. This gave them additional security, easy worldwide distribution, and the ability to incorporate graphics and video into the comparisons. The initial version was completed in one working day!

- The IBM Boca Raton site library adopted a simple database for users to browse library offerings, including periodicals, new books, and new CDs. This was a customization of a database that came with Notes.

- Usability Issues Tracking was a database on everyone's Notes desktop as a standard deliverable in IBM Boca Raton. Every site user could create a document (i.e., fill in a form) describing a usability issue or suggestion regarding the computing environment. The lead administrators monitored this weekly. The administrators could assign a specific individual to follow up with a simple name lookup and button press, put the issue on hold, or respond to the issue author via an e-mail message directly from the database. Users could easily track the progress on their issue. This created solid confidence in the information technology support team.

- Boca Raton site secretaries used a **mail-logging** database. This allowed them to conveniently record receipt of paper mail, fax, and other deliverables for the people they supported.

- IBM Personal Systems Programming established an automated user **Help Desk** using a database, Lotus PhoneNotes, and a dedicated server on the Boca Raton intranet. Administrators were able to establish a voice response dialogue for users calling in that either provided direct information or routed their calls to support personnel.

- In any medium-or large-sized business, **employee relocation** is an ongoing task that requires strong administrative coordination among several groups, including furniture movers, telephone installers, computer and networking technicians, and secretaries. To simplify information flow among these and other organizations, IBM Boca Raton developed a Notes/ Domino application called the Move database. Employees filled out a form with from and to office information. Each organization could then create the data views it needed to implement a correct move.

- Most enterprises engage in project planning for a variety of reasons. Product development is perhaps the most common. Initially, the project planning process should result in concrete, documented, high-level plans. High-level plans establish major goals for the migration and document both tactical and strategic decisions. Ideally these plans should be placed in a centrally shared database. The ideal repository for high-level plans are a Lotus Notes/Domino document database. This enables the high-level plan documents to be living documents and form the basis for regular review meetings.

- As high-level plans are formulated, detailed implementation task plans must be defined. In many cases, a schedule for the project is required. With the Lotus scheduler component, Gantt charts can be dynamically created and maintained within a document from individual tasks. This database can be used in a regular task review meeting. If only a task summary is required, creating a form to accommodate it can be done simply. When used in conjunction with a Domino-based meeting (see "Domino-Based Meetings" earlier in this chapter), this is a very powerful means of establishing information sharing among project team members, be they local or remote. Be aware that Domino is only a tool—the constancy and leadership of a team employing Domino determine the success or failure of the project.

- These and other tailored applications can drive home the value of Notes and network computing to the users. It is highly recommended that you adopt the practice of Domino application investment for your intranet.

Future Applications

With the right analysis, you should be able to select applications for a Domino intranet that will provide a solid base for a 3-to 5-year period, and perhaps beyond.

Looking beyond the short term, future applications based on leading technology and development advances should be anticipated. A broad category of future applications is **multimedia** (an application that combines at least two of the following: text, graphics, image, sound, and video). The technology behind multimedia includes denser storage media and faster processors. The approach is to digitize multimedia information rapidly, store it efficiently, and reproduce it rapidly. To digitize multimedia information means to convert it to a sequence of 0s and 1s, the fundamental way all information is encoded in a computer system. With sound, images, and especially video (a rapid sequence of images), a very long sequence of 0s and 1s results! If we consider an 8 by 11 page with regular text, about 3000 bytes of storage are needed to store the information (3000 bytes equals 24,000 bits of 0s and 1s). If we scan this same page and convert the result to a compressed, digitized image, the information load increases to about 60,000 bytes—an increase of 20 times! This affects not only the storage meant to hold the image, but the capacity of communications links over which the image is to be transmitted. [IBM, 1990].

A hot subcategory of multimedia applications is person-to-person videoconferencing. Person-to-person videoconferencing is exciting because it is the next logical step in improving person-to-person communication in a large organization or among organizations. What is involved is providing the user the software application, a video camera (to capture the user's image), supporting software services, and, optionally, a video processing card to compress, decompress, and transmit video data over the network. Another related subcategory is called video-on-demand, in which users can select video information from a central server to play on their PCs. This is exciting because it can provide an improved means of delivering user education directly to a person's office, among other applications. Both of these application subcategories are highly dependent on the network infrastructure and may be infeasible today for wide deployment in a large organization. It was estimated recently by a noted industry expert that with today's leading edge technology, person-to-person videoconferencing among 500 people could be supported on a single network, but supporting 5000 people was infeasible. [Semilof, 1993]. If the application deployment can be carefully monitored and controlled, you can introduce these new applications to many of your Domino intranet users, as Domino supports personal video-conferencing applications such as Intel's Proshare.

Another very interesting multimedia application category is **visualization**. Applications that replace numerical tables and low-resolution graphics with images of high information content are called visualization applications. These applications enable users to see complex information and data relationships quickly and easily. Today, this technology is usually associated with scientific supercomputing or high-end graphic workstations. However, it is expected that as the cost of computing continues to fall, visualization applications will start to appear on future PCs with enhanced graphics displays. In the future, a large visualization application may result in "movies" that range in length from seconds to minutes, again with very high demands on your intranet's data transmission capacity.

Finally, applications themselves will be transformed in the future by the advances being made in intranet and Internet technology. The notion of a universal computer program source language, such as Java, implies that applications will be packaged in larger and larger code packets, ready for network transmission. The IBM Network Station, a medialess, high-performance network computer, assumes that all software will arrive over the network on the fly for efficient execution at the user's desktop. It supports terminal emulation, Web browsing, and Java applications. This implies that application platforms on full-function PCs, such as Lotus Domino, must be ready for dynamic software arrival, which Lotus is now providing with native Java support.

Critical Success Factors

Application selection is a linchpin activity in your intranet. Select well and many of the critical challenges to follow—in particular, winning the hearts and minds of your users—will be easier. Following are two critical success factors to focus on.

- You should invest in standard applications to promote interoperability, reduce training costs, and reduce support costs.

- You should provide committed, accessible application support for all vendor and internal applications.

Summary

Understanding your application requirements and making good choices for your users is vital to building a successful intranet. With Lotus Notes and Domino you can deliver an application suite for your intranet that will satisfy most, if not all, of your users' needs. Domino is an outstanding platform for development of team applications. It combines ease of use and ease of programming to drastically shorten development of new applications. These applications can be readily delivered to Notes clients or Web browser clients with Domino servers. When you decide to develop customized applications, Domino provides the platform and APIs necessary. In addition to these tools, understanding how best to use them in conjunction with your legacy environment (if any) and other unique tools requires analysis and planning.

5

Building Domino Applications

After investigating and determining your application program requirements, as described in Chapter 4, you might have decided to build some of them yourself or with the help of a development team. First, this chapter will walk you through an overview of software development in general, relating your requirements to software configurations and considering Domino functionality, and will provide a few real-world examples. Next, Domino Designer is introduced along with the components of its toolkit for application creation and a little how-to. Finally, a recommended development and management program is provided as you embark on perhaps a new investment in software creativity.

A Brief History of Software Development

Groupware applications, unlike personal productivity applications, have many business-unique requirements, in particular in the data and process areas. You need to have an understanding of how to build these applications when the need arises and have the resources on hand to do so. This means software developers, development tools, development schedules, and testing.

Boar [1993] observes that software development has evolved through three stages:

1. The craft stage, in which artisans and brute force predominate.

2. The commercial stage, in which business needs add procedures and training as additional elements.

3. The engineering discipline stage, in which science, standards, and professionalism are introduced.

The craft stage of software development was the 1950s and 1960s. There were no well-defined programming development practices until the very end of this period. The 1970s and 1980s roughly correspond to the commercial stage. During these decades **structured programming** (a strict method of writing code without **goto** statements), **code inspection** (a team review process of software before testing), and other methods were combined to become the discipline called **software engineering.** Software development management insisted on these practices and trained their programmers in them.

The trends toward the use of **object-oriented design** and **open system standards,** introduced in the late 1980s, appear to have brought software development into the engineering discipline stage. Object-oriented design is a method of software development in which code and related data are developed and treated like self-contained objects. In many cases, these objects can be adapted to the new requirements with only minor modifications. This approach promotes software reusability and simplifies development. Open system standards are well-defined software interfaces and protocols (data exchange formats, for example) that promote interoperability among software and hardware systems.

Database management systems (DBMSs) provide a framework (a relational database is an example) and platform (software services to interface to the database) to standardize and simplify software development. Application development platforms that combine DBMS and object-oriented tools foster very **rapid application development.** Domino is an obvious example. Another interesting trend is the movement to more end-user software development versus central information system development. The Domino database platform generality and ease of programming are making this happen to great success at many companies around the world.

What is interesting to note here is the rapid application development approach used to create and deploy useful Domino applications. Traditional application development followed a **waterfall model** (see Figure 5.1), in which one development phase cascaded into the next. A typical sequence was, from start to finish, requirements definition, functional specification, detailed specification, design, coding, testing, installation, and maintenance. Cycles tended to be long because all software was built from the ground up. With the new tools, multiple, shorter development cycles occur in the same time period as a single traditional waterfall cycle would occur. The approach is to quickly create a prototype, test it, deploy it, and then go into a new cycle with refinements to the previous prototype. With Domino in particular, this approach is producing useful applications very quickly with great user satisfaction. Another interesting trend is the movement to more end-user software development rather than central information system development. The Domino database platform generality and ease of programming is well adapted for end-user development and is working with great success at many customer locations today.

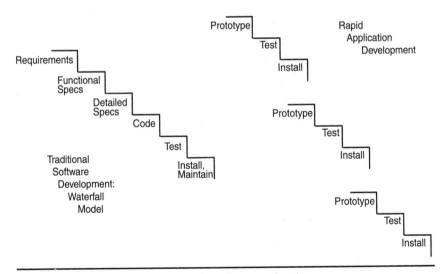

Figure 5.1. Traditional vs. rapid application development.

Application Requirements

This section examines the application program landscape with an eye toward development and support. First, applications are assessed with regard to their organizational impact, their operating environment, and their relationship to legacy systems. Some real-world examples are described, and a methodology for application development and deployment is discussed. The section winds up with a recommendation for ongoing application management.

The Organizational Impact of an Application

It is important when designing a new application to have an understanding of its potential impact on the organization. By analyzing and classifying your applications, you help determine the standards of care for administration (including change management, configuration management, and security), support (Does the Help Desk need to know about this puppy?), documentation (Do I need a separate manual?), and training (a special class?). The organizational impact of an application will depend on a combination of variables, including:

- The number of users it will serve.

- The life span of the application. (Will it support a permanent process or a one-time project?)

- The extent to which those users will rely on the application in order to perform their daily duties.

- The extent to which the application supports revenue generation.

- The extent to which the application supports strategic decision making.

- The extent to which senior management is willing to fund the development and maintenance of the application.

Taking such variables into consideration will help you to classify the application according to three useful types: Focused Workgroup, Business Unit, and Enterprise.

Focused Workgroup Applications

If an application has a small, specific audience, a limited life span (i.e., the length of a short project), or both, it should not require the very formal development and test processes discussed earlier. Such applications are called Focused Workgroup applications. Typically, these applications will be complete Domino applications (as per our previous definition) and a reuse of a standard Domino application template. For example, this type of application may be created from a Discussion design template, be used by members of a project team, and have a life span equal to the duration of the project. Focused Workgroup applications will generally not require special support or training. However, they may require replication if their users are geographically dispersed. The IBM Real Estate division's meeting/document database used to track its Domino deployment is an example of a Focused Workgroup application (Figure 5.2).

Business Unit Applications

Business Unit applications will usually have a specific audience with a long life. An example of a Business Unit application might be a market analysis application or a revenue/cost tracking application for your sales department. Business Unit applications require that a support structure be implemented and will most likely require user training. The IBM Real Estate division's Telecommunications Profile database is an example of a Business Unit application (Figure 5.3).

Enterprise Applications

Enterprise applications are similar to Business Unit applications but differ in the size of the intended audience and intended value to the organization. The audience of an Enterprise application is your en-

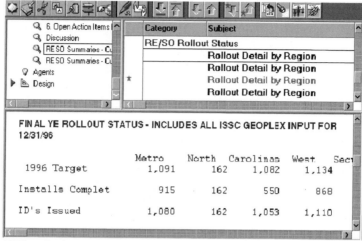

2000 Lotus Development Corporation. Used with permission of Lotus Development Corporation.

Figure 5.2.   Focused Workgroup application example.

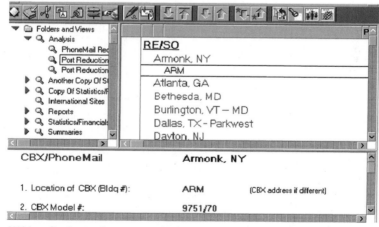

2000 Lotus Development Corporation. Used with permission of Lotus Development Corporation.

Figure 5.3.   Telecommunications Profile database example.

tire company. Having such a large audience, these applications require detailed documentation, replication schedules, and user training, as well as a support structure.

In general, Focused Workgroup applications will have a relatively low organizational impact, whereas Enterprise applications will have the highest impact. The organizational impact of Business Unit applications will vary from application to application and fall somewhere between the other two types. Figure 5.4 summarizes and contrasts these three application types.

Applications by Their Components

Because of Domino's base platform capabilities, its APIs, its companion products, and its interface standards, it can serve as the platform for many of your applications as delivered to Notes and Web browser clients. Let's examine four major categorizations by constituent parts or component to better understand this idea: complete Domino applications, front-end applications, back-end applications, and combination applications.

	Focused Workgroup	Business Unit	Enterprise
Replication required?	Rarely	Few servers	Many servers
User training required?	No	Yes	Yes
Number of Users	Few	Few to many	Many
Lifespan	Short	Long	Long
Support	Minimal	Full	Full
Funding	Minimal	Yes—business unit	Yes—corporation
Deployment	To all users at once	Incrementally as user education proceeds	Incrementally as user education proceeds
Developers	Reuse existing template or end users	Trained Notes developers	Trained Notes developers
Pilot testing	No	Yes	Yes

Figure 5.4. Organization impact: Application comparison.

Complete Application

In a complete application the user interface and data are implemented completely in a Domino database (see Figure 5.5). The Domino database is a document database—think forms, think lists, think word processor files, think graphics. If the data required fits these formats and user access is occasional (e.g., hourly, daily, weekly), then a complete Domino application should fit. You will find that an amazing number of very useful applications fit these rules of thumb! If an application is for a small team (10s to 100s), for a project of limited duration, or when requirements are not yet complete but a quick solution is needed, then starting with a complete Domino application is also a good choice. Domino's Rapid Application Development (RAD) can create a useful tool within hours or days in most cases. Again, as requirements solidify, Domino's RAD abilities make modifications quick and easy.

Here are some examples in which the complete Domino database is the best choice:

- **Tracking** applications with a combination of subjective and objective information that are updated by one or more users. Examples are sales account histories, project status reports, employee tracking, product forecasts and results, and service tracking.

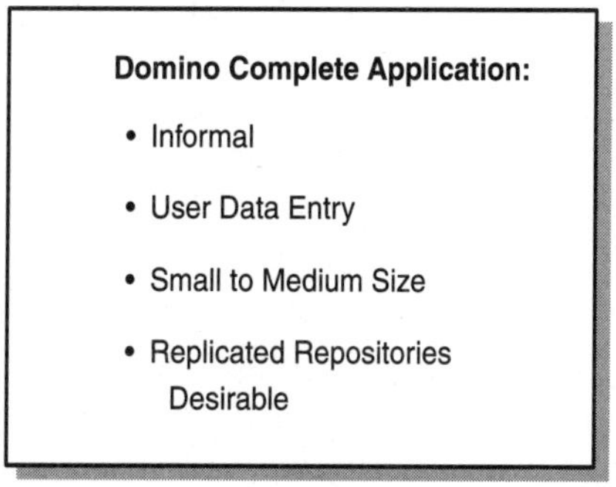

Domino Complete Application:

- Informal

- User Data Entry

- Small to Medium Size

- Replicated Repositories
  Desirable

Figure 5.5. Domino complete application.

- **Broadcast** applications, which provide time-critical static information to a variety of users. Examples are industry current events, meeting agendas and minutes (Notes-based meetings), and newsletters.

- **Reference** applications, which are similar to broadcast applications except that the documents are used as a consolidated reference library. Examples are policies and procedure databases, market research databases, and software code libraries.

- **Discussion** applications, which support structured and unstructured group communications. Examples are brainstorming databases, feedback or opinion databases, and customer support databases.

- **Workflow automation** applications, which automatically route forms, mailing reminders, and batch updates on documents at various intervals. Examples are conference room scheduling, purchasing databases, and compensation and benefits databases.

Another way of identifying complete Domino applications is to examine your business processes. A well-defined **business process** is a repeatable and cost-effective formalization of the activities of people working together to perform business tasks. Based on many well-documented experiences, including the author's own, a well-defined complete Domino application serves as the embodiment of a business process. In fact, the Domino application becomes the heart and soul of the business process over time, allowing easy improvements and preventing lapses in operation as personnel come and go. These processes have different requirements from **operational applications** (discussed later), including the need to share, track, and route many types of information. Applications that support business processes often require the following features, which are completely supported with Domino:

- Managing unstructured information, including text, image, voice, and video.

- Supporting communication and collaboration among users (i.e., e-mail integration).

- Providing multiple levels security.

- Allowing remote and mobile access.

- Providing means to track and manage tasks and workflows.

Front-End Application

Because of Domino's ability to support easy creation of customized control and data interfaces, it is natural to build a user interface, or front end in which data and application processing may occur in another application platform (see Figure 5.6). In some cases, the back-end database is more appropriate to satisfy user requirements then the Domino database (e.g., when a large relational database is required. IBM's MQ Series and CICS Link allow Domino to act as a front end to existing transaction-oriented legacy systems. With release 5.0, Domino will support direct, real-time connectivity to external databases such as DB2, Oracle, Sybase, and SAP.

Back-End Application

Because of the flexibility of the Domino database in supporting multiple data types, such as multimedia, it is frequently used as a repository for an application front end on another platform (see Figure

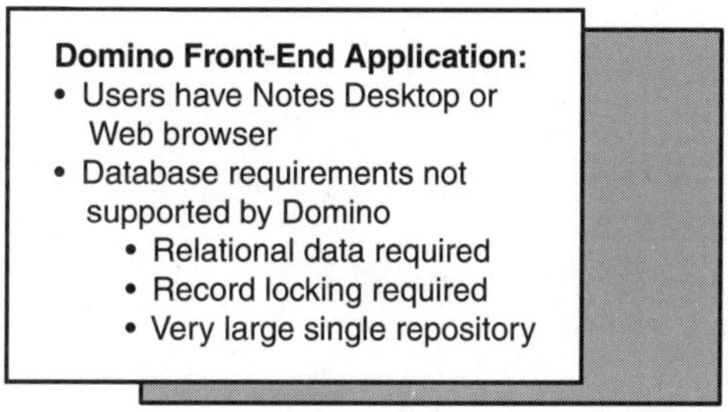

Domino Front-End Application:
- Users have Notes Desktop or Web browser
- Database requirements not supported by Domino
  - Relational data required
  - Record locking required
  - Very large single repository

Figure 5.6. Domino front-end application.

5.7). A good example is a Web application, in which the front end is a Web browser over the Internet. The new Domino server stores documents and serves them to remote users who request them with their Web browsers. At the same time, your internal users use your intranet and retrieve the same document using native Domino access.

Combination Application

This is defined as an application in which a Domino database is linked with one or more applications to make a complete application (see Figure 5.8). Let's start with an application in which you use a spreadsheet to produce useful work. This output is then linked or embedded in a Domino database for your department's access to the spreadsheet data. Thus, Domino and the companion spreadsheet combine to create a complete application. A more sophisticated example would be to embed a Java Spreadsheet applet directly into a form in the Domino application. In many cases, two or more complete Domino applications can be linked to make a combination application. Domino document routing can be used to distribute documents from Domino database to Domino database over your intranet. For example, updating a document in a Domino database will trigger a mail message to an administrator needing to take some important action (a workflow application). Also, document links can be established between two Domino databases. A document in one Domino database will have a button that, when pressed, will bring up the document from a second database.

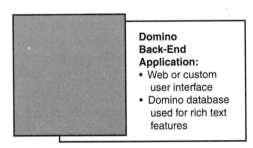

Domino Back-End Application:
- Web or custom user interface
- Domino database used for rich text features

Figure 5.7. Domino back-end application.

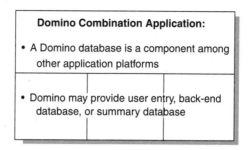

Figure 5.8. Domino combination application.

When deciding if a combination application is necessary, you should consider the following areas in which a complete Domino application will *not* meet your requirements:

- *Applications with a great deal of numerical calculations.* Domino's formula language can support mathematical calculations, but it does not have the range of financial and mathematical functions found in spreadsheet or financial modeling programs. For applications developed in Lotus 1-2-3, for example, the spreadsheets can ultimately be embedded in a document as an OLE (Object Linking and Embedding) or **DDE** (Dynamic Data Exchange) object. In this way, changes to any spreadsheet made in Lotus 1-2-3 are dynamically reflected in the document.

- *Domino databases do not lock a particular document when it is requested.* More than one user can simultaneously request a document, edit it, and store it back in the database. Collisions such as these, called replication conflicts, are resolved by user intervention. Applications that depend on automated control of such conflicts are not appropriate for Domino. A good rule of thumb is this: If a process can tolerate information processing delays of 2 hours, Domino is appropriate for the task/process, otherwise not.

- *Very large database applications.* Domino databases can be large—over 4 billion bytes and hundreds of thousands of records. However, if many users are simultaneously accessing the database and requesting divergent views, performance can be a problem. In these cases, a relational database may be more appropriate as the main repository, with a Domino front end, a data entry tool, and/or a review/reporting tool for data summaries pumped in by Lotus Enterprise Integrator (LEI, formerly NotesPump), or linked to in real-time by Domino Enterprise Connection Services (DECS).

You should assess whether the application is an operational application or a business process application. In general, Domino will not meet the requirements for an operational application all by itself. Operational applications are designed to capture and analyze business transactions such as order entry, inventory control, and payroll processing. The focus of these applications is on the data they capture, maintaining the integrity of the data's relationships, and consistent real-time transaction processing. The applications themselves typically provide continuous data access and tend to be transaction oriented. As a result, most implement a technique called database **file locking**, in which the database locks out the second requester for a specific record.

Real-World Examples

The IBM Real Estate division is employing complete Domino and combination applications to solve real business problems. An example of a complete Domino application is the Telecommunications Profile database (see Figure 5.3). It tracks all aspects of telephony data for the division, including switches, cellular phones, pagers, and telephony services. It is used by financial analysts as an asset and services tracking tool and by all managers to help track telephony processes. It was developed and populated in less than a month by the programmer.

The division is using a combination application to evaluate real estate properties. A standard Lotus 1-2-3 spreadsheet is used by real estate analysts to evaluate each property. All completed spreadsheets are stored in a Domino database as attached files for easy group access and version control. When each property's individual analysis is complete, the spreadsheets are imported into Lotus Approach and summary reports are generated for management.

When the IBM Real Estate division upgraded all of its computing facilities, providing high-performance PCs and Lotus Notes to each employee as part of IBM's network computing rollout, it managed this effort with three Domino databases: a simple Meeting/document database for weekly Domino-based meetings, a Rollout Planning database containing planning/status for each division employee, and a database containing detailed employee computing requirements surveys. Weekly telecons were conducted by the project's leadership, regional representatives for the over 50 locations involved, and support personnel, with the Meeting database containing minutes and critical documentation. The Rollout Planning database was updated monthly with the employees planned for rollout. Employees completed the detailed surveys in the survey database. On a weekly basis, a batch process was run to create links between the planning database and completed surveys in the survey database. This allowed convenient tracking of survey completion status, which was a key indicator of the coming month's installation success. As each employee was rolled out and linked to IBM's intranet, the installer completed an installer checklist form in the planning database from the employee's system. The installer checklist form was linked to the employee's record and provided positive confirmation of successful installation. Finally, an installation approval box on the installer checklist form was used by a coordinator at each site to validate a quality installation. Figure 5.9 illustrates the installer checklist form.

The division is incorporating all four types of applications into a complete architecture as illustrated in Figure 5.10. An **information warehouse** is a database that contains critical information from all key divisional applications. The IBM Real Estate division is building an information warehouse using relational database technology (IBM DB2) in a network computing environment. Each operational application contributes critical information to the information warehouse using standard data interfaces. Data for planners, analysts, and management are extracted from the information warehouse and will be placed in Domino database for convenient access. Domino applications are used, where appropriate, as complete applications and in conjunction with other components of the architecture.

Customer's Profile:

Customer's Name: Krantz, A.S. (Steve)

Customer's Ceris City: BOCA RATON

Date: 12-30-96 11:45:30 AM

Installer's Name: Chazz Chiamardas

**ISSC Installer's Total
Effort: (Hrs/Mins)**   5:00

Nbr	Task	Status	Problem
1	Shutdown and Reboot Customer's Machine	OK	
2	All Data and Applications Backup Complete	Yes	
3	All Data and Applications Migration Complete	Yes	

2000 Lotus Development Corporation. Used with permission of Lotus Development Corporation.

Figure 5.9. Installer checklist form.

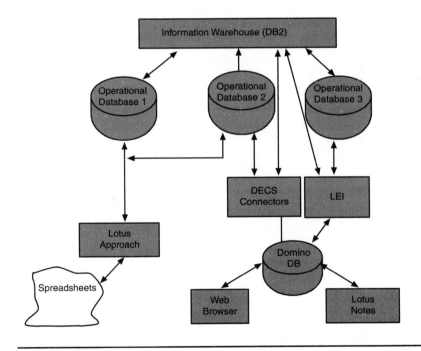

Figure 5.10. Enterprise application example.

The Programmer's Toolkit: Domino Designer

Lotus offers a large toolbox, called Domino Designer, for the Domino application developer. Domino Designer, previously known as Notes Designer for Domino, is an integrated application development environment that enables you and your developers to create, manage, and deploy secure, interactive Notes and Web applications. Key features of Designer include:

- Rapid visual development of Notes and Web applications.

- Programmable object store and access to external databases.

- Web site management using core Domino services such as document management, security, routing, and replication.

- Flexible integration with third-party tools.

Domino Designer incorporates support for the traditional tools, such as Domino formula language and LotusScript, as well as supporting HTML 4, Java, and JavaScript. Industry-standard interfaces, such as CORBA (Common Object Broker Request Architecture) and IIOP (Internet Inter-ORB Protocol), are supported for use of objects from JavaSoft's JFCs (Java Foundation Classes). With CORBA/IIOP support in Domino 5.0, you will be able to write thin Java client applications and Java applets for browsers that remotely access services and data residing on the Domino server. This feature offers developers the capability to create applets that can be downloaded to the client and can remotely invoke Domino services, such as initiate a workflow process. Following is a list of some of the tools in the Domino Designer kit bag:

- **Java JDK.** With the Domino JDK (Java Development Kit), you can build applets, agents, and servlets. Applets are small Java programs that are typically created to perform tasks at the Web browser when invoked by the current Web page. Developers can build Domino software programs, called **agents**, written in Java. They create these programs to automate tasks on both Notes clients and Domino servers. With Domino Mail, for example, a set of predefined agents can do the following:

- Automatically create a mail message archive at a designated time.

- Return a message to a sender that the recipient is out of the office.

- Help a user save sender e-mail addresses to a Personal Address Book for convenient mailing in the future.

  A servlet is the equivalent of an applet that runs on a server instead of a client. Servlets are programs that are started on the server to perform a specific task, such as link to an external database, and persist in an active state at the server for repeated requests by the clients. This persistence improves overall performance and response time to the clients.

- The **eSuite DevPack** is a set of Java-based applets that can be used as modular building blocks by your developers to create Web applications served by Domino. The DevPack includes the following applets: spreadsheet, word processor, presentation graphics, project scheduler, chart, SQL/JDBC (Structured Query Language/Java DataBase Connectivity), and CGI gateway. These applets are the equivalent of Lotus Components, developed using ActiveX technology, but now platform independent.

- **JavaScript.** A scripting language used to add programmability to applications for Web browser clients, JavaScript executes on the client.

- **LotusScript.** An object-oriented language for Notes and Web application enhancements, LotusScript has an integrated browser and integrated debugging facilities included with Domino Designer. This has been the tool of choice for large and complex Notes and Web applications in prior releases and is being updated with Domino 5.0. However, it is recommended that Java be used for new development projects where platform portability is important (maybe all of your new applications!).

- **Formula Language.** For small to mid-sized applications and where a quick prototype is desired, previous and current Notes versions offer the Domino formula language, which is similar to Lotus 1-2-3 macro language. For example, a developer might write a formula that formats text by capitalizing the first character of a word, or one that combines two or more independent fields to create a single field that is displayed to the user. The formula language is sometimes referred to as the *@functions,* because each language command begins with an @ sign.

Linking to External Data

As introduced in Chapter 4, the Domino database can be linked to non-Domino (or external) data according to three primary models: point in time, real time, and extended transaction. Let's examine each model in more depth associated with the appropriate tools.

Point-in-Time Data Duplication Model

Point-in-time data duplication is a model that implies data duplication either into or out of the Domino environment. One or more databases, Domino or otherwise, act as the data source. Similarly, one or more databases act as the data target.

The Lotus Enterprise Integrator (LEI) is an example of a tool that fits this model. It supports the periodic copying of data from Domino databases to other data stores that are relational databases or ODBC-enabled databases. ODBC stands for Open DataBase Connectivity and is a de facto interface standard for accessing data in relational and nonrelational database management systems (**DBMSs**). The movement of data is scheduled, polled, or manually initiated. On a periodic basis (hourly, daily, etc.) data is taken and copied to the target platform. Selection criteria are available to limit the amount of data copied. LEI allows the user to define conditions to monitor in Domino or the non-Domino sources. When a condition is satisfied, LEI immediately initiates a specified data exchange activity to accomplish data exchange. Data in this model is copied in two ways, either full copy or delta copy.

Full copy completely replaces all the data, requiring more processor cycles and network bandwidth. Delta copy is economical from a resource usage perspective, but there is a risk that the data may be out of synch. The business requirements of the application should be the determining factor in selecting full or delta copy of data.

The methods that use this model create a point-in-time view of the source data. This means that changes made to the source data after the copying occurs are not available in the target data until the next copying cycle is run. If a relatively small amount of data is copied during each cycle, it is feasible to run the cycles fairly frequently. However, if a large amount of data is copied, frequent running of cycles becomes difficult. In any case, it is always possible that there are different data stores and that the local data store is out of date. Any product that uses this method has this problem.

Real-Time Data Access Model

Real-time data access is a model that allows immediate access to data in a database either from the Notes user interface or from a Domino agent. The simplest form of real-time data access is the native facility that the Notes user interface provides to access data stored in Domino documents. An extension of this is the ability to access documents in databases other than Domino directly from the Notes user interface or agents.

@DBLookup, a formula language command, is a good example. In one form, the command allows access to data stored in a Domino database. An extension of the **@DBLookup** command allows access through ODBC-compliant databases. Please note that in this implementation, only read access is allowed to the ODBC-compliant database. It can be used to generate keyword lists, perform lookup operations, or launch stored queries. Performance tends to be relatively slow because with each use the connection to the database is opened and closed.

Domino Designer provides Java classes (e.g., Java DataBase Connectivity, or JDBC, APIs) and LotusScript classes (LotusScript Data Object or LS:DO), which allows ODBC access (ODBC stands for Open DataBase Connectivity, Microsoft's interface for accessing data in relational and nonrelational database management systems). The LS:DO provides three classes (programs) for accessing external databases: **ODBCConnection, ODBCQuery,** and **ODBCResultSet.** In essence, the LS:DO allows extensive read/write access to a database. With these tools, the application can perform read and write operations to the database. Data access is real-time. Operation can be optimized to cache results and create multiple queries and results.

Access to nonrelational data is not available with these interfaces. If a nonrelational database is available to Domino, a batch job is required to load a relational database with an image of the nonrelational data. Although this approach does work, it presents the same issues and concerns as the point-in-time data duplication model.

When starting from an ODBC-compliant database management system (DBMS) or other query tool, NotesSQL enables these tools to access and query data in Domino databases as if they were stored in a relational database. NotesSQL is the Notes ODBC driver for Windows. With NotesSQL, the external DBMS can easily combine (join) data from both Domino and the relational source for a consolidated report, for example.

Object Linking and Embedding, or **OLE**, a standard established by Microsoft to dynamically link data between two applications, is another major example of real-time data access. Domino supports this method both as a client and as a server application for the Windows environment. First, this means that in creating a document, the user can paste (as in the Edit/Copy/Paste Special commands or drag and drop) a non-Domino object, such as a Lotus 1-2-3 spreadsheet at any point in a **rich text** field in the Domino document (a rich text field is a place in a Domino document that can contain text, graphics, scanned images, audio, and full-motion video data). After the document is saved, another user can access the document, and if the Lotus 1-2-3 spreadsheet has been updated in the meantime, the changes will be visible. Even more interesting, if the second user wishes to edit the spreadsheet, he or she can do so from within Domino and the User Interface (UI) dynamically changes to the Lotus 1-2-3 user interface for ease of use. Correspondingly, users of Windows applications that support OLE can create links to documents residing on Domino servers.

Be aware that accessing data in real time raises performance concerns. If the host database is very large or if queries are complex, response time may be slow and host resource utilization may skyrocket. In the case of OLE links, there may be considerable end-user delay until a linked application is successfully launched.

The most recent addition to these assorted tools is called DECS, or the Domino Enterprise Connection Services. It offers seamless, high-performance access to enterprise data from a Notes client or Web browser via a Domino server. Native connectivity is provided out-of-box to DB2, Sybase, and Oracle databases. No programming is required as a visual mapping interface is part of the product. DECS consists of a Connection Server Administrator with which you create Connector and Activity form definitions (i.e., define the enterprise data linkages with your Domino applications), a server add-in task to start/stop Connector activities, and the Connector programs themselves, which retrieve/save data in real time as required.

As you can see, over time a variety of solutions for developing real-time integration with external systems have been released for Domino, including custom LSX's, LS:DO, @functions, NotesSQL, ODBC, Java support, and most recently DECS. The Lotus strategy is to pursue a common connector architecture and provide access to these systems via applications developed through a choice of tools, as illustrated in Figure 5.11.

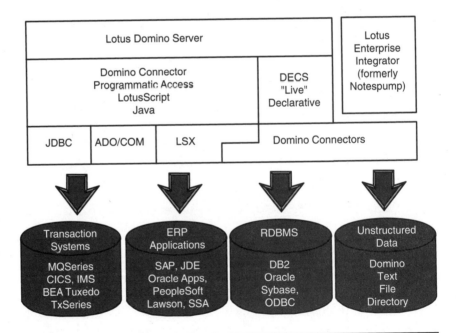

Figure 5.11. DECS (Domino Enterprise Connection Services).

Extended Transaction Model

The Extended Transaction Model (ETM) is a third model for accessing enterprise information from the Domino environment. The principal difference between the ETM model and the point-in-time and real-time models is that ETM allows access to enterprise processes whereas the other two models allow access just to enterprise data. In ETM, the *only* way to access data is through a transaction.

The Extended Transaction Model allows access to enterprise transactions from the Domino environment. Transaction-based applications typically process a large number of similar, distinct pieces of data, each of which must be securely recorded in a database. An example is an accounts payable system. By definition, a transaction is a data transfer or information request between applications that has the properties of atomicity, consistency, isolation, and durability, or ACID. However, applications built in the Domino environment do not meet ACID requirements, as Domino is not a transaction-oriented system. The ETM allows Domino to participate in transaction-oriented systems by acting as a front end or as a data repository. The enterprise-critical data is managed by the transaction system, not Domino.

The tool available that implements the ETM is the MQSeries plug-in for Domino (also called the MQSeries LSX). The tool allows access from the Domino environment to transactions running on an enterprise network. In the case of the MQSeries plug-in, the transaction may be a program running on any of the platforms supported by MQSeries. The list includes MVS/ESA, CICS/ESA, IMS, AIX, OS/2, and OS/400. For example, MQSeries link can allow access from Lotus Notes to a transaction running on CICS/ESA and in an IMS environment at the same time. Figure 5.12 illustrates the software components and their relationships for MQSeries for Domino.

Three Models Compared

The three models do not compete against each other, they are complementary. The criteria for selecting a particular model should be guided by the business requirements of the application. It is possible that in a single application, all three models might be used! Of course, these are general guidelines.

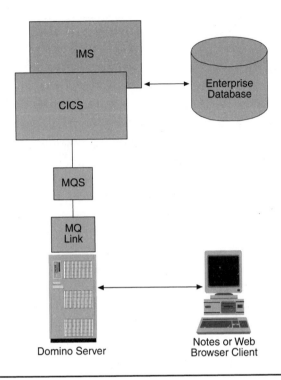

Figure 5.12. MQSeries.

The data duplication model is best suited for applications that are not sensitive to the currency (timeliness) of the data. Data duplication gives good performance to the Notes user interface because a local copy of the data is available in a Domino database. Data duplication is best suited for reference data or nonvolatile data (such as a list of customer numbers, names, and address) and historical data (last month's information).

Data duplication could consume significant storage on the Domino server. It is best used for applications in which it is likely that a significant amount of the data will be used. For example, if a database of 10,000 parts is duplicated into a Domino database in support of an order entry application, but only 100 of those parts are typically referenced during the course of business, it might be better to duplicate those 100 parts and use direct data access for the 9900 parts that are infrequently accessed.

Care should be taken when using data duplication for updating relational databases from Domino. Transaction systems have been put in place to ensure that certain business rules are executed to protect the integrity of the relational data. For example, a simple business rule might be in place to ensure that no order is placed on a new order database without also putting a billing record in a customer billing database. If data duplication is used to populate these databases, the Domino programmer must ensure that the same business rules are in place in the Domino application. Often, the business rules are much more complicated than this simple example and might be difficult, if not impossible, to implement in Domino.

The real-time data access model should be used when the timeliness of the data is important or pieces of data are infrequently accessed. The real strength of this model lies in its ability to dynamically query a large relational database. In cases of very large tables (i.e., hundreds of thousands of rows), a relational database engine provides better query support than a Domino database.

The ETM model should be used when it is desirable to link Domino to an existing host-based or legacy software system. This may occur when it is difficult or undesirable to rewrite the business logic of this system into a Domino application. The enterprise may wish to keep the core business logic in one system (host) and not distribute it out to many Domino systems. Better control is realized, ensuring that out-of-date business logic is not being run in the servers. Also, if the current software system is mission critical, the properties of atomicity, currency, isolation, and durability (ACID) are compelling for its transactions. This leads to the selection of a robust transaction manager interface between Domino and any back-end system or process.

In some cases, the resource that the Domino application needs to access is not supported by the other models. For example, if the customer needs to access data from a nonrelational legacy database, such as IMS, ETM is a way to access this information. Figure 5.13 provides a summary comparison of the data access tools described in this section.

Linking to SAP

Of special mention is the SAP R/3 application, which is an industry-leading transactional system for business operations. Data can be in-

	DECS	Java, LS:DO NotesSQL	Lotus Enterprise Integrator (LEI)	MQSeries Plug-in
Data sources	DB2, Oracle Sybase, plus ODBC-compliant data sources	All ODBC-compliant data sources	DB2, Oracle, Sybase, plus ODBC-compliant data sources	18-host systems via MQSeries, e.g. IMS, AS/4500, etc.
Read and write	Yes	Yes	Yes	Yes
Data volatility	High	High	Low	High
Response time	Real-time	Real-time or batch	Batch	Real-time and asynchronous
Data volume	Moderate	Moderate	High	Moderate
Programming	No	Yes	No	Yes

Figure 5.13.   Comparison of tools.

terchanged between Domino and SAP in several ways:

1. Real-time data interchange using the LotusScript Extension (LSX) for SAP R/3 and the Domino Connector for SAP (part of DECS).

2. Batch data interchange using Lotus Enterprise Interchange.

3. Domino Workflow Integration for R/3. A customized Domino Mail template is used to transfer workflow requests between the two systems.

4. SAP R/3-Domino Mail Integration using Domino SMTP MTA (Messaging Transport Agent) and the SAPConnect API.

5. MQSeries Link for R/3. The Link technology works to transfer R/3 Intermediate Document (IDoc) data from the Application Link Enabling (ALE) layer of the R/3 Server to MQSeries Inbound and Outbound Servers. These processes deliver assured transfer of R/3 data to and from MQSeries Queue Managed processes. Figure 5.14 graphically illustrates the linkages from Domino to SAP.

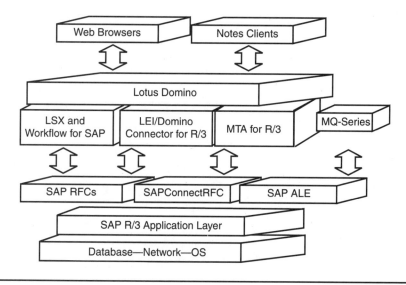

Figure 5.14. Domino and SAP integration tools.

Domino Applications for the Web

For applications requiring high-volume lookup, information broadcasting, status reporting, and high visual impact, combining a Web browser client with a Domino application is a good choice. In general, the Domino database features alone will be sufficient for all function. For more precise control over appearance on the Web, you can create HTML code and paste it directly in Domino documents.

Documents define the layout of your Web pages. When we build a form into a Domino document or change an existing document, these changes are propagated to all documents in the database. Similarly, all Web pages generated from the documents are automatically modified as a result of a change to the document format. The user creates documents destined for Web browser clients without having to know anything about creating HTML. Editing a document and saving it results in an updated page being presented to Web clients.

In interpreting documents, Domino evaluates the formula language encountered on the fly. Formula language is the integrated, fundamental Domino application development language. By handling formula language, Domino supports dynamic customization of generated Web pages in terms of user identity, user authorization, and time of document creation (e.g., **@Created**), among others.

Views display collections of documents in many different, easily determined ways. They offer excellent human factors features, such as "drill-down"-style expansion to lower-level or more detailed view information. With Domino, these same features, which include view categorization, sorting, expansion, and collapse among others, are available to Web browser users. Full-text search can be provided. Very long views are automatically broken down by Domino into smaller "view" pages as they are transmitted to the Web browser client. Next and Previous buttons are added to each "view" page for the browser user to navigate through the overall view. Figure 5.15 illustrates a database view as rendered by Domino to a Web browser.

The Domino database action bar buttons translate to the Web user interface as well. You can decide to hide or show buttons and

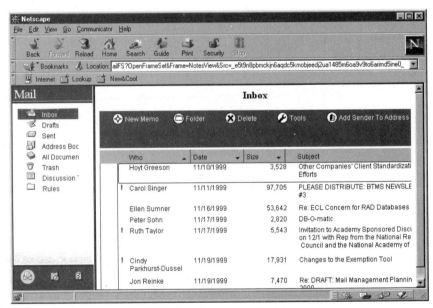

2000 Lotus Development Corporation. Used with permission of Lotus Development Corporation.

Figure 5.15.   Database view in Web browser as served by Domino.

control which buttons take you to different forms. Figure 5.16 is a screen shot illustrating how buttons appear in a Web browser when rendered by Domino.

With Domino, both Notes and Web clients can be served. If desired, an application can be easily programmed to vary its behavior depending on whether the client accessing the database is a Web client or a Notes client. This can be done using the **@UserRoles** function of the Domino formula language.

You can embed HTML text into Domino forms and documents to control the appearance of the Domino Web pages. However, many HTML tags aren't necessary—the appearance of the Domino document is automatically rendered into appropriate HTML. For example, if you center something in a Domino document, it will automatically present itself that way in HTML to a Web client. If you need to link two parts of a single document, you can add an anchor link and jump to it from anywhere else in the document.

You can add CGI programs, LotusScript agents, or Java applets into Domino documents to be executed, or you can invoke other CGI programs using the Domino server. A CGI directory in which your

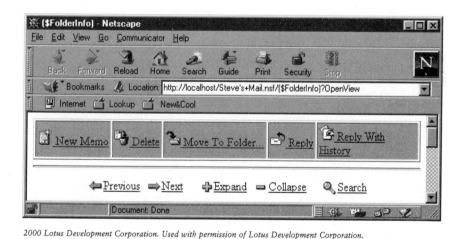

2000 Lotus Development Corporation. Used with permission of Lotus Development Corporation.

Figure 5.16. Database controls in Web browser as rendered by Domino.

CGI programs can be stored and executed when referenced can be set up on the Domino server. Similarly, LotusScript agents and Java applets can be invoked on the server as a result of Web user interaction (Figure 5.17).

Creating Links

Links created in a document, view, or database are recognized and supported by Domino. For example, you can present the links to Web clients by actually creating all the different types of hotspots you can in Notes with its navigator capability. Because Domino links are based on the unique, internal identifier of the object of the link, the link is more stable than traditional HTML links. Ordinary HTML links are file based. If the HTML file is renamed or moved, the link is broken. By contrast, if you recategorize a linked document or move it to a different view, its link will still work.

If you need to specify a URL (Universal Resource Locator) to create an off-site link, Domino supports this with a convenient function from its formula language. You first select the text or graphic to be the button or hotspot for the end user. Then select the Create Hotspot command and enter the **@URLOpen** function in the formula editing panel.

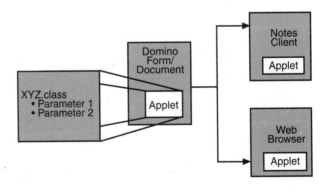

Figure 5.17. Applet runs in both Notes and browser.

Developing for Both Notes and Web Clients

Domino application development has gone through four major iterations over a period of more than 10 years with a single development group in charge. This has resulted in a mature and rich application suite, as we have previously discussed. By comparison, Web applications are fairly immature and not as rich from a functionality or user interface perspective. In general, you can easily extend the reach of a Notes client application by enabling Web browser clients to use it. The flip side of this is modifying a Domino application originally targeted for Web browser clients to take advantage of functionality only found in the Notes client. With Domino 5.0, the differences between client functionality and look and feel are diminishing, leading to a write once, use everywhere approach. However, by standardizing your development approach using Java and/or JavaScript, this goal is achievable.

It is important for the developer to recognize the differences between the Web and Notes client environments to get the best results. Forms in Domino differ from typical documents on the Web. Web forms typically have backgrounds; Domino forms typically do not. Web forms often have navigational tools at the top or the bottom of the form; Domino applications will have an action bar above the body of the form. These action bars can be passed to the Web client as on screen controls. Domino uses columnar views to indicate a set of like documents. This format is not typically displayed at Web sites but, again, is readily supported with Domino. Be aware that alignment support is partial for Web clients; that is, left, right, and center functions are supported, but full justification and no wrap is not supported. In addition, Domino does not support all HTML features, such as indentation, interline spacing, and tabs. For applications for both Web and Notes, the following steps are recommended:

- Use Domino native design elements, but HTML authoring tools can be employed to provide Web-specific information if necessary.

- Take advantage of unique features in Domino, such as discussion threads and collapsible and expandable views, that are not available in the Web environment.

- Exploit Domino support for tables in Domino format. HTML support for tables does not support column width and automatic resizing of columns to the width of the widest entry.

- Create a searchable Web site by setting up the Domino full-text search engine on the database.

- Use Domino support for background colors and background graphics for Web clients. Domino has the ability to overwrite the form color and background color on a document-to-document basis (**$Papercolor**).

- Domino formatting support such as text color, bullets, numbered lists, and named styles will add variety for Web clients.

- Caution should be used in using the underline text feature of Domino. Normally in the Web environment, underlined text represents a hypertext link. It should not be used in dual-client environments.

- Build prototype forms and view them in both environments to evaluate their differences and adjust as necessary.

Application Development Methodology

As your development team and your more innovative end users create applications with Domino, the development of those applications should go through four phases: end-user prototyping, formal development, development test, and production deployment.

End-User Prototyping

Your Domino developers and some adventuresome end users will have access to Domino Designer. These users will have achieved a certain level of proficiency with Domino application development. In some cases, they will be Lotus Certified Domino Application Developers or Lotus Certified Domino Specialists. Their application prototypes start out on their personal workstations for demonstrations and initial tests. This constitutes the end-user-prototyping phase of development. When the prototype is deemed satisfactory by the ultimate end-user community or their representatives, it should be migrated to the formal development environment for further enhancement.

Formal Development

The formal development environment is reserved for your programming and Domino administrative staffs. The formal development environment should consist of a separate Domino domain, distinct from those of the test and production environments (see Figure 3.12 for IBM's implementation). This means at least one server must be dedicated to completing your prototypes, which will ensure that problems encountered during the development process will not affect other areas of your intranet. In programming parlance, this is where the programmer completes any missing features and performs initial tests to ensure functionality. Typically, design and code reviews will occur during this period to ensure that the design is sound, that it meets requirements, and that development standards are met.

It is a sound practice to carefully review each Domino application at this stage—as it is for any important software application. This review should be performed by peer developers and, at times, administrators, to provide a mechanism for knowledge transfer and produce applications of higher quality much faster than would have otherwise been possible.

Development Test

Once formal development is complete, an independent test team (sometimes called Quality Assurance) should test the Domino application in a separate Domino domain. This domain should mimic the production environment as far as possible so that realistic test scenarios can be developed and applied. However, to ensure the integrity of the production intranet, the sharing of data between the two environments should not be automated in any way (e.g., replication of databases/templates, sharing of certifier IDs, etc.). Your Domino test team should consist of a group of experienced developers and representatives of your Domino administrative staff. They will ensure that all applications moving to production adhere to the your application development standards.

Production Deployment

When the initial development and testing is complete and users are ready for the application, it should be placed into the production intranet by your Domino administrators. At this point, it is hands off for the developers and testers. Your Domino administrators get ready to provide support for your intranet. For example, they ensure that only authorized users can access Domino servers and that replication has occurred.

The administrative tasks for Domino applications are often shared with their users or owners. The owner of a Domino application is the person responsible for ensuring the integrity and security of the data within the database. This includes managing the Access Control List and resolving replication conflicts.

Now let's look at a suggested procedure to follow before you place your Domino applications into the production environment for the first time:

- **Guideline Review.** The developer reviews the Domino application development guidelines and standards.

- **Estimate.** The developer estimates the time needed to develop the application, train the users (if training is required), and deploy the application.

- **Estimate Review.** The development estimate is reviewed by the administrative staff for support implications: test time, server space, and replication impact.

- **Development.** The developer creates the Domino application and tests it on a PC.

- **Demonstration.** The developer demonstrates the application with prospective end users for their approval. If improvements are necessary, they are made by the developer.

- **About/Using/Help Documentation.** Complete documentation is created (About document, Using document, etc.).

- **Application Review.** The application code and documentation are reviewed by peers and representatives of the Domino administrative staff. If necessary, corrections are made by the developer. Details such as a unique Domino design template name are resolved at this step.

- **Formal Test.** The application is moved from the developer's PC to the test domain, formal testing by the Domino administrative staff is performed, and corrections, if they are needed, are made by the developer.

- **Data Migration.** If the application is a rewrite of a previous one on a legacy platform, for example, this is the time to migrate old data to the new application. This might be done using a quick and dirty data export procedure for the old data (e.g., convert it to flat ASCII files) and a Domino macro to import it into the new application.

- **Pilot Test.** Depending on the complexity of the application or its organizational impact (e.g., any Business Unit or Enterprise application would qualify), volunteer users are identified to shake down the application before general deployment. A well-defined test period is scheduled, pilot users only are given application access, they test and provide feedback, and, again, corrections are made by the developer, if necessary.

- **Final Checks.** The Access Control List should be checked for adherence to standards and completeness by your Domino administrative staff. For example, you might want to remove the application developers from the ACL and you may always want a staff member to have manager rights. Required groups should be added to the Directory by the Domino administrative staff, if necessary.

- **Production Deployment.** The application is placed on the production hub server, the application stub is placed on the spoke servers to enable replication from the production hub, the database is replicated according to the schedule from the hub to the spokes, the owner and manager are notified, an entry is made in your database catalog, and the Domino administrative staff announces application availability via an e-mail message or a special announcement database. A good approach to application announcement is to send an e-mail message to your users with a button that, when pressed, automatically adds the Domino application to the user's desktop.

A similar procedure should be followed when changing an existing application. Figure 5.18 illustrates such a procedure. Note the differences between new deployment, described earlier, and the changed application deployment.

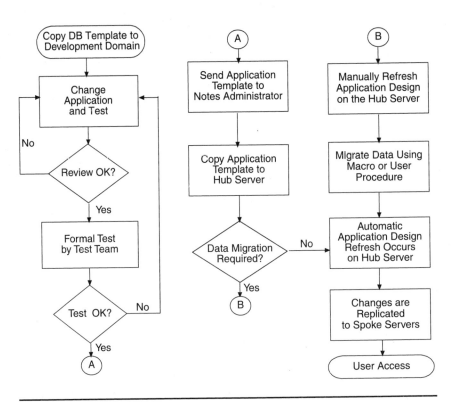

Figure 5.18. Domino application change management.

Ongoing Application Distribution and Management

After you have created your customized groupware, the next step is delivering it to your user community. A simple approach is to use a Domino database as a catalog for these and any other applications. Placing a copy on every Domino database server will let users easily add the catalog to their Notes desktops. The catalog describes each application in a Domino document with selection buttons for adding and opening. Your Domino Database Catalog should be created with the following objectives:

- Provide an easy-to-use catalog for users seeking application access.

- Identify all the applications in your enterprise, their owners, and other pertinent support information. This includes the Business Unit and Enterprise applications, as discussed previously.

- Focused Workgroup applications should not be listed unless they represent examples of "best-of-breed" implementations.

- Provide a reference for developers of "certified" Domino database templates for their reuse. These would be drawn from best-of-breed Focused Workgroup applications and any other well-implemented and general-purpose applications. Figure 5.19 shows the main view of the IBM Application Catalog, the primary means of delivering Notes and Web applications to IBM employees worldwide. It organizes applications functionally and by business unit for easy access.

Controlling application development, procurement, and development is a task that is fraught with controversy. On one hand, one of Domino's major selling points is ease of development. This rarely fails to ignite sparks of innovation in more than a few novices, hackers, and would-be programmers in a large organization! This innovation can result in new and very valuable tools with great grassroots support—clearly something not to be snuffed out. However, without suitable controls, the spirit of Domino programming can create a swamp of marginally developed and redundant applications, which

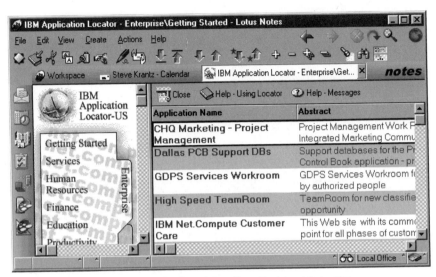

2000 Lotus Development Corporation. Used with permission of Lotus Development Corporation.

Figure 5.19. Main view of the IBM Application Catalog.

can create a maintenance and deployment nightmare on your intranet. Clearly, a middle-ground approach is called for:

- Encouragement of local Domino application development.

- Enforced development standards.

- Standard applications.

- A well-defined application testing and deployment process.

Establishing a focal point for these activities at the inception of your intranet is a good approach. A major success story for the IBM Real Estate division was the early establishment of an Application Review Board during its network computing rollout. The board's job was to promote standardization of application usage across the division as the users changed from mostly host-centric applications and roll-your-own PC applications to a common, networked environment. First, it was staffed with representatives from each major region in the division. Next, a skillful leader was named to administer and adjudicate disagreements. Then a Domino database was created to be the embodiment of the application review process. The database was a classic Domino workflow application that combined nomination forms and response forms so that the entire process of nomination, evaluation, and decision making was tracked and public. This approach has kept the division on track toward a low-cost, interoperable set of standard applications and productive users.

Your Application Review Board should

- Review application requirements on a weekly or monthly basis.

- Provide guidance in the development or procurement and deployment of applications to promote good practices, avoid duplicate development, and data duplication.

- Ensure consistency with any other applications in your enterprise and any Information Warehouse activities.

- Ensure integration with your business processes.

Summary

A well-defined development process and ongoing application management plan is critical for long-term success. You should consider establishing an Application Review Board to control acquisition, development, and deployment of new applications. This is a very cost-effective decision in the long run. Supporting the process with an easily accessed team application will solidify its use.

6

Rolling Out Your Intranet

This is the "how to do it" chapter from an intranet deployment perspective. The majority of the chapter describes a phased methodology to transform a business from midrange or mainframe-centric computing to a Notes/Domino intranet infrastructure. The chapter ends with a perspective on overall project management and how to evolve to ongoing information technology (IT) management.

Rollout Methodology

Successful intranet rollouts have the following characteristics in common:

- Top management support.

- Empowered project management.

- Dedicated team members with clearly articulated roles.

- Business unit involvement in planning and execution.

- A structured methodology with defined milestones and deliverables.

Building an intranet in a business with an existing LAN environment is relatively easy—you should be able to bridge from your existing infrastructure. If, however, you have a host-centric base, the effort is considerable. Change requires a commitment across the entire organization. New skills must be learned. The building process is very much like a large development project, in which an overall methodology is critical to success. This chapter assumes that you are starting from the host-centric base. Those of you with an existing LAN should focus more specifically on the later rollout phases.

An intranet rollout can be managed by breaking it into five phases. Phase 1 ("Getting Started") includes team formation, information gathering, and action plan definition. Phase 2 ("Build the Bedrock") establishes the network, client, and server infrastructures. Education courses are prepared, user support is organized, and user communication goes into full swing. Phase 3 ("The Rollout Engine") delivers client PCs and NCs in synchronization with education delivery, server setup, and support delivery. In Phase 4 ("Planting the Seeds of Productivity") groupware applications are developed for specific user areas. Applications are tailored to meet local needs, and tools are deployed to encourage migration from the legacy environment. In Phase 5 ("Steady State") long-term processes are initiated and rollout activities and staffs are scaled down. Figure 6.1 depicts the time relationship of the phases graphically. Note that phase overlap and elapsed time will vary considerably based on resources available and the scale of the rollout. It is recommended that Phases 1 through 3 occur sequentially with relatively little overlap. Phase 4 can occur at any time through the start of Phase 3, and probably never ends! Depending on the number of users and the state of the network (its readiness to support an intranet), a rollout may take from 6 to 24 months.

Phase 1—Getting Started

Getting started is the hardest part of any major project. All the people involved are learning their roles and responsibilities. Interpersonal

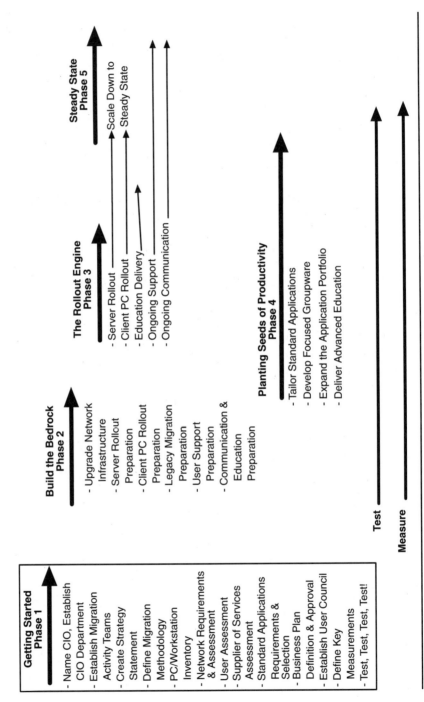

Getting Started
Phase 1

- Name CIO, Establish CIO Department
- Establish Migration Activity Teams
- Create Strategy Statement
- Define Migration Methodology
- PC/Workstation Inventory
- Network Requirements & Assessment
- User Assessment
- Supplier of Services Assessment
- Standard Applications Requirements & Selection
- Business Plan Definition & Approval
- Establish User Council
- Define Key Measurements
- Test, Test, Test, Test!

Build the Bedrock
Phase 2

- Upgrade Network Infrastructure
- Server Rollout Preparation
- Client PC Rollout Preparation
- Legacy Migration Preparation
- User Support Preparation
- Communication & Education Preparation

The Rollout Engine
Phase 3

- Server Rollout
- Client PC Rollout
- Education Delivery
- Ongoing Support
- Ongoing Communication

Planting Seeds of Productivity
Phase 4

- Tailor Standard Applications
- Develop Focused Groupware
- Expand the Application Portfolio
- Deliver Advanced Education

Steady State
Phase 5

- Scale Down to Steady State

Test

Measure

Figure 6.1.   Intranet rollout methodology outline—Phase 1.

relationships are just being formed. The Phase 1 activities encompass basic personnel organization and information gathering that allow the actual rollout to begin. These baseline activities include naming a **Chief Information Officer (CIO)**; establishing a CIO department; establishing rollout activity teams; creating a clear statement of strategy; defining a rollout methodology, a PC/workstation inventory, a network infrastructure assessment, a complete user assessment, a supplier of service assessment, standard application requirements, and a business plan; establishing a user council; and defining measurements. Now let's look at each of the steps listed in Figure 6.1 under Phase 1—Getting Started.

Name a CIO and Establish a CIO Department

The acronym CIO stands for Chief Information Officer. The CIO is the individual responsible for management of a business unit's information technology infrastructure, ongoing investments, and ongoing support. The CIO department is a staff organization empowered to carry out the CIO's mission. It should consist of strong leaders with critical skills, including:

- Finance.

- Networking.

- Computer Systems Operations.

- Business Processes.

- Communications and Education.

- Application and Database Programming.

- Project Management.

A computer science background (software or hardware) is desirable, but business acumen and interpersonal communication skills are the most important.

Technological change is very rapid for the intranet environment. By examining the extensive glossary at the end of this book, you can get a feel for the pace. There are over 600 definitions, of which perhaps 100 are new terms that emerged only in the past two years! Therefore, to be on the leading edge of this volatile environment, you should invest in a team of technologists to formulate investment plans in addition to the core CIO team.

Establish Rollout Activity Teams

Empowered teams with proactive leadership can make an intranet rollout fly. An empowered team is a team able to execute all required actions without approval from any other party. Such teams are effective because there are no process delays once a course of action is chosen. Teams should be made up of both CIO and information technology support staff.

You should form the following eight teams (depicted in Figure 6.2) to cover the bases:

1. **Network Team.** This team should focus on documenting the current network infrastructure, identifying new requirements, creating a comprehensive plan, and making things happen. It must be staffed with network administrators and planners who have the deep knowledge necessary to make the right decisions. Outside consultants may be required to join the team periodically.

2. **Standard Tools Team.** This team should define a standard operating system and application suite for the **office client** (a PC with e-mail, calendar, phone directory, and, optionally, word processing, spreadsheet, and business graphics applications installed in an office), and **mobile client** (a client system with access to the enterprise network, but not present on-site) PCs based on user requirements. It should define the minimum PC hardware configuration to support the standard operating system and applications based on careful benchmark testing. It should also survey legacy (host-based) applications requirements to guarantee convergence.

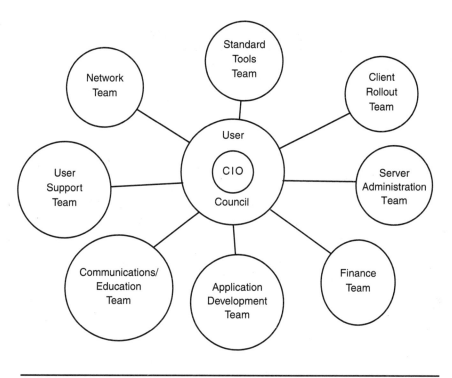

Figure 6.2.   Intranet rollout activity teams.

3. **Client Rollout Team.** This team should define and execute processes to deploy office and mobile clients. This involves hiring the required staff, setting up the required client configuration facilities, and working with users to upgrade or replace their PCs. This workgroup should be staffed with skilled coordinators and people with strong PC support skills.

4. **Finance Team.** This team should create and sell the business case for Domino intranet computing to upper management, negotiate contracts with suppliers of services, track to budget, and create long-range financial plans. Individuals with a strong financial background and knowledge of information technology fit on this team.

5. **Application Development Team.** You should staff this team with application programmers. Its mission should be the creation of Domino groupware applications and other tools to meet specific user needs. Initially, hiring outside consultants to jump-start this team may be required. Chapter 4 provides several examples where key groupware applications built on Domino and other special-purpose tools improved user productivity and acceptance of the new environment.

6. **Communications/Education Team.** You should staff this team with strong communicators and writers. Its mission should be development of an education delivery system for the new applications, synchronized with the client rollout. It should also be responsible for development and execution of a business-wide communication plan to win the hearts and minds of all site users and keep them regularly informed of rollout progress.

7. **Server Administration Team.** This team is responsible for the acquisition, configuration, setup, and support of server systems, including Domino. This includes installation of all application, operating system, and services software, as well as support of server data management, security, backup, and recovery. Server deployment needs to be carefully coordinated with the client rollout process. Staffing necessary skills is a major challenge in this area. In an installation with a large number of users, several key staff must be knowledgeable in server hardware, software, and applications.

   Key to a successful server administration team is including a Notes/Domino architect who will be responsible for the overall planning and design of the Domino server environment and network plan. This includes the definition of the standards, policies, and procedures for building and maintenance.

8. **User Support Team.** This team is responsible for defining and executing a complete user support plan. It should include phone-based and hands-on support for user problems for Domino, all other applications, PCs, and workstations. Lead-

ership must be flexible and proactive if a large rollout is in progress, due to the tremendous user impact of new tools.

Figure 6.3 provides an example of support staffing team by team, assuming 5000 users. Note the inclusion of two project leaders to coordinate team activity and make key overall rollout decisions along the way. This data was based on actual staffing at a typical IBM site.

Create a Strategy Statement

Your project leaders should create a strategy statement in the form of a presentation. This accomplishes three vital purposes. First, it establishes goals for all participants. Second, it helps wins the hearts and minds of the user community (when effectively presented). Most important, it gains executive support for the financial and people investments required. A more elaborate strategy document is useful for the long haul to benchmark results and keep things on track. It should be created in parallel with all five phases. Note well that yesterday's strategy becomes tomorrow's policy.

	Total
Network Team	10
Standard Tools Team	2
Client Rollout Team	32
Finance Team	2
Application Development Team	10
Communications & Education Team	5
Server AdministrationTeam	18
User Support Team	10
Project Leadership	2
Total	91

Figure 6.3. Support staffing example.

Define Rollout Methodology

The project leaders should customize the rollout methodology phases discussed in this chapter to fit your business' requirements and produce an appropriate plan.

PC/Workstation Inventory

Performed by the Client Rollout Team, a complete PC/workstation inventory to understand the magnitude of any intranet rollout should be an initial activity. The results of the inventory will be the basis for many assumptions in the business case. The inventory should encompass all PC and workstation hardware and software, including any remotely located systems. A database should be established to house the information to become the base for ongoing asset management.

The information gathered includes operating system (level included), PC machine type, processor, coprocessor, total memory, total hard disk storage, display type, and communication adapter. User identification, such as name and department, should be included as well.

To maintain a current inventory, your Client Rollout Team should consider adding a software agent to each PC's configuration that can automatically report system software and hardware to a central database over the network. The Tivoli Inventory Manager provides this network-based capability, using the TME Endpoint Agent to gather the necessary data for your PCs.

Network Requirements and Assessment

Your Network team should complete a statement of requirements for the intranet network infrastructure and an assessment of how the existing network must be enhanced to meet it. This should include a proposed configuration of the physical network, with networking components such as switches, hubs, bridges, routers, gateways, and cables.

This work demands a dedicated team of network experts. The team must have a complete understanding of the existing infrastructure and the technical depth to modify the network as required. This is an area in which consultants must be employed if the skill is not available in-house.

User Assessment

A complete count of users with associated organizational and job responsibilities is critical to scope the intranet rollout and fuels the business case. This can be completed by the Finance or Client Rollout Teams. You should include all information technology users, including regular and nonregular employees (i.e., contractors and vendors). This information should be placed in a database and kept current as a base for measurements.

User requirements for an office client, either a PC or an NC (network computer), or a mobile client (a notebook computer), must be determined at this stage. A good rule of thumb for determining an office client is if the user travels (leaves his or her desk) less than 25% of the time. In deciding between the less costly NC versus a PC, you should consider the user's application requirements. If the user needs only e-mail and access to corporate applications available via a Web browser, then an NC is the right choice. If the user needs to create complex documents or business charts, or requires access to a standalone application, then a PC is the right choice.

When considering mobile users, determine if they are traveling to external locations or to other corporate internal locations. For outside salesmen or travelers to other external places, a notebook computer is a good choice. However, if a large percentage of travel is to another internal location or to different spots within a large business complex, the use of publicly available NCs should be considered as a less costly alternative.

Supplier of Services Assessment

Your project leaders should gather information on each supplier of service to capture the company name, key contacts, type of work performed, breadth and depth of skills, fee structure, and availability. Key services are information systems support, application development, and information technology consulting (e.g., network analysis and design, application deployment).

The typical information technology shop may be too mainframe-centric to provide the kind of unbiased and broadly experienced advice necessary to guide a successful intranet rollout. Depending upon the situation, establishing a relationship with an experienced consulting firm may provide critical near-term guidance.

Boar [1993], in his book *Implementing Client/Server Computing,* leads the reader to the conclusion that an in-house, dedicated information technology shop is clearly preferred. If this is not feasible, then a long-haul partnership is recommended with a primary vendor. Outsourcing is an alternative for minor utility functions only.

Standard Application Requirements and Selection

User requirements for intranet application programs need to be understood so that the right programs are selected for deployment. These selections are critical because they drive PC, workstation, server, and network investment decisions. When selecting applications, it is important to define a standard suite for deployment to minimize cost and promote interoperability. Therefore, the Standard Tools team should complete a survey of users regarding what applications they use in the current environment and how often (daily, weekly, monthly, yearly, infrequently) they use them. They should analyze the data to determine the sequence in which applications should be available in the intranet environment to meet the users' needs. It is highly recommended that access to all legacy applications continue to be available to users for a defined period after they are migrated, if possible.

Business Plan Definition and Approval

The Finance team should create an intranet information technology business plan. The business plan should present a complete picture of intended expenditures over a defined period (typically 5 years) and contrast them against other alternatives. The goal is to be able to demonstrate a positive return on the investment and gain approval to proceed. The business plan is a critical piece of analysis and communication. Without its timely creation and delivery, the rollout is impossible.

Establish a User Council

A user council with participants representing every major business unit at your site is a forum for information sharing, user feedback, and critical decision making. With the right participants (committed, technically astute), it broadens the communications channel so necessary to win the hearts and minds of the user community. Regular meetings should be held—monthly is recommended. The meeting should be chaired by the site CIO. The agenda should include reviews of all current activities provided by team leaders, presentations of ongoing measurements by the provider of information technology services, and presentations of proposed additions or changes to the intranet computing environment.

To support the operations of the user council consider creating a Requirements database in Domino. Each document could contain an initial user requirement section followed by an evaluation section for implementation status by the responsible support team. As a requirement is processed through the stages of evaluation, acceptance, and implementation, automatic user notifications could be e-mailed to the requestor. This is precisely the method used by IBM's CIO staff as the centerpiece of its evolving network computing environment.

Define Key Measurements

The business plan should be the source of many important measurement targets. These include the capital budget target, expense budget targets, rollout population versus total population, number of new PCs required, number of upgraded PCs required, and number of servers required. A CIO database should be established to capture measurements on a regular basis. Each rollout phase includes the keeping and reporting of key measurements.

Test, Test, Test, Test, Test!

Testing new applications and processes *before* they are deployed to the general population should be standard practice throughout the entire rollout process. Call them pilot tests, alpha tests, or beta tests, they are needed before deploying applications, services, and infra-structure upgrades. For example, the stability of each individual's desktop system should be a major concern before the rollout. Informal pilot testing should be performed with individual applications before deployment. An early testing process will improve stability for the office client users. This is a highly recommended practice for any client rollout project and for ongoing maintenance.

Phase 2—Build the Bedrock

This phase establishes the network infrastructure, the client preparation area, and the server farm. Education courses are prepared, user support is organized, and user communication goes into full swing. Now let's look at each of the main tasks in phase 2 (see Figure 6.4).

Upgrade the Network

The network team should execute the site network upgrade plan developed in Phase 1. This may include acquisition and installation of new wiring and network hardware (**switches, bridges, routers, hubs, management consoles, gateways, cables**—these terms are defined in the glossary at the end of this book).

The network team should make sure that each site is able to communicate with all other sites in your enterprise and complies with enterprise-wide standards for intersite connectivity. This includes the integration of existing WAN and LAN connectivity (**WAN** stands for Wide Area Network, the connections among systems at distant geographic locations; **LAN** stands for Local Area Network, the connections among local systems). The team should ensure that there is sufficient network bandwidth between sites. Firewalls for interenterprise connectivity should be established through the implementation of a separate physical and logical domain for this traffic.

As with any other large effort, setting the right objectives is important. In an intranet design, the traditional elements of Reliability, Availability, and Serviceability, or RAS, should be a major focus item. Your intranet architecture should provide a reliable computing environment, meaning that users should be able to rely on a consistently

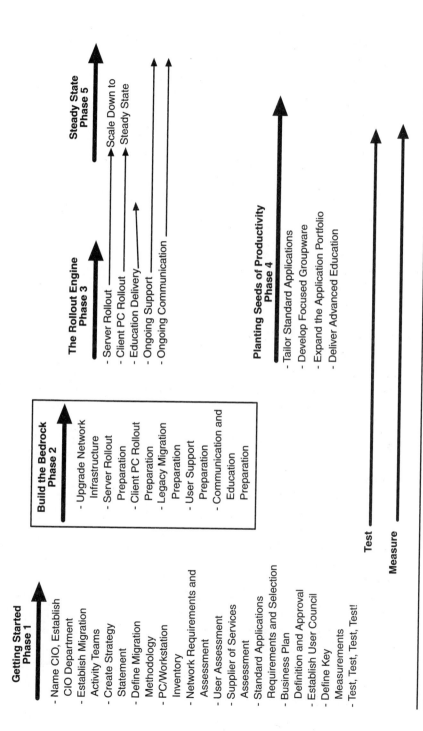

Getting Started Phase 1
- Name CIO, Establish CIO Department
- Establish Migration Activity Teams
- Create Strategy Statement
- Define Migration Methodology
- PC/Workstation Inventory
- Network Requirements and Assessment
- User Assessment
- Supplier of Services Assessment
- Standard Applications Requirements and Selection
- Business Plan Definition and Approval
- Establish User Council
- Define Key Measurements
- Test, Test, Test, Test!

Build the Bedrock Phase 2
- Upgrade Network Infrastructure
- Server Rollout Preparation
- Client PC Rollout Preparation
- Legacy Migration Preparation
- User Support Preparation
- Communication and Education Preparation

The Rollout Engine Phase 3
- Server Rollout
- Client PC Rollout
- Education Delivery
- Ongoing Support
- Ongoing Communication

Planting Seeds of Productivity Phase 4
- Tailor Standard Applications
- Develop Focused Groupware
- Expand the Application Portfolio
- Deliver Advanced Education

Steady State Phase 5
- Scale Down to Steady State

Test

Measure

Figure 6.4. Intranet rollout methodology outline—Phase 2.

high level of service being provided to their PCs. For example, when a user sends e-mail it should arrive at its destination(s) within a reasonable length of time. The potential impact of system outages on end users should be minimized as much as possible. Hardware failures are inevitable in any large system. Therefore, the chosen architecture should identify potentially critical points of failure and either eliminate them or provide appropriate recovery strategies. When system outages do occur, the architecture should provide the means to diagnose and resolve the failure quickly and with minimal interruption to end users. Network management must be in place to handle problems, performance, change, capacity planning, and configuration management.

Server Rollout Preparation

The server team needs to complete pilot tests of critical applications in a controlled intranet environment. This provides a means to identify application problems prior to wide user deployment. A pilot test is the setting up of a fully configured application server with a small group of users (5 to 20) for a defined period. This should be done in conjunction with the client team. A typical pilot test should take from 1 to 4 weeks to complete.

Ordering hardware and software for application and gateway servers should occur in parallel with pilot tests. Orders should lead the client rollout so that adequate server capacity is available as clients are rolled out.

A well-designed site network will centralize access to all major LAN connectivity equipment. The **server farm** should be located at this central access point to allow flexibility in connectivity as the intranet environment evolves (a server farm is an area reserved for a large number of server computing systems). This allows for performance optimizations to occur easily, if required. Adequate server farm space should be reserved, allowing for reasonable growth. Ideally, the server farm area should have racks or cabinets for server systems, above-average cooling, line-conditioned power (incoming power is filtered for spikes and surges) with an uninterruptible power supply, and a raised floor to avoid wiring clutter. Office space for server administration and the network control center should be nearby. Spare parts should be located nearby as well.

You should prepare to support hands-on server administration with display and keyboard access on the server farm floor. To minimize cost and space, a single display and keyboard can be set up to service a cluster of servers in a common server farm rack or cabinet. If remote control is required, network-based tools and procedures need to be in place not only to allow for checking and controlling healthy, running servers but also to allow for remote system restart, including system power off and power on. This is a common feature of major network management systems. In addition, localized network failures may require out-of-band, remote communications directly to a problem server. This means a dial-up direct connection over the public telephone network via modem to each server system. Consider also utilizing automated administrator paging, driven by your network management system, to create server failure alerts.

Server availability is a critical requirement that should be considered during this phase. In solving this requirement, it is important to balance availability with cost. Figure 6.5 illustrates a three-dimensional set of alternatives that should be considered when making these decisions. The vertical axis, labeled Availability, focuses on increasingly expensive alternatives in improving server uptime. Spare parts

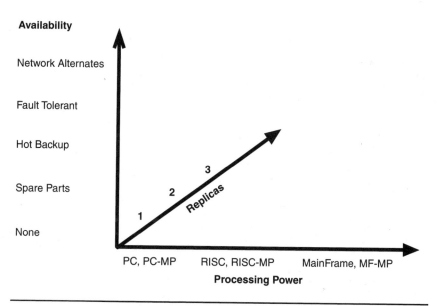

Figure 6.5. Server availability vs. processing power.

is the least expensive but, subject to parts availability, may result in user downtime of 30 minutes to hours to days! Next, you can invest in a hot backup system that can be substituted for any server in your farm within 30 minutes. Hard disk storage can be swapped in or recovered from your backup tapes. Investing even more, you can purchase fault-tolerant servers, with dual processors, RAID storage, dual power supplies, and so on. This virtually eliminates specific server failure. An even more expensive choice is providing network alternates, that is, completely duplicated systems, available online on your network. If the primary system is going down, the client user's system is automatically redirected to communicate with the alternate server. This last approach may dovetail nicely with your Domino replication strategy; that is, you have replicated specific databases for improved response times to large user groups. Your business's unique requirements will determine if one or all of these choices should be made.

The horizontal axis, labeled Processing Power, focuses on increasingly expensive alternatives in improving server responsiveness or server capacity. The base number of users and their proximity are two criteria for selecting a server by its processing power. A small enterprise of 500 or fewer employees could start with a PC-class server, making sure that it can be upgraded to MP (multiprocessor) capability as the number of users increase. Ratcheting up to 2000 to 3000 users, a RISC-class server, such as an IBM RS/6000, could be selected, again making sure that an MP upgrade was viable. A large enterprise should consider the Domino server for the IBM System/390 platform, estimated to support up to 10,000 users. As you make these selections, don't forget to consider desired response time during peak business hours, nonstop versus daytime operation requirements, the Domino replication schedule, and the impact of periodic system backup, cleaning, and restart.

Server backup is essential for protection against data loss. Backup needs to include Domino control files, system databases, and user databases. Depending on update cycle and value, information should be backed up daily or at least weekly. It might be necessary to run backup when the server is down. For example, some of the Notes control files are open while the server is running, and most backup tools are not able to handle open files. Besides the backup of data to tape, which is usually the least expensive solution, a simple but expensive way is to do it by using RAID disks. **RAID** stands for Redundant Array of Inexpensive Disks, a de facto standard that defines how two or more inexpensive hard disks can be combined to provide enhanced fault tolerance or performance in a computer system. They allow for online backup and can switch seamlessly between disks if problems occur.

The Tivoli Storage Manager, or TSM (formerly ADSM), is a network-based backup and archive application for workstations and servers that offers unique Domino-specific features that reduce cost and improve backup and recovery time. TSM's Domino Backup Agent can be utilized to perform incremental backup and recovery of documents in a Domino database.

Server storage space policies should be established in this phase. With adequate storage on each user's desktop, it is recommended that each user be responsible for archival of personal data. Policies should be set up regarding allocation of server storage by organization, personal e-mail data space allocation and policing, requests for additional space, and backup service requests. A good policy is to make each user responsible for personal data archiving.

Client Rollout Preparation

The client team needs to run pilot tests of new office applications in conjunction with the server team. At a minimum, these should include e-mail, a calendar, a directory for both office and mobile clients, and print services. (An office client is a PC or NC installed in an office. A mobile client is a PC that is not office-bound; it can be a truly mobile notebook PC or a home-bound desktop system.)

Your efforts will be greatly simplified by your up-front analysis into user requirements. If most of your users' computing needs can be satisfied with a Web browser, then providing NCs rather than PCs will dramatically reduce both your capital investment in client systems and your ongoing support costs. According to the Gartner Group, the 5-year cost of ownership of a full-function PC is around $43,000, and NC 5-year cost is estimated by industry sources as $8000 to $12,000. NCs require minimal software preload and setup—equivalent to that of a dumb terminal. The installation process is essentially just a connection to the network. Your server preparation should reflect your PC–NC mix, of course.

A plan and process for upgrading or replacing client systems should be created and tested. An office and mobile client configuration area should be established to set up new client systems with standard applications, operating system, and services. An office client rollout schedule should be created whereby departments or teams are rolled out in close time proximity. In that way, sharing the rollout pain will become a group effort. Further, Phase 4 efforts to create and deploy targeted Domino groupware will be enhanced. Other scheduling factors to consider are availability of hardware and business need. Hardware and software should be ordered according to the rollout schedule. Based on the number of clients to be rolled out and the time objectives involved, a staff of trained installers should be hired to upgrade or replace client systems. Temporary employees should be considered for this role.

A client rollout is extremely challenging, requiring a highly synchronized "manufacturing" process, worthy of a case study in industrial engineering! Many things can go wrong, and will (according to Murphy's Law), unless careful planning is performed. Several elements require synchronization, including

- **Gathering and Logging Customer Data Profiles and Requirements.** A comprehensive questionnaire should be completed for each user, containing all information necessary for a successful client rollout. This data should be consolidated in a Domino database for the downstream in-office installation process.

- **Inventory Delivery, Staging, and Control.** Hardware delivery schedules can be unpredictable. Problems can be minimized through flexibility in schedule management, establishment of a 3- to 4-week inventory of readily accessible hardware, and support by a (Lotus Notes) tracking database.

- **Work-in-Process Management.** Well-laid-out processes make the difference.

- **Technical Requirements Changes.** This is inevitable, as software levels change or last-minute user requests filter in. The rollout team must be flexible and responsive to properly handle these changes.

- **Workload Balancing.** The client installation team must be well trained and proficient in their tasks to accommodate this.

Installers should be PC-familiar at least, with application and some operating system modification experience.

- **Network-Based Software Delivery.** This is a critical technology for a large-scale client migration.

- **Setting Customer Expectations.** Customer expectations for each phase of the process should be appropriately set. A mass client migration takes a good deal of the "personal" out of a user's personal computer. This is increasingly inevitable as network computing technology matures.

- **Scheduling with the User.** This is a delicate matter. If your installer is late, the installation opportunity may be missed and the user will be angry. If the user doesn't show, again, the installation opportunity is missed, jeopardizing the overall schedule. This problem can be minimized through use of the airlines' method of overbooking (a key insight) and up-to-the-minute scheduling communication with the user.

- **In-Office Installation Experience.** The overriding objective should be to minimize user work disruption. This means maximizing software preloading and minimizing in-office installation time. The installer's guarantee should be that the user will have full capability after the installation. Preservation of all current user data should be a given.

- **Additional User Visits.** Installation problems requiring additional user visits by installers add schedule pressure. These are inevitable given a large and complex rollout. They can be minimized through the use of carefully documented procedures and up-front testing by the installation team.

The assignment of user focal points is highly recommended for your rollout. The focal point should be a person in each area or department to serve as your local agent to communicate directly with each person to receive a new or upgraded PC. The goal should be to have a focal point in each department (10 to 20 clients). The focal point key duties should be these:

1. Ensure completion of client questionnaires. The questionnaire should be taken online by most clients. It gathers comprehensive information of client requirements.

2. Order network identifiers and key software licenses.

3. Track new PC orders and gather complete data on PCs to be upgraded.

4. Communicate with the client rollout team and the clients throughout the rollout period.

A well-defined group-by-group rollout process should be initiated once a focal point is identified.

Domino applications can play a critical behind-the-scenes role for your client rollout process. A document library database can contain procedures, processes, and forms documents specific to the rollout. User questionnaires can be readily maintained in a consolidated Domino database. Users not yet on Notes can complete a survey in their own environment (e.g., OfficeVision/VM), and the result can be imported if it requires conversion to the Domino format. A Domino database can easily be employed to schedule and track user PC installations. For the IBM Boca Raton rollout, three Domino databases were set up to inform users of their migration schedule, provide a migration checklist and, most important, track purchase orders for new equipment.

Your approach to client installation or upgrade should be comprehensive. It should be based on the Golden Rule (do unto others as you would have others do unto you), because each office client upgrade has a significant psychological, intellectual, and physical impact on a new user.

Legacy Migration Preparation

Your company's information technology legacy may be a mainframe environment, a midrange system infrastructure, another LAN-based e-mail system, or a Notes Release 4.x intranet. In all of these cases, you will need methodologies and tools to migrate your users to the new Notes/Domino intranet.

Experienced mainframe application users sometimes require coaxing to take the leap onto a Notes/Domino intranet. Specialized tools to migrate key data files from the mainframe to useful versions on the intranet platform are very helpful. User-friendly tools to reduce space used on the mainframe, archive files for safekeeping, or download them to the PC give that extra boost as well.

The legacy environment determines the scope of any migration activity. In this context, legacy means applications, tools, and data that require conversion to a new base as part of the establishment of the intranet. In most cases, this means converting e-mail and calendar functions, together with their associated directories to the new base. Figure 6.6 summarizes the coexistence and migration steps discussed. Three key areas should be addressed when preparing for a legacy migration effort—coexistence requirements, end-user requirements, and availability of migration tools.

Coexistence Requirements

If the number of end users is large enough that the migration duration is more than 3 months, then coexistence with the legacy environ-

	Mail Files	Calendars	Directories
Coexistence	Gateway systems for message transfer between legacy and new mail system	Gateway systems for meeting scheduling interoperability (mutual free-time search, viewing)	Manual or automatic synchronization
Migration	Transfer, convert old mail messages, forward new mail, terminate legacy access for end users	Transfer, convert old calendar data and terminate legacy access for end users	Transfer, convert old distribution lists, nicknames for end user Convert legacy directory to new directory

Figure 6.6. Migration/coexistence considerations.

ment must be addressed. With some users in both the old and the new environment, it is important that the migrating applications (e-mail, calendar, directory) interoperate.

Coexistence for e-mail means that legacy e-mail system end users can send messages to the new e-mail system and vice versa. Either a gateway server system or a **backbone switch** that will perform the necessary e-mail message translations must be installed on your intranet, as previously discussed.

Coexistence for calendars means that legacy and new calendar system end users must be able to view each others' calendars and/or free and busy times and exchange meeting notices. A specialized gateway system that performs this function between the two calendar systems may be required. An example of such a product is the Lotus OfficeVision Calendar Connector (LOVCC), which supports free-time searches and exchanges of meeting requests/accepts/rejects between Domino Calendaring & Scheduling and IBM's OfficeVision calendar function.

Coexistence for directories between two e-mail or calendar systems means a synchronization program that ensures that, as one directory changes, the other directory is updated correspondingly. An investment in such a tool is warranted for migrations with large numbers of users or for a protracted coexistence period even if there are relatively few users. The Lotus Messaging Switch, a backbone switch for large e-mail coexistence requirements, provides such cross-directory maintenance and synchronization. Even if synchronization tools may not be required, an automated directory jump-start tool may save considerable time and effort. For example, tools are available to convert legacy format directories to the Domino Domain Directory from Lotus.

End-User Migration Requirements

From the end-user perspective, legacy migration typically means file transfer and conversion of current, personalized mail, calendar, and directory files from the old environment to the new environment. This can be very difficult or easy depending on the legacy environment and how long it was used. In the case of IBM Boca Raton, over 2000 end users migrated from OfficeVision/VM to Notes in 1995. Some had been OfficeVision/VM users for a decade and had many large, important files in that environment that required considerable time and effort in migration. End users require tools to perform their personal migration or will depend upon system administration to perform the migration for them. These tools are discussed in the next section.

End users also require communication, education, and support to survive the migration process. In IBM Boca Raton in 1994–1995, the CIO team developed a specialized migration workshop class and a Domino application to help its users complete their journey to Notes. The migration workshop provided an overview of Notes and hands-on experience with the migration tools. A record was created in the Domino application for each user to be migrated. It contained the user's e-mail address and date of migration class and was programmed to automatically generate e-mail reminder messages periodically before scheduled workshops. After the workshop, it sent messages reminding the users to terminate their OfficeVision subscription within 10 days or it would be automatically revoked by system administration. This process was highly successful—over 2000 OfficeVision/ VM IDs were terminated within a 5-month period.

Engaging end users effectively throughout a migration is very important, as was just described. Once end users have Notes, sending them e-mail messages with instructions and buttons to perform migration steps is a great approach. This was precisely what IBM's information technology support did to migrate thousands of Notes 3.x Mail users to Domino 4.x Mail servers after they had received the Notes 4.x client.

Availability of Migration/Coexistence Tools

Under the umbrella term "Domino Upgrade Services," the Domino Administrator includes several built-in e-mail migration tools, including the ability to migrate mail, calendar, directory and archive information administratively. See Figure 6.7 for details.

Coexistence between Domino and cc:Mail/Organizer, Exchange/ Outlook, MS-Mail and Schedule Plus, Groupwise, Netscape, Eudora, and Banyan mail and calendar environments are available from Lotus, Binary Tree, and Wingra.

Migration and coexistence tools from IBM's OfficeVision/VM, OfficeVision/MVS, and OfficeVision/400 to Notes/Domino are available from Lotus, Binary Tree, and TBS Software companies. Because of the large numbers of OfficeVision clients migrating to Notes/

Convert	Mail	Directory (user/groups)	Calendar/ Tasks
cc:Mail—DB6 and DB8 post offices (all "modern" versions)	Yes, with full fidelity. Support of rich text (cc: Mail R8) planned for 5.01+	Yes—users who are local on the source post office and groups	N/A
Lotus Organizer—2/x group scheduling version used with cc.Mail.	N/A	N/A	yes
MS-Mail—3.2 and above	Yes	Yes—users and groups	N/A
Microsoft Exchange–all versions	Yes	Yes	Yes
Novell Groupwise 4	Yes	Yes	Yes
Novell Groupwise 5	Yes	Yes	Yes
Netscape Mail Server	Yes	Users Only	N/A

Figure 6.7.   Built in migration tools in Domino upgrade services.

Domino, Lotus and IBM have announced the ability of the Notes client software to directly access OfficeVision data (VM, MVS, and OS/400 environments). This provides an easy way for end users to familiarize themselves with Notes/Domino in advance of actual data migration.

Upgrading from Notes/Domino 4.x to Notes/Domino 5.0

Lotus has simplified the upgrade from the prior Release 4.x to its current Release 5.0. There is full interaction between Release 4.x and 5.0 clients and servers. However, Release 4.x users will not have full use of Release 5.0 databases that use advanced Release 5.0 features. You need to carefully plan the steps necessary to upgrade your servers and clients with minimal disruption to ongoing work. In general, the Domino application program interfaces (APIs) between the two releases are compatible. The recommended sequence is to prioritize your current Release 4.x servers and convert them to Release 5.0 first, then address your end users in a staged manner. This means converting advanced Notes users (early adopters) first to help test the environment.

User Support Preparation

User support means that if a user has a question or a problem, he or she has a quick and cost-effective means to get an answer or resolve the problem. To support a large organization (500+ users) using intranet tools requires an organized approach to user support. This organized approach is usually called a **Help Desk**. A typical Help Desk includes a centralized staff of experts, a user-friendly voice response unit, a centralized problem-tracking database, a well-managed user-communication process, a well-defined service-level agreement on responsiveness, and a communication process for network and server status.

A centralized staff of application and system experts should be ready to answer questions and solve problems for a well-defined portion of the working day. The trend is to provide 24-hour-a-day, 7-day-a-week support. The staff should treat each and every user with patience and respect. According to a *PC Week* survey, the most important attributes of a help desk support staff from a user's perspective are (1) technical expertise, (2) speed in responding to reported problems, and (3) attitude and (4) consistency of phone support. [Schneider, 1993].

An intelligent phone service interface for users, sometimes called a **Voice Response Unit (VRU)**, is the first point of user contact for the Help Desk. A single, easy-to-remember phone number should be available for users to call and receive support. The VRU should offer a menu of choices to speed users to either automated responses (e.g., status of a common server) or an application expert.

A central database should be used by support personnel to enter and track problems through to resolution while referencing user profile information. This is useful to ensure problem closure, measure responsiveness, identify recurring problems, and identify users' personal information and problems' history quickly. Help Desk staff should obtain a standard set of information from the caller (name, location, problem description, etc.).

A process for identifying users, classifying and recording their problems, seeking additional expertise if necessary, communicating results to the users, and closing their problems must be defined. Seeking additional expertise may involve contacting backup support personnel or visiting the user's office for hands-on support. This can be handled by information technology or CIO team members identified to the Help Desk staff as on-site support personnel.

A well-defined policy of responsiveness based upon problem severity is key. For example, a showstopper problem should be resolved within 24 hours, a serious problem with a workaround should be resolved within 72 hours, and a minor problem with a workaround should be resolved within 7 days. A well-defined process for communicating network and server status among support staff, network administrators, server administrators, and the users is a must. Ideally this is an automated process linked to the network management system of alerts.

The following facilities are less common, but should be sought out as part of a comprehensive Help Desk system:

- **User direct access** to the central problem database for entry, review, and update. This will reduce the load on the Help Desk and increase user satisfaction.

- **Online query capability** of a comprehensive information database for support personnel and users. This can be considered to be a "self-help-desk" application.

- **Remote client system access by support personnel** to correct user problems. The IBM NetFinity application for Intel-based systems provides this capability when NetFinity Services is installed on the user's system and the NetFinity Manager is installed on the support person's system.

- **Expert system assistance** to support personnel. An expert system is an application capable of rapidly searching an expert **knowledge base** to derive an answer to a complex question or problem. A knowledge base is a database containing rules (or rules of thumb) about a complex subject based on experience or simple reasoning (e.g., "If the program returned an '0C1' return code, it is defective").

User productivity and user satisfaction are the most important benefits of a well-run Help Desk. Some secondary benefits come from downstream uses of Help Desk data accumulation. By analyzing the problem database, problem areas of the network or problem applications can be identified. This can help in replacement and new purchase decisions.

Computing the number of Help Desk staff required is based on the expected volume of calls, which depends on the number of users. A baseline can be achieved by measuring call volume and average call duration for a defined period (e.g., 5 to 10 days). Dividing call volume by the number of users derives a calls-per-user factor. This factor can then be applied to predict call volume as the rollout proceeds and new users are added to the total. The predicted length of an average user call helps determine the number of calls per day a support person is expected to handle. The call volume can then be used to estimate the number of personnel required. It is a good idea early on in a rollout to estimate high in case there are startup problems encountered. Office PC access to a problem report and network status database should be developed during this phase. This will reduce the load on the Help Desk and increase user satisfaction.

Communication and Education Preparation

The move to a Domino intranet is a culture shock to large organizations used to mainframe-based applications and workflow. Careful communication and demonstration is required to win users' hearts and minds. Human intellectual inertia is a barrier as well. Your new standard applications with graphic user interfaces (GUIs) require initial education, active practice, and ongoing support. A shift in daily operations and applications is hard for many people to adapt to quickly. Also, many users will be engaged in hot projects, preventing them from migration. Once beliefs are changed, intellectual inertia can be overcome. Once high-quality, stable tools are delivered, the transition to an intranet computing environment can occur smoothly.

The communications and education team should develop a communication plan to address user buy-in and ongoing awareness. Another key element is developing tools to capture end-user satisfaction with the new environment and thereby improve the transition process. The communication plan should address (1) user community analysis, (2) strategy, (3) deliverables, and (4) education audience analysis.

User Community Analysis

Within any large working population are specific groups that require a special communication focus. Executive management is especially important for early buy-in and participation. A clear and effective overall strategy statement and business plan presentation is the critical deliverable here.

Next, the CIO department and suppliers of service, that is, the members of the rollout teams, need to be solidly behind the new environment. They need to become early adopters of the tools, despite missing pieces, bugs, and performance problems. They also need to become an empowered team to execute the migration plan under time and budget constraints.

Unless your site has other special groups requiring early or special attention, the remaining users should be handled on a department-by-department basis, according to their rollout schedule.

Communication Strategy

Based on your user community analysis, a clear communication strategy can be built. It should have both a top-down and bottom-up approach. Top-down means gaining executive backing. Bottom-up means gaining grassroots user community support. The former allows the migration to start; the latter makes sure it succeeds.

1. Win early executive-level and critical user group support through focused, personal communication.

2. Win broad user support through frequent positive communication deliverables, user feedback mechanisms, demonstration of productivity and cost gains, and consistent quality responsiveness.

3. Win user support department by department with focused communication before and after departmental rollout.

Communications Deliverables

Communications deliverables are the documents, presentations, and programs "delivered" to the users in the execution of your communication strategy. They must be timely, highly accurate, sensitive to your audience, and consistent. Following is a suggested list of communications deliverables with a recommended delivery schedule:

- Publish **executive memos** to all managers and all users at migration kickoff and key checkpoints during the rollout.

- Publish **internal articles, newsletters, or technical reports** at least bimonthly to all users. Online softcopy and hardcopy versions should be provided to assure the widest possible distribution.

- Hold **well-advertised public presentations**, open to all users, monthly to present migration status.

- Present **the strategy and rollout details** to each department well before their rollout date (8 weeks preferably). This is valuable for setting expectations properly and handling individual concerns and questions.

- Conduct **postrollout feedback sessions** with a regular sample of departments. These provide valuable feedback to all team members.

- Conduct **frequent CIO Council meetings**. Attendees should include the CIO, service support leaders, and user representatives. Rollout status and upcoming events (checkpoints and decisions) should be on the agenda.

- Establish **Domino databases for user communication**. For example, an Important Bulletins database should be established to communicate upcoming intranet changes.

- Create a **user's guide**. It should be available as a Domino database for online access to both Notes and Web browser clients (and consider a printed version when a user is just rolled out).

- Consider a **custom poster or calendar** for all site users with a Notes intranet theme.

- Don't forget to kick off your communication activities with a **media blitz** just before the rollout begins!

Training staff and users is vital to the success of a Notes/Domino intranet rollout. A rollout is costly to fund and costly in impact to the employees undergoing training. A survey of Fortune 1000 companies estimated that almost one third of the total cost of intranet application acquisition and successful deployment was retraining expenses. [McFadden, 1994]

Education Audience Analysis

The key audiences that should be addressed are the CIO team, the information technology support staff, the site's secretaries, the executives, and the general users. The first audiences that must be educated in the new environment are the CIO team and any information technology support staff. It is assumed that the CIO team brings strong motivation and significant computer user experience to the table. It is further assumed that the information technology support staff brings skill and experience in intranet technology, support, and application development, but may require education in specifically selected user applications (if not, you selected the wrong supplier). If an inexperienced, internal information technology staff is employed, you should consider outsourcing or postponing the migration. The bedrock support for an intranet requires knowledge, skill, and experience across a broad set of technical areas.

Client Rollout Education Requirements

Education requirements for an intranet rollout are:

1. **Effectiveness.** Skills must stick with the user after education.

2. **Timeliness.** If education occurs in close time proximity to client system delivery, it is more likely that lessons will stick with the user.

3. **Convenience.** Education should last long enough to transfer critical skills but not so long as to impact current work assignments. Scheduling should be flexible to accommodate individual user requirements, but not violate the timeliness requirement.

   4. **Affordability.** The cost of education must be within budget
      limits.

Education Delivery Alternatives

The major education delivery alternatives are video tapes,
Computer-Based Training (CBT), traditional classroom instruction,
and multimedia intranet-based educational offerings such as streaming audio/video services.

   Videos can be very cost-effective if used with groups, but they
offer no customization or Q&A (question and answer) interaction.
Used as a supplementary delivery mechanism for individual applications or available on a long-term basis during steady state, they can
be valuable.

   Interactive CBT packages are very good for individual study. Recent packages incorporate CD-ROM and motion video technology
for improved quality and interactivity. For a large-scale rollout, lack
of individualized Q&A and lack of customization may be an obstacle,
as it is for videos. Also, some packages are quite expensive (up to
$2500) and may actually cost more than classroom instruction. How-
ever, CBT delivery should be seriously considered for both rollout
and steady state if it is cost-effective.

   Traditional classroom instruction coupled with hands-on interaction is the best alternative for a large-scale rollout. The opportunity for individualized Q&A and local customization makes this a
standout. However, this can be a costly selection. A high-quality instructor can cost over $2000 per day. Assuming a 20-student class,
this is a $100 daily charge per student. Don't forget to throw in the
costs of class materials and technical and administrative support. If
your users are primarily mainframe users with limited exposure to
GUIs, you need to invest in this form of education delivery. Your
Education team should acquire or develop course material on the
primary office applications—Notes and your productivity applications—at a minimum. This should include hands-on education with
handout materials. Class schedules should be synchronized with the
client rollout team. Courses should be customized to user requirements in terms of course content and class duration. The ratio of
customers who completed the education to the total target rollout
population should be tracked.

Network-based courses that provide dynamic, on-demand delivery of end-user education have recently become available. They offer multimedia features such as audio and video in addition to traditional text information. More important, they offer simplified end-user access via a Web browser with minimal delivery overhead. Time- and space-consuming installation steps such as those required for a CBT course are avoided. Course customization or correction is simplified because data need to be corrected only on the data delivery server. With sufficient intranet bandwidth and multimedia-capable client systems (e.g., a sound card and high-resolution graphics), these new tools are a valuable alternative to consider. IBM's internal rollout in the United States provided this "education-on-demand" for Notes to thousands of users.

Phase 3—The Rollout Engine

This phase is the critical path of the entire project. A critical path is that part of a plan in which problems must be solved rapidly or the plan will not achieve its target end date. Server rollout (setup and installation of servers in the server farm) should lead client rollout (PC installation in user offices). As organizations receive their new or upgraded clients, users should attend introductory education sessions. The project leadership should be ever-present, communicating early and late with users to gauge satisfaction and react to problems (see Figure 6.8).

Server Rollout

Server rollout is the installation of servers in the server farm to coincide with the requirements of the client rollout. E- mail servers and any supporting gateways (e.g., OfficeVision/VM to Lotus Notes) are likely the most critical here--they are very sensitive to the number of users assigned. You should develop a solid understanding of the number of users per server for this and other key applications.

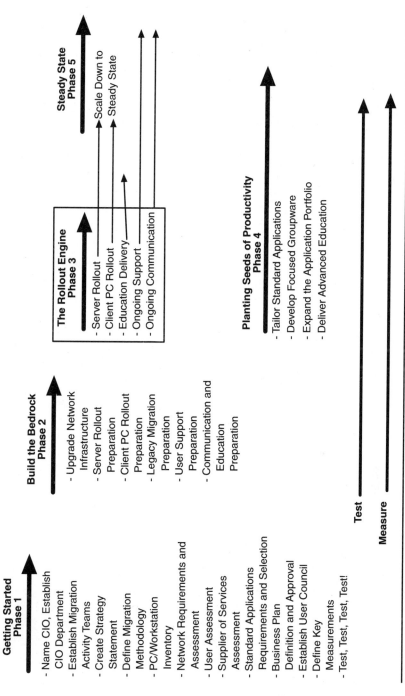

**Getting Started
Phase 1**

- Name CIO, Establish
  CIO Department
- Establish Migration
  Activity Teams
- Create Strategy
  Statement
- Define Migration
  Methodology
- PC/Workstation
  Inventory
- Network Requirements and
  Assessment
- User Assessment
- Supplier of Services
  Assessment
- Standard Applications
  Requirements and Selection
- Business Plan
  Definition and Approval
- Establish User Council
- Define Key
  Measurements
- Test, Test, Test, Test!

**Build the Bedrock
Phase 2**

- Upgrade Network
  Infrastructure
- Server Rollout
  Preparation
- Client PC Rollout
  Preparation
- Legacy Migration
  Preparation
- User Support
  Preparation
- Communication and
  Education
  Preparation

**The Rollout Engine
Phase 3**

- Server Rollout
- Client PC Rollout
- Education Delivery
- Ongoing Support
- Ongoing Communication

**Planting Seeds of Productivity
Phase 4**

- Tailor Standard Applications
- Develop Focused Groupware
- Expand the Application Portfolio
- Deliver Advanced Education

**Steady State
Phase 5**

- Scale Down to
  Steady State

Test

Measure

Figure 6.8.   Intranet rollout methodology outline—Phase 3.

The server administration team, supporting the server rollout, will see a leap in their responsibilities in the day-to-day operations of the servers (Domino, gateways, etc.) and network environment:

- They must ensure that daily, weekly, and monthly lists of tasks are completed on a timely basis and ad hoc requests are efficiently handled.

- They must maintain the Domino Domain Directory, certify servers and users, and oversee database replication.

- They must maintain server integrity through virus checking.

- They should control remote access, external customer access, and server access and deny lists.

- They must monitor many events: Domino server logs, thresholds, server statistics, pending mail vs. dead mail, and server-to-server connectivity.

- They must maintain software levels according to software maintenance guidelines for new releases and fixes.

- They must manage hard file space and perform data backup and recovery.

- Finally, they should identify and resolve Domino-related problems and report problems not under their control to the appropriate support team.

Client PC Rollout

Client PC rollout is the scheduled, managed process of installing PCs or NCs in user offices. Scheduling PC installations with busy users under considerable time pressure requires solid preparation, a smooth process, acute communication skills, and technical competence. This includes migration from legacy environments as well as delivery of new capabilities.

Education Delivery

Users unfamiliar with the basics of the new intranet interface need basic education just prior to client PC upgrade. Assuming that users still have access to legacy applications (in order to be able to continue to perform their jobs), education on new applications should occur within two weeks after rollout.

Ongoing User Support

The Help Desk, covered in the Phase 2 discussion, must be armed and ready when the bell sounds for the rollout.

Phase 4—Planting the Seeds of Productivity

This phase is motivated by the need to accommodate local user requirements, to tailor the new tools with functional or human factor improvements where needed. It is motivated by the need to bring some beloved features from the past (the legacy) into the present while encouraging users to leave the past behind where appropriate. Most important, it is motivated by the need to exploit the power of the intranet tools in targeted ways to improve productivity. It is also a phase that never ends! Phase 4 is where the application development team earns its stripes (see Figure 6.9).

A UCLA/Arthur Andersen study surveyed users of Notes and determined that although most were using e-mail, only about half used discussion or knowledge databases. Further, just 14 percent used workflow applications--deemed the most valuable to a business by the study. The study recommended that "companies use small experiments to expand groupware competencies," because "insights can be gained and risk can be contained." [Anonymous, 1996]

Tailor Standard Applications

Most PC applications offer some form of customization: default values, parameter settings, switches, smart icons (user- or application-

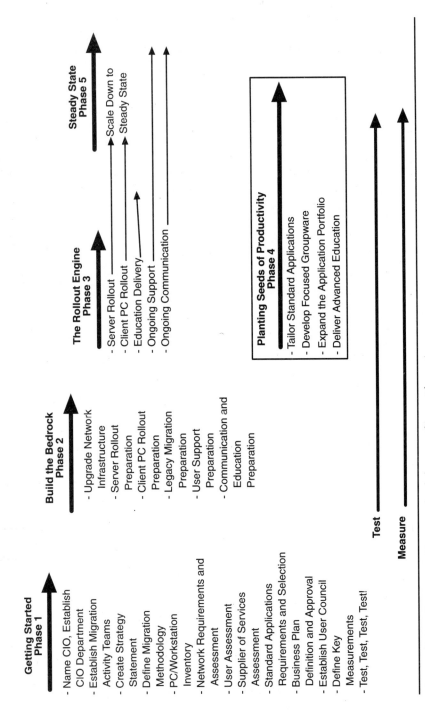

Getting Started Phase 1
- Name CIO, Establish CIO Department
- Establish Migration Activity Teams
- Create Strategy Statement
- Define Migration Methodology
- PC/Workstation Inventory
- Network Requirements and Assessment
- User Assessment
- Supplier of Services Assessment
- Standard Applications Requirements and Selection
- Business Plan Definition and Approval
- Establish User Council
- Define Key Measurements
- Test, Test, Test, Test!

Build the Bedrock Phase 2
- Upgrade Network Infrastructure
- Server Rollout Preparation
- Client PC Rollout Preparation
- Legacy Migration Preparation
- User Support Preparation
- Communication and Education Preparation

The Rollout Engine Phase 3
- Server Rollout
- Client PC Rollout
- Education Delivery
- Ongoing Support
- Ongoing Communication

Steady State Phase 5
- Scale Down to Steady State

Planting Seeds of Productivity Phase 4
- Tailor Standard Applications
- Develop Focused Groupware
- Expand the Application Portfolio
- Deliver Advanced Education

Test

Measure

Figure 6.9. Intranet rollout methodology outline—Phase 4.

supplied icons that are optional) and APIs. If user requirements and legacy application experiences are understood, application customization can play a key role in user acceptance of and satisfaction with new Notes intranet applications.

Develop Focused Groupware

In a large organization, there are many teams with unique work processes as well as processes that affect the entire user community. With a powerful groupware development platform, such as Domino, focused groupware applications can be quickly developed. Like seeds planted in a garden, these applications sprout and blossom to create compelling examples of productivity for all to see.

The rollout leadership should identify a set of key business application areas that are candidates for initial groupware development. Internal or external groupware experts should then set up short, focused group meetings with each business area to understand requirements and suggest a groupware application solution. If the reaction is positive, a prototype application should be created for evaluation. If this is accepted, the final application should be quickly deployed. In many cases, the prototype *is* the final application! This is where your Application Development team earns their pay.

Expand the Application Portfolio

New applications and enhanced versions of current applications are part of a never-ending stream of evaluation, acceptance or rejection, testing, and deployment. Establishing a user-driven application review board aided by a workflow application greatly smoothes this process.

Deliver Advanced Education

As users digest the new applications, become comfortable with them, and develop expertise, advanced courses should be available to enrich their use of the applications and, if possible, develop new groupware applications. A key objective for your Notes/Domino intranet should be to educate a reasonable percentage in Domino application development. Percolating this application development skill in your organization will pay rich dividends in user satisfaction and productivity. Also, the basic education should be expanded to include support for any new or enhanced applications.

Phase 5—Steady State

After a major rollout, the rollout teams should be reduced in staff to reflect a steady-state process (see Figure 6.10). Support, communications activities, delivery of legacy migration tools, development of Domino groupware, and expansion of the application portfolio should continue as in Phase 4.

Overall Planning and Project Management Processes

A well-thought-out planning and project management process must accompany the rollout's execution. Regular, formal meetings are required to guarantee that the requirements, the plan, the financial model, buy-in, processes, and the organization remain on track throughout the rollout. Note that meeting frequency and duration must be balanced against the need to get real work done (see the task management meeting approach discussed later in this section).

The planning process should result in concrete, documented, high-level plans. High-level plans establish major goals for the rollout and document both tactical and strategic decisions. Ideally these plans should be placed in a centrally shared database. A good approach is to place high-level plans in a Domino document database. A common title page format, containing summary information, is easily followed by a free-form in-depth section.

The high-level plan documents should be living documents and form the basis for regular review meetings. For example, quarterly high-level plan reviews can be initiated from the project's inception. The planners can present their work to representatives of each team. Key external consultants can be invited to provide guidance and fresh opinions.

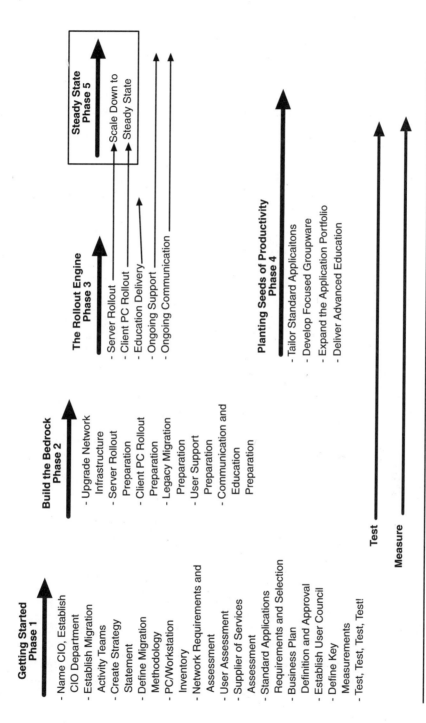

**Getting Started
Phase 1**

- Name CIO, Establish
  CIO Department
- Establish Migration
  Activity Teams
- Create Strategy
  Statement
- Define Migration
  Methodology
- PC/Workstation
  Inventory
- Network Requirements and
  Assessment
- User Assessment
- Supplier of Services
  Assessment
- Standard Applications
  Requirements and Selection
- Business Plan
  Definition and Approval
- Establish User Council
- Define Key
  Measurements
- Test, Test, Test, Test!

**Build the Bedrock
Phase 2**

- Upgrade Network
  Infrastructure
- Server Rollout
  Preparation
- Client PC Rollout
  Preparation
- Legacy Migration
  Preparation
- User Support
  Preparation
- Communication and
  Education
  Preparation

**The Rollout Engine
Phase 3**

- Server Rollout
- Client PC Rollout
- Education Delivery
- Ongoing Support
- Ongoing Communication

**Planting Seeds of Productivity
Phase 4**

- Tailor Standard Applications
- Develop Focused Groupware
- Expand the Application Portfolio
- Deliver Advanced Education

**Steady State
Phase 5**

- Scale Down to
  Steady State

Test

Measure

Figure 6.10. Intranet rollout methodology outline—Phase 5.

As high-level plans are formulated, detailed implementation task plans should be defined. The framework surrounding this effort should be a comprehensive project planning application leading to Gantt chart (the rollout methodology figures are examples) or PERT analysis for the project. **PERT** stands for Program Evaluation and Review Techniques and is a method of deriving plans of action from a set of individual tasks. PERT analysis is key to understanding critical paths and intertask dependencies. You can easily place detailed tasks in a Domino database. The goal should be to make things easy for your rollout teammates. The Domino database contents can then be automatically converted into input for the CASuperproject application, for example, which can create the PERT diagrams. For a small-scale project, the Domino task database itself, with suitable views, can suffice.

The Domino task database should be used in a weekly task review meeting, run by a single project leader whose role should be to follow up and coordinate all participant task entry and status information prior to the meeting. Have a set agenda by major activity area (e.g., Client Rollout, Server Rollout, etc.). In this way, individuals only have to attend the portion of the meeting that reviews their tasks. This approach minimizes the impact to their work schedules. Keep the meeting to a maximum duration of two hours. Insist that tasks not last longer than a week. If an activity takes longer than a week, have it broken up into weekly tasks for checkpointing purposes. The project leader can then step through each weekly task to determine if it has been completed. Minimal side conversations should be allowed during task status reviews.

It is important to note that, in addition to all of the technical concerns and activities, personnel management issues and group dynamics play a major part in the success of a project of this nature. Only seasoned leaders need apply.

From Rollout Management to Information Technology Management

As you move from rollout management to steady state, you must consider ongoing management of your overall information technology investment. Following is a set of objectives that should be considered:

- **Users in Control.** It is very important to have the users in control of the information technology infrastructure. This means that user representatives should be contributing to the information technology investment, deployment, and support processes on an ongoing basis.

- **Team-Oriented Management Structure.** The information technology management organization must be empowered and flexible to make short- and long-range decisions, and to deal with problems as they arise.

- **Processes in Place.** Well-defined processes for investment, deployment of facilities, security of assets, disaster recovery, and ongoing support of the information technology infrastructure should be in place.

- **Measurements.** A comprehensive measurement system for the information technology infrastructure, including operational status, financial status, security, and customer satisfaction, is key. Measurements should be reported regularly in summary form for decision-making purposes.

- **Skilled Support Partners.** A dedicated, highly skilled support organization should be in place for long-term information technology infrastructure support.

- **Management Tools.** Tools, including workflow and measurement databases, must be available to control information technology processes.

These goals are strongly recommended for effective information technology management. They achieve the overriding objective of a user-controlled information technology environment. The fallout from a well-executed rollout will lead to accomplishing the rest of the goals as well.

Summary

The five-phase methodology described in this chapter is a proven approach based on the author's experience in IBM Boca Raton in 1994 and 1995. [Krantz, 1995] It has since been applied in other IBM divisions (e.g., IBM Microelectronics Division) and other companies (e.g., Bezeq–Israel Telecom). With its guidance, a good organization, and appropriate funding, you, too, can establish a Notes/Domino intranet in your organization.

Appendix A

Lotus Resources

The purpose of this appendix is to offer a brief guide on how to get more information in pursuit of a Notes/Domino infrastructure for your business.

Resources on the Web

- **Iris Associates, Inc.** (the developers of Notes and Domino) at URL *www.iris.com*. Its main purpose is to offer contact with the company and provide a directory to major Notes/Domino sites.

- **Lotus Development Corporation** (Iris's parent company and developers of SmartSuite, including Lotus 1-2-3, Freelance, Organizer, cc:Mail, and other products). URL is *www.lotus.com*. It is a full-function site containing product, service, and related information for the company.

- **Notes.Net Web Site.** Notes.Net is staffed and maintained by the folks at Iris Associates, the developers of Notes and Domino. Its main appeal is to Notes and Domino developers. It can be found at URL *www.notes.net.*

- **NotesNIC Web Page.** Provides information about NotesNIC, a Notes directory service on the Internet that provides a way for Domino-driven sites to locate and communicate with each other. This is accomplished by grouping all NotesNIC servers into one Domino domain called the NET Domain. As a result, all NotesNIC servers share a replica copy of the NET Domain Directory, which provides the information needed to locate and communicate with Domino Internet sites. Its URL is *http://www.lnn.com/notesnic.nsf.*

- **Lotus Notes FAQ Web Page.** A FAQ that addresses commonly asked Notes questions taken from the comp.groupware.lotus-notes.misc news group and the LNOTES-L mailing list. Its URL is *metro.turnpike.net/kyee/NotesFAQ.html.* If you are not into today's Notes/Domino administration or programming details, it's not for you.

- **Lotus Notes on Netscape.** Netscape has a special category for Notes-related companies and products. The URL is *http://directory.netscape.com/Computers/Software/Groupware/Lotus_Notes/.*

- **Lotus Development Support.** Lotus offers a complete suite of support alternatives, customizable to most business needs. This includes telephone access and online "knowledge base" access for questions and problems. On the Web, visit URL *http://www.support.lotus.com* for information. Lotus Knowledge Base contains information on Lotus products: Notes, cc:Mail, SmartSuite, and Developer Tools. It is available for queries over the Web from the support page. A recent, innovative support offering is called Personal Page, a Web-based service with which you can create individual Web pages to access personalized Lotus support information. The customizable Web pages are continuously updated with user-service with which you can create individual Web pages to access personalized Lotus support information. The customizable Web pages are continuously updated with user-selected topics. Either a Web browser or Notes client can be used for Personal Page.

Other Resources

- **Business Partners.** Hundreds of national and local companies, including consultants, resellers, and developers, are business partners with Lotus Development. Lotus lists them in its Business Partners Catalog database (Notes of course), available on the Web for queries from the Lotus home page (select "Business Partners").

- **Certifications.** In the Certified Lotus Professional programs, consultants, developers, and administrators can become Notes certified in four areas of specialization. Go to the Lotus home page on the Web, select "Education," and then "Certifications."

- **Education.** Lotus education services include:

  - Instructor-led, hands-on training at Partners Worldwide.

  - Professional and instructor certification (CLP, CLS, CLI).

  - Media-based training (including CBTs, ScreenCam, etc.).

  - Lotus Authorized Education Centers (LAECs) located all over the world.

  - Lotus Education Academic Partners (LEAPs), a global alliance of accredited colleges and universities that give technical education to students on all levels.

- LearningSpace, a tool for developing, deploying, and delivering courses and for augmenting classroom training. LearningSpace course materials include a class schedule, links to readings, assignment, and quizzes. LearningSpace encourages interaction through its facilitation of discussions among each other and with the instructor in teams. The URL to find out more is *www.lotus.com/ learningspace.*

- See URL *http://www.lotus.com/home.nsf/welcome/education* for more details.

- **Lotus Consulting.** Lotus Consulting is a worldwide organization available to provide a jump start to Notes, Domino, or other Lotus product investments. More information can be found at URL *http://www.lotus.com/home.nsf/welcome/consulting.*

- **LotusSphere.** Annual five-day conferences in the United States and Europe, including in-depth technical sessions and trade demonstrations.

Appendix B

Glossary of Terms

Following is a glossary consisting of Notes/Domino, Internet, and general computing terms for the reader. For additional Internet definitions refer to RFC 1983 at URL *http://www.cis.ohio-state.edu/htbin/ rfc/rfc1983.html.*

ACL   Access Control List. Data that controls access to a protected object. An access control list specifies the privilege attributes needed to access the object and the permissions that may be granted. Notes uses access control lists for individual databases.

ACK   Acknowledge. A network packet acknowledging the receipt of data.

ActiveX   Microsoft's ActiveX consists of Active Controls, which are downloadable programs, and Active Documents, which allow a browser to host a file with all of its editing tools and functions available. ActiveX is based on the Component Object Model (COM) standard and provides object-based interoperability between development tools, components, applications, and operating systems. It is a direct proprietary competitor to Java.

ADSL   Asymmetric Digital Subscriber Line. A new modem technology that converts existing twisted-pair telephone lines into access paths for multimedia and high-speed data communications, ADSL transmits more than 6 Mbps to a subscriber and as much as 640 Kbps in the opposite direction.

Agent A portion of a network management system that reports information about conditions and accepts commands to alter the state of one or more managed objects. Typical commands are GET, SET, CREATE, DELETE, and ACTION.

Aggregation and Delegation Object-oriented programming terms. Although multiple inheritance is more flexible than single inheritance, it can add a significant amount of complexity to an object model. An alternative to multiple inheritance is a model called aggregation and delegation. An aggregate object can be created that exposes an interface combining the behaviors of multiple objects. The aggregate object itself does not implement these behaviors. Instead, it delegates the requests to a set of other delegation objects.

AIX IBM's version of UNIX, available on the PS/2, RISC System/6000, and other platforms. AIX on the RISC System/6000 is based on OSF/1 and meets 1151 of the 1170 elements of SPEC1170.

Alert A network management term for data sent from a network management agent to a manager indicating that some action is to be taken or a problem has occurred.

Alias A name, usually short and easy to remember, that is translated into another name, usually long and difficult to remember.

Alpha test The first test of a software application or operating system performed by an external, volunteer organization.

Analog Telephone transmission and/or switching that derived from the word "analogous," which means "similar to."

Anonymous FTP A method using the FTP program to download or upload files from a server over a TCP/IP network without a password.

ANSI American National Standards Institute. The U.S. standardization body. ANSI is a member of the International Organization for Standardization (ISO).

API Application Program Interface. A functional interface supplied by the operating system or by an application program that allows an application program written in a high-level language to use specific data or functions of the operating system or the licensed program.

AppleTalk   A networking protocol developed by Apple Computer for communication between Apple Computer products and other computers.

Applet   In general, a small application program. An applet is a unique type of compound document component. It is a mini Java application that is designed to run within a Web page container in a browser. The Java applet is downloaded into the browser at execution time. In the original model, applets were confined by some very strict security features. An applet was restricted by a "sandbox." The sandbox prevents an applet from accessing any file or network resources on the browser client machine. A number of people found the sandbox too restrictive, so it is now an optional feature for applets.

Application layer   The topmost layer in the OSI Reference Model, providing such communication services as electronic mail and file transfer.

Application server   A server system that runs application code in response to a client system's request.

Archie   An Internet application for locating publicly available files using anonymous FTP.

ARP   Address Resolution Protocol. A method to translate an IP (Internet Protocol) address into a MAC (Media Access Control) address.

ARPAnet   The first network of computers, funded by the U.S. Department of Defense Advanced Projects Agency.

ASCII   American Standard Code for Information Interchange. A 7-bit code representing 128 discrete characters without using a shift code. It defines 96 printable characters (A through Z in upper- and lowercase, 0 through 9, and punctuation marks) and several control characters (carriage return, line feed, and backspace). An eighth bit called a parity bit is sometimes added for error checking. IBM developed an Extended ASCII with 8 bits per characters for the IBM Personal Computer in 1981. The lower 128 characters (0 through 127) are standard ASCII; the higher 128 characters (128 through 255) are for international punctuation and other special characters.

Async   Asynchronous. Operating without precise clocking. Also, a method to transmit data that sends a single character at a time.

ATM Asynchronous Transfer Mode. A method of high-speed data transmission that can dynamically allocate bandwidth to multiple data streams of different types by breaking each stream into 53-byte cells (5-byte header, 48 bytes of data) of information. It is intended to support many different types of traffic on a single network (e.g., voice, video, and data). ATM is planned to be used as a basic data transport technique for high-speed WAN and LAN applications. Operating speeds are from 25 Mbps to 155 Mbps for individual connections today. Gigabit-range transmissions are predicted within the next 5 years.

Attribute A term used for a data item for a network management system or a directory service (such as X.500). An attribute consists of a type identifier along with one or more values.

Authentication Verifying that a data transmission from a person (or a process) is indeed from that person (or process).

Automatic routing Routing of fax documents to the addressed individual on a LAN or centralized system automatically. There are several methods of accomplishing this using DID, OCR (optical character recognition), or DTMF techniques.

BISDN See *Broadband ISDN*.

Backbone That portion of a network used to interconnect major subnetworks. For example, the cable used to connect the networks of two buildings on a site could be called a backbone.

Backbone switch A gateway system that supports multiple mail protocols, including industry standards such as X.400, and is designed for high levels of traffic. It will sometimes include e-mail address directory synchronization features. Also called an e-mail switch.

Backplane A board in a hub or router system that contains one or more buses that carry all network communications. This enables networking among the various modules that directly connect different LAN segments. It is analogous to a PC bus to which various interface cards are connected.

Bandwidth The amount of data that can be transmitted across a particular network. Token-ring has a 16 Mbps bandwidth. Technically, bandwidth is defined as the difference, in Hertz (Hz), between the highest and lowest frequencies of a transmission channel.

Baseband A network technology that uses a single frequency for data transmission. All communicating stations participate in every transmission.

Baud The number of modulations of an analog signal in one second, typically referring to data transmission speed over a telephone line.

BBS See *Bulletin Board System*.

Berkeley Software Distribution (BSD) UNIX operating system and its utilities developed and distributed by the University of California at Berkeley. BSD is usually preceded by the version number of the distribution; e.g., 4.3 BSD is version 4.3 of the Berkeley UNIX distribution.

Beta test The second major test phase performed on an unreleased version of a software application or operating system by an external volunteer or internal organization. Because beta test follows alpha test, it is assumed that the software is basically stable and will only have a few minor bugs left. A very common practice in the PC software industry is for software vendors to recruit a large number of external volunteers to participate in a beta test of an update to an existing application or the release of a new one.

Big-endian A format for storage or transmission of binary data in which the most significant bit (or byte) comes first. The reverse convention is called little-endian.

BOC Bell Operating Company. A more common term is RBOC, for Regional Bell Operating Company. The local telephone company in each of the seven U.S. regions.

Bps Bits per second. The rate of data transmission across a network.

Bridge A device that transparently interconnects two LANs that use the same logical-link control protocol but may use different Media Access Control (MAC) protocols. This is performed in a manner transparent to higher levels on the protocol stack. Only data destined for the other LAN is transferred. Bridges can usually be made to filter packets, that is, to forward only certain traffic. Related devices are repeaters, which simply forward electrical signals from one cable to another, and full-fledged routers, which make routing decisions based on several criteria.

Broadband The multiplexing of multiple independent network data streams onto a single cable. This is usually done using frequency division multiplexing. Broadband technology allows several networks to coexist on a single cable; traffic from one network does not interfere with traffic from another because the "conversations" happen on different frequencies in the "ether," rather like the commercial radio system.

Broadband ISDN   BISDN. Digital data transmission standard to handle high-bandwidth applications, such as video. The architecture supports wide area transmission at speeds of 51, 155, and 622 Mbps per channel. Eventually 2.4 Gbps will be supported. Fiber-optic cable is required.

Broadcast   A packet delivery system in which a copy of a given packet is given to all hosts attached to the network (e.g., token-ring).

Broadcast storm   Condition when an incorrect packet is broadcast onto a network, which causes multiple systems to respond all at once (typically with equally incorrect packets, which causes the storm to grow exponentially in severity).

Brouter   A combination bridge and router device that transmits data between networks at both the data-link and network layers.

Browser   A graphical software interface that enables you to look at information on the World Wide Web.

Bulletin Board System   BBS. A computer, and associated software, that typically provides electronic messaging services, archives of files, and any other services or activities of interest to the bulletin board system's operator. Although BBSs have traditionally been the domain of hobbyists, an increasing number of BBSs are connected directly to the Internet, and many BBSs are currently operated by government, educational, and research institutions.

Cable   The wires used to interconnect one or more network components. Cable types include twisted pair, coaxial, and fiber-optic.

CASE   Computer-Aided Software Engineering. Software products that aid software developers with data modeling, library management, and code generation.

CCITT   International Consultative Committee for Telegraphy and Telephony. Now known at the ITUT, it is a unit of the International Telecommunications Union (ITU) of the United Nations. CCITT produces technical standards, known as Recommendations, for all internationally controlled aspects of analog and digital communications.

CDI   Compact Disk–Interactive. A format developed by Philips Consumer Electronics Co. for recording and playing interactive multimedia program on 120-mm optical (compact) disks.

CDDI   Copper Distributed Data Interface. FDDI over shielded or unshielded twisted-pair copper wire.

CDPD Cellular Digital Packet Data. A wireless communication standard transporting digital data packets at 19.2 Kbps across idle channels on cellular telephone networks.

CDR Compact Disk–Recordable. A 120-mm optical (compact) disk on which data can be recorded once and read many times.

CD-ROM Compact Disk–Read-Only Memory. CD format for text, graphics, and high-fidelity stereo sound.

CD-ROM XA CD-ROM eXtended Architecture. CD enhanced format that supports concurrent audio and video. This was originally supported by Sony, Philips, and Microsoft.

CERN The research center in Switzerland that is the home location of the World Wide Web.

CERT A cooperative venture that collects information about vulnerabilities and disseminates it to systems managers, sponsored by the Defense Advanced Research Projects Agency and Carnegie Mellon University.

CGI Common Gateway Interface. An interface for external programs to communicate with information servers, such as HTTP servers.

Channel An electrical path of communication between two or more points. Also called a circuit, facility, line, link, or path. Typically, what a subscriber rents from the telephone company.

Checksum A calculated value that depends on the contents of a packet. This value is sent along with the packet when it is transmitted. The receiving system computes a new checksum based upon the received data and compares this value with the checksum of the packet. If the two values are equal, the receiver is assured that the data was received correctly.

CIO Chief Information Officer. The individual responsible for management of a business unit's information technology infrastructure, ongoing investments, and ongoing support.

Circuit A direct data stream between two systems on a network.

Circuit switching A communications model in which a dedicated communication path is established between two hosts. The public telephone system is an example of a circuit-switched network.

Circuit-switched service A category of long-distance telecommunication service in which the equipment dials a connection, transfers data, and hangs up when it completes the transmission. [Derfler and Freed, 1993]

CISC Complex Instruction Set Computer. A computer whose processor is designed to sequentially run variable-length instructions, many of which require several clock cycles, that perform complex tasks and thereby simplify programming.

Class A class is a template that defines the structure of an object. The structure consists of the member variables and the methods supported by the object. Multiple instances of an object may exist, each conforming to the class template. Each instance will maintain its own unique values for the variables. For example, you might have two instances of the client object, Jim and Joe. Both objects use the same class template, but they maintain different data values. All Java objects are defined through a Java Class. The JDK provides a set of Java Core Classes.

Client A computer or process that accesses the data, services, or resources of another computer or process on the network.

Client/server computing A computing model in which clients' systems (usually intelligent PCs and workstations) run user applications. The applications use a combination of their resources and a portion of the storage and computing resources of one or more server systems (e.g., high-performance PCs) to perform useful work. The application portion on the client requests server resources by communicating over a network.

Client/server network A computer network in which client systems use the network to request services and data from network-attached server systems.

Collapsed backbone A collapsed backbone is formed when the midplane/backplane of a box (hub, bridge, router) is used as the backbone. Performance on a collapsed backbone is often better than performance on a normal backbone.

COM Common Object Model. Microsoft's binary standard for specifying interfaces between objects as well as a language for describing those interfaces. The Common Object Model is a language-independent model that defines both an object model and a component model. COM objects support encapsulation, polymorphism, and multiple interface inheritance. COM uses aggregation and delegation to simulate multiple implementation inheritance. The COM runtime model provides basic ORB functions, including object location, object activation, and object destruction. COM objects communicate using events and interfaces. Interfaces are defined using IDL. COM objects are also components. COM supports development components (ActiveX controls), compound document components (DocObjects), and service components (automation and native COM objects). COM components can be implemented in Java. The Microsoft JVM dynamically generates COM interfaces for all Java applications and JavaBeans. Therefore, all COM applications can interoperate with Windows-resident Java applications.

Common Gateway Interface   See *CGI*.

Communication services   The software and protocols that move data across the network.

Compiler   A computer program that converts source programs (e.g., C or FORTRAN) into executable (or binary) programs.

Component   A component is a reusable software building block. It is analogous to an electronic component. A component may or may not strictly conform to the academic definition of an object, but it looks and feels a lot like an object. All components are encapsulated, but they may or may not support the other two defining characteristics of an object: inheritance and polymorphism. Three characteristics differentiate a component from an object:

- A component is designed to be used within another application, known as a container.

- A component may consist of only one class, or it may be a composite of many classes, or it may be an entire application.

- A component is designed to be reused without modification of its source code.

This third point is really critical. In general, it's pretty hard to reuse an object without access to the source code. Components, on the other hand, are designed to be reused as is, without modification of source. Many components are customizable, but they are customized through property manipulation or customization methods. If you need to muck around in the source code of an object to make it suit your purposes, then it is not a component; it is more likely a foundation class.

Component Model   There are many different types of components. A component model defines how a component is defined, how it is used, and how it interacts with its container or with other components. Some components are designed to be used within application development tools (development components). Some components are designed to be used within a compound document framework. Others are designed to be used as application services (service components).

Compound document   A document or a part of a document that contains text, graphics, scanned images, audio, and full-motion video data.

Compression   Changing the storage or transmission scheme for information so that less space is required to represent the same information (i.e., fewer bits).

Confidentiality   A term used in computer security to mean encryption of transmitted data.

Connectionless service   A data transmission service in which each frame of data can be broken up into one or more independent packets, each containing both a source and destination address. The packets may be delivered out of sequence or dropped. Sometimes called datagram service. Examples are LANs, Internet IP, and ordinary postcards.

Container   A container is the application that contains a component. A container provides an application context and management and control services for the component. For development and compound document components, a container is often some type of visualization device, such as a form, frame, or compound document. For service components, a container provides a set of execution services. In practical terms, a container provides an operating system process in which to execute the code within the component.

CORBA   Common Object Request Broker Architecture. A set of specifications to enable objects to transparently make requests and receive responses across a computer network. The Object Management Group's (OMG's) CORBA is a language-independent object model and a specification for a distributed ORB. CORBA objects support encapsulation, polymorphism, and multiple interface and class inheritance. CORBA object servers are service components. Numerous vendors have implemented CORBA-compliant ORBs. The OMG has also defined a set of related object services (CORBAservices), although the vendors have been less consistent in implementing these services. CORBA objects communicate using interfaces defined through IDL and optionally using events. If the specific CORBA implementation being used provides IDL mappings for Java, then CORBA clients and objects can be developed in Java. Originally, each CORBA vendor developed its own communication protocol. Recently OMG defined a standard interoperability protocol, the Internet Inter-ORB Protocol (IIOP). Most vendors now support IIOP. Java IDL provides a generic mechanism to map Java requests to CORBA IDL and the IIOP protocol.

Corporate network   Connects two or more geographically distant sites, where each site connects several hundred users.

CSMA/CD   Carrier Sense Multiple Access with Collision Detection. The media access control method employed by Ethernet networks.

Cyclic Redundancy Check   CRC. A number derived from a set of data that will be transmitted. By recalculating the CRC at the remote end and comparing it to the value originally transmitted, the receiving node can detect some types of transmission errors.

Daemon   An event-triggered program, equivalent in function to an agent.

DASD   Direct Access Storage Device. A hard disk is an example.

Data model   Describes the data that a computer process works with and produces.

Datagram   A data packet transmitted through a network with prior connection being established between the source and destination systems.

Data-Link Layer   Layer 2 of most network architectures. Defines the method to transmit data between two network entities across a single physical connection or a series of bridged connections.

DBMS   DataBase Management System.

DCE   Distributed Computing Environment. A distributed computing foundation that helps create a single system out of all the diverse resources distributed on the network. This includes directory services, naming services, authentication services, and remote procedure calls, among other facilities.

DCOM   Microsoft's Distributed COM (DCOM) provides distribution services for COM. DCOM automatically constructs proxy objects on the client and server machines to represent the remote objects. DCOM uses an object-enhanced version of the DCE RPC for its communications protocol.

DDE Dynamic Data Exchange. A standard for dynamic data sharing between two desktop applications, DDE is supported in the Windows and OS/2 operating environments.

Decision Support System DSS. A software product that provides services, such as an interactive query of a database, or functions, such as statistical routines, that give meaning to information. A DSS presents the information to the end users.

DECS Domino Enterprise Connection Services. Access to enterprise data from a Notes client or Web browser via Domino server. Native connectivity is provided to DB2 (IBM's flagship relational database offering), Sybase, and Oracle. A visual mapping interface is provided, requiring no programming.

Dependent display terminal Typically a combined CRT (cathode-ray tube) OK. display and keyboard device connected to a network that transmits keystrokes to a multiuser system running a desired application. The multiuser system returns updated user interface screens to the terminal. These were most commonly employed by mainframe multiuser systems.

DES Data Encryption Standard. A widely used, government-sponsored, data encryption method that scrambles data into an unbreakable code for transmission over a public network. The encryption key has over 72 quadrillion combinations and is randomly chosen.

DHCP Dynamic Host Configuration Protocol. An IP-based protocol that dynamically assigns an IP (Internet Protocol) address to a host upon request.

Dictionary/Directory An inventory of data resources that controls the totality of data elements within an application and that serves as the repository of all descriptive information about each data element, including location information.

DID Direct Inward Dialing. The method of dialing inside a company directly without going through the telephone attendant.

Digital signal processor A specialized digital microprocessor that performs calculations on digitized signals that were originally analog (e.g., voice) and then sends the results on.

Digital signature An identification mark provided by the sender/composer to prove that he/she really sent the message. It meets the following conditions: (a) unforgeable, (b) authentic, (c) unalterable, (d) nonreusable. Digital signatures have the potential to possess greater legal authority than handwritten signatures. Notes uses digital signatures when mailing documents and section signing using RSA's MD2 (Message Digest 2) algorithm.

Digital switch See *Switch*.

Directory In DCE, the directory contains information about resources, services, objects, and users on the network. This makes it simple to find each of these things by using only the name and makes it possible for each component to be moved in the network as business or technology requirements dictate without needing to change applications.

Distributed computing A type of computing that allows computers with different hardware and software to be combined on a network to function as a single computer to share the task of processing application programs.

Distributed database A collection of several different data repositories that looks like a single database to the user.

Distributed Directory Services A DCE service that provides a single naming model throughout the distributed computing environment, enabling users to identify network resources by name. With this universal naming system, users can locate and access servers, files, disks, or print queues without specifying their physical location in the network.

Distributed Relational Database Architecture See *DRDA*.

Distributed services Permits transparent sharing of files and other system resources among systems.

DME The Distributed Management Environment, developed by the OSF, defines a set of APIs for writing applications to manage distributed computing environments.

DNS Domain Name System. The distributed name/address mechanism used in the Internet.

Document compiler A software program that translates a document and a set of tags into final printed output. The IBM document compiler, BookMaster, used tags of the form **:P.** and **:H1**, where **:P.** indicated the start of a paragraph and **:H1** indicated a new title for a page.

Domain (1) That part of a network in which the data processing resources are under common control. (2) In TCP/IP, the naming system used in hierarchical networks. In Lotus Notes, a collection of Domino servers. The Domain Directory contains the contents or definition of the domain in terms of servers, their mail routing connections, replication schedules, and user names and addresses.

Domain controller   A designated server in a client/server network responsible for control of a set of data processing resources, such as a group of file servers or printers. Clients will gain access to these resources by logging on to the domain controller.

Domain Directory   The Notes/Domino name of the Domino database stored on Domino servers containing the contents or definition of the associated Domino domain in terms of servers, their mail routing connections, replication schedules, and user names and addresses.

Domino Enterprise Connection Services   See *DECS*.

Dotted decimal notation   The syntactic representation for a 32-bit integer, which consists of four 8-bit numbers written in base 10 with periods (dots) separating them. Used to represent IP addresses in the Internet, as in 192.67.67.20.

Download   The transmission of data from a mainframe to a PC or from a server to a client. See *Upload*.

dpi   Dots Per Inch. A measure of output device resolution. The number of dots a printers can place in a horizontal inch. The higher the number, the higher the resolution.

DRDA   Distributed Relational Database Architecture. IBM's architecture for allowing relational databases on a network to interconnect and share data.

DSAP   Destination Service Access Point. The network (MAC) address of the destination of a data transmission.

DSOM   Distributed Systems Object Method. A complete implementation of CORBA. DSOM works transparently with SOM.

DTMF   Dual Tone MultiFrequency. A term describing pushbutton or touch-tone dialing.

e-Commerce   Electronic commerce over the Internet.

EDI   Electronic Data Interchange. A computer sends required data in electronic form over telecommunication lines directly to the receiver's computer. [Tapscott and Caston, 1993]

Electronic mail   E-mail. A system that allows users to send messages on a network.

Empowered team   A team of workers who are able to make any and all decisions necessary to accomplish their mission and are accountable for the results.

Empowerment   A management approach to give technical professionals more autonomy and decision-making power in the organization.

Encapsulation The technique used by layered protocols in which a layer adds header information to the Protocol Data Unit (PDU) from the layer above. As an example, in Internet terminology, a packet would contain a header from the physical layer, followed by a header from the network layer (IP), followed by a header from the transport layer (TCP), followed by the application data. In object-oriented technology, packaging data variables and all of their related methods into a single object entity is called encapsulation. Encapsulation hides the details of an object's implementation from the user. A user does not need to know how the object performs its functions, only how to invoke the functions using a published interface. Because an object can be manipulated only through its interfaces, encapsulation ensures the basic integrity of an object.

Encryption The method of encoding messages/fields/forms/networks/data, using keys to scramble the data so that only the proper individuals possessing the appropriate key can decrypt and read the messages/fields/forms/networks/data. The end result is secured data. The keys are usually a string of alphanumeric digits that have a mathematical relationship to a corresponding key (a Public Key/Private Key relationship), so one is used to encrypt, the other to decrypt. The key also can have a relationship to itself (called a symmetric key—e.g., RC2, RC4) in which the same key is used to encrypt and decrypt.

Enterprise JavaBeans Enterprise JavaBeans (EJBs) are nonvisual service components. EJBs can be assembled into application systems. An EJB is similar in concept to an OLE Automation server, a native COM server, or a CORBA server. EJBs run in a special container called Beanstalk.

Ethernet A 10-Mbps standard for LANs, initially developed by Xerox, and later refined by Digital, Intel, and Xerox (DIX). All hosts are connected to a coaxial cable and contend for network access using a Carrier Sense Multiple Access with Collision Detection (CSMA/CD) paradigm. Adopted as an IEEE standard (802.3).

Event driven Refers to an application that can respond to events occurring in its environments (such as a keystroke or a message from another application).

Events Events provide an asynchronous mechanism of communication between objects. An object can create an event, and other objects can listen for the event.

Expert systems   A form of artificial intelligence (AI) technology composed of highly structured, rule-based computer programs that attempt to re-create the knowledge of human experts to perform a particular function.

EXtensible Markup Language   See *XML*.

EXtensible Stylesheet Language   See *XSL*.

Extranet   A network connecting independent companies, such as customers to suppliers.

Facsimile   Fax. Facsimile equipment allows information (written, typed, or graphic) to be transmitted through the telephone network and printed at the receiving end. The sending fax scans the material to be sent, digitizing it into binary bits and sending them through a modem to the receiving fax. The receiving fax reverses the process and sends the data to a printer.

Fast Ethernet   An emerging new set of protocols that can transmit data over most conventional cables at 100 Mbps. Two versions are in the proposal stage: 100VGAnyLAN and 100BaseX.

Fax (facsimile)   See *Facsimile* and *Group III Standard*.

FCS   Fiber Channel Standard. A draft ANSI standard that provides a fiber-optic replacement for the SCSI and HiPPI copper channel standards.

FDDI   Fiber Distributed Data Interface. A high-speed (100-Mbps) protocol for fiber-optic LANs.

Federation of databases   A set of internally consistent databases all tied together by another database "designed to meet the needs of senior management." [Vaskevitch, 1993]

File server   A server system that stores files created by application programs and makes them available for sharing by clients on the network.

Filtering   When applied to a network bridge, filtering refers to recognizing the type of a data packet and redirecting it to another path on the network or rejecting it.

Firewall   A computer-controlled boundary that prevents unauthorized access to the network for transmitting and receiving data. A firewall usually consists of one or more routers capable of accepting, rejecting, or editing transmitted information, placed between an organization's internal network and an external connection, such as the Internet.

Flame To express a strong opinion about and/or criticism of something, usually as a frank inflammatory statement in an electronic message.

Form A dialogue box with check boxes, radio buttons, pull-down menus, and fields for editing.

Fractional T1 A WAN service that provides one or more 64-Kbps channels of a T1 line.

Frame A set of data bytes transmitted or received by the data-link layer of the network protocol stack. A frame consists of a header, information, and trailer bytes. When physically transmitted, it may be broken up into one or more packets. In the Web browser sense, a frame is feature that provides multiple "windows" or frames in the browser's user interface.

Frame relay A WAN service protocol for high-speed, long-distance digital data packet transmission. It is a simplification of the X.25 protocol on a faster channel. Therefore, it is ideal for interconnecting two LANs over a WAN and is replacing X.25 commercial services. It is designed to provide high-speed packet transmission, very low network delay, and efficient use of network bandwidth. Speeds of from 64 Kbps to 1.544 Mbps are defined.

Frequency The number of complete oscillations per second of an electromagnetic wave.

FTP File Transfer Protocol. A protocol (and program) used with TCP/IP to send files over a network.

Full-duplex transmission The transmission of data across a network in both directions at the same time.

Fuzzy logic A form of logic that allows for the partial membership of sets. Instead of viewing everything as black and white, it allows for the existence of shades of gray.

Gateway A program or system that converts and routes data from one application to another. E-mail programs typically contain gateways so that they can exchange messages with other messaging programs and services.

GIF Graphics Interchange Format. A standard graphic format supported by World Wide Web standard browsers.

GML Generalized Markup Language. A document-tagging language used to create formatted documents when interpreted by a document compiler such as BookMaster.

Gopher A distributed information service that makes available hierarchical collections of information across the Internet. Gopher uses a simple protocol that allows a single Gopher client to access information from any accessible Gopher server, providing the user with a single "Gopher space" of information. Public-domain versions of the client and server are available.

GOSIP Government OSI Profile. The subset of the OSI protocols endorsed by the U.S. government.

Group III Standard A standard for compressed transmission of fax data developed by the ITUT, it allows high-speed, reliable transmission over voice-grade phone lines. It specifies a format of 203 horizontal dots by 98 vertical dots per inch in standard resolution mode, or about 1,400,000 dots, or pixels, for a page of text.

Groupware A new classification of application software that allows users to conveniently share data across a telecommunications network.

Guardbanding A term used to describe an engineering practice of designing the parts of a system to operate with sufficient tolerance in a performance band so that the system will operate successfully even if new parts are substituted.

GUI (GOO-ee) Graphical User Interface. A pictorial way of representing to a user the capabilities of a system and the work being done on it.

Half-duplex transmission The transmission of data across a network in which only one side can send at a time.

Header The portion of a packet, preceding the actual data, that contains source and destination addresses, and error checking and other fields. A header is also the part of an electronic mail message that precedes the body of a message and contains, among other things, the message originator, date, and time.

Help Desk A user problem support service. A staff of application and infrastructure experts are available by phone to resolve user problems in real time.

Hierarchical routing The complex problem of routing on large networks can be simplified by reducing the size of the networks. This is accomplished by breaking a network into a hierarchy of networks in which each level is responsible for its own routing.

HiPPI High-Performance Parallel Interface is a draft ANSI standard that provides high-bandwidth, point-to-point transmission for the efficient transfer of large blocks of data over copper wires. It provides a point-to-point transmission with a peak data rate of 800 Mbps for a 32-bit bus and 1.6 Gbps for a 64-bit bus. The distance limitation is 25 meters.

Home page A document that serves as the entryway for all the information contained on a Web site.

Hop A term used in routing. A path to a destination on a network is a series of hops, through routers, away from the origin.

Host In the TCP/IP sense, a computer that allows users to communicate with other host computers on a network. Individual users communicate by using application programs such as electronic mail and FTP. Also used to refer to a large computer system, such as a mainframe.

Hot Java A Web browser produced by Sun Microsystems written entirely in Java and designed to run on JavaOS or a Java-based Network Computer.

HSM Hierarchical Storage Manager. A data backup system that stages data on different storage devices, typically based on frequency of use.

HSSI High-Speed Serial Interface. The physical-layer interface between a DTE and a DCE at speeds in the SONET STS1 range.

HTML HyperText Markup Language. A coding language used to create hypertext documents for use on the World Wide Web.

HTTP HyperText Transport Protocol. A protocol for moving hypertext files across the Internet that requires an HTTP client program on one end and an HTTP server program on the other. The HTTP is the most important protocol used on the World Wide Web.

Hub A central point for the cables attached to one or more network interface cards on a LAN or a computer system that serves as a central point of data interchange with other systems.

Hypertext Documents with links to other documents, which let a user follow related ideas from one place to another.

IAB Internet Activities Board. The technical body that oversees the development of the Internet suite of protocols (commonly referred to as TCP/IP), the IAB has two task forces (the IRTF and the IETF), each charged with investigating a particular area.

ICMP Internet Control Message Protocol. The protocol used to handle errors and control messages at the IP layer, ICMP is a part of the Internet Protocol (IP).

IDL Interface Definition Language defines the structure of an interface. An IDL compiler generates the interface routines from the IDL. Language-independent object models, such as COM and CORBA, require a means to represent the input and output parameters in a language-independent form. These models provide a rich set of data types to represent the parameters. Java provides a set of APIs, called Java IDL, which map to CORBA IDL. Java IDL enables Java applications to interoperate with CORBA objects.

IEEE Institute of Electrical and Electronic Engineers. A professional society and standards-making body.

IETF Internet Engineering Task Force. Part of the IAB, the IETF is a volunteer group of engineers responsible for Internet standards development.

IIOP The OMG has defined a standard interoperability protocol, the Internet Inter-ORB Protocol (IIOP) for software objects communicating over the Internet. Most vendors now support IIOP.

IMAP Internet Message Access Protocol. A method of accessing electronic mail or bulletin board messages that are kept on a mail server that permits a client e-mail program to access remote message stores as if they were local.

Information Technology IT. The computing and networking systems used by a business to process and store its information (data).

Information technology architecture The underlying framework that defines and describes the technology platform required by a business to attain its objective and achieve a business vision. [Tapscott and Caston, 1993]

Information warehouse A central repository of information for an enterprise, spanning all important operational applications. Information is organized in a systematic manner, typically in a relational format.

Inheritance Inheritance provides a mechanism to allow objects to share definitions. An object can inherit the characteristics and behaviors of another object. Objects can inherit interface and class definitions and/or implementations (code). For example, our insurance company might have an abstract object called client for which it has a class definition and a set of interfaces. (Because it is an abstract class, there is no code written to implement the methods.) Both the HMO client and the major medical client objects can inherit the class definition and interfaces from the client object. An object can inherit from a single superclass (single inheritance) or from multiple superclasses (multiple inheritance).

Interface   An interface defines the messages that are used to invoke methods in an object. Depending on the object model, an object may have one or more than one interface.

Interface routine   Interface routines automate the process of sending a message to an object. These routines construct outgoing messages and break down incoming messages (a process called marshaling). Based on the function requested, the interface routine dispatches the appropriate method in the object. Interfaces are often used to send messages across the network, and they manage all interactions with the networking system. If appropriate, these routines automatically translate the message data as they are passed between different application languages or platforms. An interface is defined using IDL.

Internet   A set of connected networks. The term "Internet" refers to the large and growing public-domain internetwork developed by DARPA (Defense Advanced Research Projects Agency) that uses TCP/IP. It is shared by universities, corporations, and private individuals. To be on the Internet you must have IP connectivity (i.e., be able to telnet to or ping other systems). Networks with only e-mail connectivity are not actually classified as being on the Internet.

Internet address   A number that identifies a host in an internet, it is a 32-bit address assigned to hosts using TCP/IP. See *Dotted decimal notation.*

Interoperability   The ability of unlike systems to work heterogeneously. Computers of different sizes and brands can communicate together, sharing resources, information, and software applications. [Tapscott and Caston, 1993]

Intranet   An internal corporate network employing Internet and World Wide Web technologies, such as TCP/IP, HTTP, and HTML protocols.

IP   Internet Protocol. The network-layer protocol for the Internet protocol suite.

IP datagram   The fundamental unit of information passed across the Internet, it contains source and destination addresses along with data and a number of fields that define such things as the length of the datagram, the header checksum, and flags to say whether the datagram can be (or has been) fragmented.

IPng IP next generation. Under development by the IETF IPng committee, IPng is intended to upgrade the current IP to greatly increase the number of networks and nodes beyond the current 4 billion addresses and provide other enhancements to support future high-speed internetworking requirements.

IPX Novell's Internetwork Packet eXchange network communication protocol.

IRTF Internet Research Task Force. The mission of the IRTF is to promote research of importance to the evolution of the future Internet by creating focused, long-term and small Research Groups working on topics related to Internet protocols, applications, architecture and technology.

I/S Information Systems. The in-house information systems organization that provided IBM mainframe system installation, support, and application development until 1992 in Boca Raton.

ISDN Integrated Services Digital Network. A standard architecture, specified by ITUT, for integrating different types of data streams, such as data, video, and voice, on a single network, ISDN is just now being offered by the telephone carriers of the world.

ISO International Organization for Standardization. An organization in Paris devoted to developing standards for international and national data communications. The U.S. representative to the ISO is ANSI.

ISP Internet Service Provider. A business that sells services to other companies for purposes of establishing a presence on the Internet.

ITUT International Telecommunications Union–Telecommunications. One of four parts of the International Telecommunications Union, located in Geneva, Switzerland, the ITUT issues recommendations for standards applying to modems, packet switched interfaces, etc. Formerly known as the CCITT.

JAR A Java ARchive (JAR) is a compressed format that is used to distribute Java applications or JavaBeans. A JAR file contains all of the Java classes that make up the application, along with any additional resources that are required by the application, such as icons, images, audio clips, or help files.

Java A new programming language and compiler that generates byte code rather than executable machine code as do standard programming languages. Java byte code can then be executed on any target client platform, as long as the Web browser includes the Java interpreter. Java is an interpretive object-oriented programming language. Many refer to Java as "C-plus-plus-minus-minus," or C++ without the hard stuff. Its syntax is very reminiscent of C++, but quite a bit simpler. C++ supports multiple inheritance. Java supports only single inheritance. C++ makes extensive use of pointers, whereas Java does not support pointers. Java automates memory allocation and garbage collection. Memory leaks account for approximately 30% of all C++ bugs. Memory leaks do not occur in Java.

Java applet A miniprogram that has been compiled into byte codes using a Java compiler and is typically stored as a separate downloadable file with a .CLA extension. Java applets are transmitted over a network to perform useful work on a client or server system. Typically, this will be self-contained and of limited function. Multiple applets may be included on a single HTML page.

Java application A Java application is an application program written in the Java programming language. Java is a unique programming environment in that the language directly supports the development of Web-based applications. A Java application can be implemented to run as a component within a Web browser (an applet) or a Web server (a servlet). Although many people believe that it was designed only to support Web applications, Java is in fact a full-featured programming language that also supports the development of traditional applications. A Java "application" (as opposed to an applet) refers to an application that has been implemented to run in a standalone process and not in a Web browser container.

JavaBeans A specification for Java objects developed by Sun Microsystems. A JavaBean is a reusable software component that can be visually manipulated in builder tools such as a JDK toolkit. It has a component interface, including properties, events, and methods. It will be contained typically in an applet or application.

Java byte code When Java applications are compiled, they are converted into an interpreted pseudo-code called Java byte code. Java byte code can be deployed and executed on any system that provides a Java platform.

Java IDL Java Interface Definition Language (IDL) provides a mapping between Java and CORBA IDL. Java IDL provides interoperability between Java objects and CORBA objects. Java IDL uses the CORBA Internet Inter-ORB Protocol (IIOP) to communicate between systems.

Java Object Model Java is a language-specific object model that supports components. Java supports encapsulation, polymorphism, and single-implementation inheritance. A model to support aggregation and delegation is in development. The Java Class Loader and the Java Virtual Machine provide basic ORB functions, including object activation and object destruction. Java objects can communicate using either messages or events. Java applications can be implemented as components. JavaBeans are used as development components. Enterprise JavaBeans are used as service components. Applets are used as compound document components. Servlets are used as service components.

JavaOS Sun has implemented a specialized operating system for the Network Computer market. JavaOS provides a native Java platform, and it supports only Java applications.

Java platform Because Java is an interpreted language, Java applications require an interpreter runtime environment. This runtime environment is referred to as a Java platform. A Java platform consists of a Java Virtual Machine (JVM), a Java Class Loader (a simple ORB), and a Java Security Manager. Any Java application can run on any system that supports a Java platform. Therefore, Java applications are completely portable. Java platforms have been implemented on nearly every operating system and hardware platform in the industry. Subsets of the Java platform are even available to run on smart cards (JavaCard), embedded microprocessors (Embedded Java), and personal electronic devices (Personal Java).

Java RMI Java Remote Method Invocation (RMI) provides a distribution service for Java. RMI can be used either to transfer method requests between distributed objects or to transfer actual object instances between systems. If appropriate, RMI will automatically construct proxy objects on the client and server machines to represent the remote objects. RMI uses its own protocol to communicate between systems.

Java Security Manager The Java Security Manager ensures the integrity of a Java applet or application. It verifies that the Java byte code has not been corrupted during transmission. It can check the digital signature of the creator of the applet. It can disable an applet if the creator is not on an approved list or if the download source location is not approved. It ensures that a Java applet or application behaves in a friendly manner. Java applets can be automatically contained in a "sandbox" and prevented from accessing file and network resources on the local machine.

Java servlet   A server side counterpart to a Java applet. A Java servlet will load when the Web server loads. They are gradually replacing CGI programs because of improved performance and platform independence.

JavaScript   Netscape's JavaScript is a programmable API (Application Programming Interface) that allows cross-platform scripting of events, objects, and actions. Based on the Java language, JavaScript allows the Web page designer to access events such as startups, exits, and user mouse clicks. JavaScript is interpreted, not compiled.

JDK   Java programmers write Java applications using the Java Development Kit (JDK). The JDK is available free from the JavaSoft Web site. The JDK consists of the Java Core Classes and the Java compiler. There are also a number of extension classes available free in separate development kits. These extension classes are gradually incorporated into the core classes as they are tested and released.

JDBC   The Java DataBase Connectivity (JDBC) APIs are a set of Java Core Classes that define a standard mechanism to access and manipulate a database. JDBC is roughly based on Microsoft's Open DataBase Connectivity (ODBC) standard. As with ODBC, JDBC "drivers" are required to connect the JDBC APIs with each vendor's database. JDBC support is now available for most database environments.

JIT compiler   A Just-In-Time (JIT) compiler can dramatically improve the performance of a Java Virtual Machine (JVM). A JIT compiler is called as a Java application is loaded into the JVM. The Java byte code is dynamically compiled and converted into platform-specific binary code at load time.

JPEG   Joint Photographic Expert Group. An industry format used to represent photographic images suitably compressed for efficient transport over a network, JPEG is supported by standard Web browsers.

JVM   The Java Virtual Machine (JVM) is the runtime interpreter of Java byte code.

Kerberos   The security system of the MIT Athena project, Kerberos is based on symmetric key cryptography.

LAN   Local Area Network. The interconnection of several personal computers and other hardware such as printers. Designed originally as a means of sharing hardware and software among PCs; now used as a general means of communication between PCs.

LAN adapter   Moves data to and from a personal computer's memory to transmit and receive data over LAN cable.

LAN segment   See *Segment*.

LAPS   LAN Adapter Protocol Support. A suite of network communication software for OS/2 that includes the NDIS-compliant protocol and network adapter drivers.

Layer   Communication networks for computers may be organized as a set of more or less independent protocols, each in a different layer (also called a level). The lowest layer governs direct host-to-host communication between the hardware at different hosts; the highest consists of user applications. Each layer builds on the layer beneath it. For each layer, programs at different hosts use protocols appropriate to the layer to communicate with each other. TCP/IP has five layers of protocols; OSI has seven. The advantages of different layers of protocols are that the methods of passing information from one layer to another are specified clearly as part of the protocol suite and that changes within a protocol layer are prevented from affecting the other layers. This greatly simplifies the task of designing and maintaining communication programs.

LDAP   Lightweight Directory Access Protocol. A protocol for accessing directory services with TCP/IP that provides a standard method of access for clients, applications, and servers to directory listings in complex environments and on the Internet.

Legacy applications   Widely used applications developed for large mainframe systems.

LEI   Lotus Enterprise Integrator. The new name for the Lotus NotesPump product. It's considered "middleware" to connect to and transfer information between Domino Connector enterprise sources on a scheduled or event driven basis.

LIN   LAN Internetwork. Multiple LANs interconnected within an organization.

Little-endian   A format for storage or transmission of binary data in which the least significant byte (bit) comes first.

LON   LAN Outer Network. Remote users who participate in the LAN by dialing into the network.

Local Area Network (LAN)   See *LAN*.

Logical LAN One or more physical LANs that are bridged together, representing a single name space to any client within the logical LAN. Logical LANs may be physical LANs connected with a split bridge across a WAN, or they may be all local to increase the size of the logical LAN beyond the size allowed on a single physical LAN.

Logical-Link Control LLC. The upper portion of the data-link layer, as defined in IEEE 802.2. The LLC sublayer presents a uniform interface to the user of the data-link service, usually the network layer. Beneath the LLC sublayer is the MAC sublayer.

Loop The wire that passes between your home phone and the phone company, generally a length of copper wire.

Lotus Enterprise Integrator See *LEI*.<gl>LPRMON A printer monitor utility supplied with IBM TCP/IP 2.0.

LS:DO LotusScript Data Object. Software object that provides full read and write access to external ODBC data sources from LotusScript.

LSX LotusScript eXtension Toolkit. Software tools that allow LotusScript developers to write custom programs that are integrated with Notes and Lotus Suite environments. These modules, called LotusScript eXtensions (LSXs), are separately loadable modules that implement one or more LotusScript classes.

LU 6.2 Logical Unit 6.2. A peer-to-peer (system-to-system) communication protocol that supports program interoperability developed by IBM as part of SNA. Also called APPC.

MAC Media Access Control. The process by which systems on a network control access to the network cable.

MAC address The hardware address of a device connected to a shared media.

Mail gateway A machine that connects two or more electronic mail systems (especially dissimilar mail systems on two different networks) and transfers messages between them.

Mainframe A large computer system, such as an IBM System/370 or System/390, running either the MVS or VM operating system. See *Host*.

MAN Metropolitan Area Network. A LAN-like network that covers larger geographic distances (up to 50 km), possibly crossing public rights-of-way.

Management console A display terminal that provides the status of one or more network entities and sometimes the ability to respond to network events, such as faults.

MAPI Messaging Application Program Interface. A standard software interface for message interchange provided by the Microsoft Corporation.

Media Materials that store or transmit data. Network cable, magnetic tape, and diskettes are examples of media.

Message A message is used to send a request to an object. A message contains the name of the object (or interface), the name of the method to be invoked, and a list of input and output parameters that are required for the method.

Message Integrity Checks MICs. Methods to ensure that a transmitted message has not been tampered with.

MHS Message Handling System. A server-based application to process electronic mail messages.

MIB Management Information Base. A rigorously defined database for network management information, a MIB is the conceptual repository of management information within an open system. It consists of the set of managed objects, together with their attributes. Standard, minimal MIBs have been defined, and vendors often have private enterprise MIBs.

Middleware Any set of software routines or functions that allow two dissimilar programs to interoperate. The term typically refers to software that supports client/server database applications that transparently allow clients to access data from one or more database servers.

MIME Multipurpose Internet Mail Extensions. A message representation protocol that specifies considerable detail about message headers but leaves the message content, or message body, as flat ASCII text. This document redefines the format of message bodies to allow multipart textual and nontextual message bodies to be represented and exchanged without loss of information.

Mirrored server A term used to describe a server on an intranet or the Internet containing a copy of data from another server.

MIS Management Information System.

Mobile client A client system with access to the enterprise network, but not present on the site. This includes truly mobile notebook systems as well as desktop systems permanently stationed at a user's home.

Modem A device that converts binary information into on-and-off analog tones that can be transmitted over the public telephone network. The most common speed is 28,800 bits per second. Up to 57,600 bits per second is the maximum today. Because they typically connect to a computer or terminal, an RS232C communications interface is used. [Derfler and Freed, 1993]

Mosaic An application with a GUI interface that supports easy browsing of information on the Internet. In addition to standard binary and text files, Mosaic supports multimedia information. It was developed by the Software Development Department of the National Center for Supercomputing Applications at the University of Illinois.

MTA Messaging Transport Agent. A program that serves as a gateway between two different e-mail systems to transfer messages.

Multicast A special form of broadcast in which copies of the packet are delivered to only a subset of all possible destinations. See *Broadcast.*

Multimedia The combination of text, graphics, image, sound, and video in a single application or data stream.

Multimode fibers Optical fibers that have larger cores than single-mode fibers and so can use a variety of light sources and connections. They cannot be used for long-distance transmissions.

Multiplexing Fixed assignment of the capacity of a data transmission media to several users.

MVS IBM's Multiple Virtual System operating system for mainframe computers.

Name resolution The process of mapping a name into the corresponding address, typically a TCP/IP address.

Name server A server system used in a TCP/IP network that converts TCP/IP network addresses into names and vice versa. An example of a TCP/IP name is *us.ibm.com,* which is recognizable and can be used for e-mail purposes. It corresponds to a unique number that is the actual network address. The name server performs the conversion on request.

Named pipes An interprocess protocol used by OS/2, LAN Manager, and LAN Server to communicate between server and client.

NC Network Computer. A simple device connected to the Internet or an intranet that can do many tasks associated with PCs, but at a fraction of the cost of a standard PC.

NDIS Microsoft's Network Driver Interface Standard defines a standard interface between network communication software (i.e., redirector software) and the network interface card (LAN adapter).

NetBEUI (net-BOO-ee) Microsoft's NetBIOS Extended User Interface. Client software that redirects application software requests for service across the network.

NetBIOS Network Basic Input Output System. Client software that redirects application software requests for service across the network. Originally developed in 1984 as a high-level programming interface to the IBM PC Network in 1984, it quickly became a de facto session layer standard for the LAN industry. Most major LAN vendors support NetBIOS.

Network A computer network is a data communications system that interconnects computer systems. A network may be composed of any combination of LANs, MANs, or WANs.

Network address The network portion of an IP address. For a class A network, the network address is the first byte of the IP address. For a class B network, the network address is the first two bytes of the IP address. For a class C network, the network address is the first three bytes of the IP address. In each case, the remainder is the host address. In the Internet, assigned network addresses are globally unique.

Network architecture How systems are to be interconnected in a network.

Network cable The media that carries the digital network signals.

Network computer See *NC*.

Network interface card See *LAN adapter*.

Network layer The OSI layer that is responsible for routing, switching, and subnetwork access across the network environment.

Network licensing A method of purchasing usage rights to an application over a network in which only the number of simultaneous users determines the number of licenses required to be purchased.

Network management services Software and hardware service tools that enable a network administrator to manage a network (e.g., diagnose and repair faults, measure performance, and resolve bottlenecks).

Network Operating System NOS. A family of programs that run on networked computers. Some programs provide the ability to share files, printers, and other devices across the network.

Neural networks An architecture similar to the design of the human brain, neural networks are programs that incrementally learn from data examples. They are typically employed to solve highly nonlinear problems.

NFS   Network File System. A network service that allows a system to access data stored on a different system as if it were on its own local storage. Part of the ONC standards developed by Sun Microsystems.

NIC   Network Interface Card. Another term for LAN adapter.

NMS   Network Management Station. The system responsible for managing a (portion of a) network. The NMS talks to network management agents, which reside in the managed nodes, via a network management protocol. See *Agent*.

NNTP   Network News Transport Protocol. A protocol for supporting discussion groups over the Internet.

NRPC   Notes Remote Procedure Call. The primary interface between Notes Client and Domino Server.

Object   A software package that consists of some data and a set of procedures that can perform operations on the data. The data items are called member variables, and the procedures are called methods. The variables and methods within an object are described in a class definition. Methods are grouped into interfaces. According to the academic definition, an object exhibits three basic characteristics: encapsulation, polymorphism, and inheritance.

Object identifier   An OSI concept for hierarchical naming that provides a handle by which to refer to objects. Each node in the hierarchy is assigned a value unique among its sibling nodes and so can be identified by the concatenation of the values assigned to those nodes in the path from the root node down the tree to the identified node. This facilitates "walking the MIB" functionality by an agent or network management application.

Object model   An object model describes how objects are defined and how they interact with one another. Object models may be language specific or language independent. Language-specific models include Java, C++, and Smalltalk. Language-independent models include CORBA and COM.

Object-oriented design   A method of software development in which code and related data are developed and treated like a self-contained object. A critical feature of the tools that support this method, called inheritance, is the ability to create new objects by referring to existing objects.

Object request broker See *ORB*. The mechanism that allows objects to communicate with each other over a network.

OCn Optical Carriern. SONET hierarchy for fiber-optic transmission.

SONET Level	Rate (Mbps)
OC1	51.84
OC3	155.52
OC9	466.56
OC12	622.08
OC18	933.12
OC24	1244.16
OC36	1866.24
OC48	2488.32

ODBC Open DataBase Connectivity. ODBC is Microsoft's interface for accessing data in relational and nonrelational database management systems (DBMSs). It allows applications to access data using Structured Query Language (SQL) queries as a standard.

ODI Novell's Open Data-Link Interface defines a standard interface for network communication software to interface with a network interface card (LAN adapter).

ODMA Open Document Management API standard. The ODMA standard defines how desktop applications interact with document management repositories.

Office client An office client is a PC with e-mail, calendar, phone directory, network connectivity, and, optionally, word processing, spreadsheet, and business graphics applications installed in an office.

OfficeVision An IBM VM application that supports electronic mail, calendar, document, and file management functions, also known as OfficeVision/VM, OV, or OV/VM.

OLE Object Linking and Embedding. Originally a compound document architecture, it is now Microsoft's stated direction for developing software in the Windows and Windows NT environments. It depends on OLE's fundamental approach to objects, called the Component Object Model (COM).

OLTP OnLine Transaction Processing. Near-real-time handling of incoming transactions by a computer system.

OMG Object Management Group. A standards-setting body for object-oriented design.

ONC Open Network Computing. A distributed applications architecture promoted and controlled by a consortium led by Sun Microsystems.

Open Blueprint IBM's direction for distributed products and solutions. A structure for customers to organize products and applications in an open, distributed environment, it is also a guide for developers to provide function to integrate and operate with other products.

Open system An abbreviation of the IEEE definition is "A...set of...standards...that...accomplish interoperability and portability of applications, data and people." The ISO definition is similar. Many UNIX vendors define an open system as a UNIX system.

ORB An Object Request Broker (ORB) provides a set of core services that enable a user to interact with an object. The ORB frequently performs object life-cycle services. It locates an object, loads the object executables, instantiates and activates the object, manages object or interface handles, and destroys the object. In some cases, an ORB also provides distribution services. To establish a connection between two distributed objects, an ORB creates a proxy object on the local machine to represent the remote object. Once the connection is made between the proxies, the ORB transparently transfers the object requests using a communications protocol, performing all necessary translations for platform or language discrepancies.

OS/2 Operating System/2 for the Personal System line of computers. OS/2 extended edition provides multitasking, common communications interface, integrated relational database, and query functions.

OSF Open Software Foundation. A not-for-profit organization that develops and delivers open technology to its members. There are several hundred members of OSF, including Apple, DEC, Hewlett-Packard, Hitachi, IBM, ICL, Lotus, Microsoft, Motorola, Novell, and Xerox. OSF delivers five technologies: OSF/1, DCE, DME, Motif, and ANDF.

OSI Open Systems Interconnect. Standards developed by ISO for an open network environment. The OSI Reference Model is an abstract model defining a seven-layer architecture of functions, with protocol standards defined at each layer.

OSI Reference Model A seven-layer structure designed to describe computer network architectures and how data passes through them. Developed by ISO in 1978. Also see *ISO*.

Out-of-band A communication channel other than the primary network that is carrying the data. For example, critical network management alerts should be communicated on a separate channel to guarantee their receipt.

OV See *OfficeVision.*

OV/VM See *OfficeVision.*

Packet A set of data bytes that are transmitted as a group across a data network. A packet typically contains addressing and data information.

Packet-switched service A type of telecommunication service that breaks up data into packets for transmission.

Packet switching The transmission of data in small, discrete switching packets for the purpose of making more efficient use of physical data channels.

Palladium A print management technology developed at MIT with IBM, Digital, and Hewlett-Packard that is a complete set of end-user functions to submit and control printing in an open distributed environment.

Parallel disk array PDA. A storage system in which a set of small hard disks appear to be a single, fast hard disk to the operating system or application. See *PDA* and *RAID.*

Paradigm A pattern, example, or model.

PASC Portable Applications Standards Committee. The new name for POSIX, based on the realization that it is more than UNIX.

Parity bit An extra bit appended to data for error-checking purposes. Based on the number of zero and one bits transmitted, either a zero or one parity bit is appended so that the sum of the one bits is either always odd (odd parity) or always even (even parity).

PBX A telephone switching system, purchased by a business, that interconnects telephone extensions to the public network.

PC Personal Computer.

PCI Peripheral Component Interconnect local bus. A standard internal connection in a PC for data transfer to peripheral controller components.

PCMCIA Personal Computer Memory Card International Association bus. A standard external connection that allows peripherals adhering to the standard to be plugged in and used without further system modification.

PCS Personal Communication Services. A wireless communication service operating at radio frequencies of 120 Mhz in the 2-GHz range to provide a transport for data and voice.

PDA See *Parallel disk array.*

PDU Protocol Data Unit. A formally defined data structure to contain protocol information to be passed between entities; the OSI term for a packet.

PEL Picture ELement. Contains only black and white information, no gray shading.

Peer-to-peer communication Network communication between entities at the same network protocol layer.

Performance model A software program that describes the operation of a complex system and then simulates its operation for the purpose of determining performance characteristics and bottlenecks.

PERL Practical Extraction and Support Language. A general-purpose scripting language that is commonly used to perform back- end processing on Web servers using CGI.

PERT analysis Program Evaluation and Review Techniques analysis. A method of deriving plans of action from a set of individual tasks. PERT analysis is used to identify critical paths in a complex plan.

Physical layer This OSI layer provides the procedures for transferring a single bit across a physical media.

Physical medium Any means in the physical world for transferring signals between OSI systems.

Ping Packet internet groper. A program used to test reachability of destinations by sending them an ICMP echo request and waiting for a reply. The term is used as a verb: "Ping host X to see if it is up!"

Platform A product, design, or architecture upon which applications, other products, or designs can be built.

Points of presence A term for connectivity ports in a network.

Polymorphism Polymorphism refers to the fact that multiple objects can publish identical interfaces, yet these objects could implement different methods to perform the operations. For example, a medical insurance company might maintain two different types of objects to describe its clients, one for HMO clients and one for major medical clients. Both of these objects could support the same interface containing a method called RetrieveClientInfo. When users invoke this method, they will get different results from the two different objects.

POP Post Office Protocol. A client/server protocol for handling user electronic mailboxes. POP works best when one has only a single computer because it was designed to support "offline" message access, wherein messages are downloaded and then deleted from the mail server.

Port An entrance or an exit from a network; the physical or electrical interface through which one gains access. Also, the abstraction used by Internet transport protocols to distinguish among multiple simultaneous connections to a single destination host.

Portability The freedom to run application programs on computers from many vendors without rewriting the program code.

POSIX Portable Operating System Interface. The "X" at the end denotes that POSIX is a UNIX-type specification. POSIX is a set of interfaces involved in applications portability to systems.

PostScript The de facto printer language in the client/server computing environment. Developed by Adobe Systems Inc., it is capable of printing varied fonts, graphics, image, and color.

POTS Plain Old Telephone Service. The basic service supplying standard single telephones, lines, and access to the public switch telephone network.

PPP Point-to-Point Protocol. Proposal for multiprotocol transmission of datagrams over serial (point-to-point) links (RFC 1171/1172). Based on HDLC, PPP can be used as the underlying protocol for TCP/IP transmission over telephone lines, for example, and is seen as the successor to SLIP.

Print server A server connected to the network that completes printing requests by clients on the network.

Private WAN A private, usually leased-line, WAN service. Private WAN services, such as T1 and T3, offer high-speed data transmission from 1.54 Mbps to 44 Mbps.

Protocol A formal definition of information interchange. In networking terms, protocol refers to the bits of information added to transmitted data that permit its successful receipt.

Protocol stack Usually used to refer to the OSI seven-layer protocol stack. Implies the bits of information added to transmitted data as it is passed from level to level by a well-defined series (stack) of software subroutines to guarantee its successful transmission over a network.

Proxy The mechanism whereby one system represents another system in responding to protocol requests. Proxy systems are used in network management to avoid having to implement full protocol stacks in simple devices such as modems.

PSTN Public Switched Telephone Network. The worldwide voice telephone network accessible to all those with telephones and access privileges.

Public WAN A WAN service offered by a vendor in which data traffic from several customers is interleaved.

Pull installation The delivery of software over a network to a computing system initiated by the user of the target computing system.

Push installation The delivery of software over a network to a computing system either initiated by network administration or automatically initiated by another application.

RAID Redundant Array of Inexpensive Disks. A de facto standard that defines how two or more inexpensive hard disks can be combined to provide enhanced fault tolerance or performance in a computer system. RAID level 0 defines disk mirroring. RAID level 5 defines data striping across multiple disks with checksum data.

RBOC Regional Bell Operating Company. See *BOC*.

RC2 A block cipher encryption method. Data is encrypted blocks at a time rather than one character at a time (stream cipher/RC4). Block ciphers are slower than stream ciphers because data is encrypted only when a block is full. Notes/Domino uses this method for mail, passwords, fields, and network encryption with international versions. RC2 is a DES replacement. DES was not a suitable choice for Notes due to export restrictions imposed by the U.S. government.

RC4 A stream cipher encryption method. Each plaintext symbol/character is dynamically translated to ciphertext. RC4 is used for network/port encryption between client and server.

Realm A mechanism for setting up groups of users that have authority to view certain HTML files or directories on a Web server.

Redirector Client software that accepts requests from application programs and routes them across the network for service.

Redirection A function performed by a network operating system, such as IBM's OS/2 LAN Server program, to give access to a resource on a network (such as a server hard disk) as if it were on the client's system.

Remote client A term used to describe the service to a remote workstation to share data and applications located on a common WAN/LAN server. The remote client approach supports small single-server networks but does not scale well to support large or distributed environments.

Remote node   A term used to describe the service to a remote workstation interacting with an on-site communications server. The device driver within the LAN-attached communication server enables the server to take incoming data off a WAN and put it onto the LAN and vice versa. This approach can easily accommodate growth in the number of remote LAN users.

Remote Procedure Call   RPC. The DCE communications mechanism that enables subprograms to execute on several servers in the network while an application is running. A message from the client application is sent to the remote server, requesting its services. The RPC can be represented by a program written in any computer language.

Repeater   A communication device that simply amplifies network traffic at the physical layer for further transmission of that amplified signal.

REXX   An IBM-developed programming language, available for several operating systems (including VM and OS/2), used to create applications involving high-level manipulation of operating system resources.

RFC   Request For Comment. Documents created by Internet researchers on computer communication.

Rich text   A term describing the capability of a document or a part of a document to contain text, graphics, scanned images, audio, and full-motion video data.

Rightsize   The action of a large business to move from an exclusive mainframe-centric computing environment to a best-fit-of-technology computing environment in which a mix of PCs, workstations, PC servers, workstation servers, minicomputers, and mainframes interoperate in a client/server computing network.

RIP   Routing Information Protocol. Early BSD UNIX routing protocol used within a small network.

RISC   Reduced Instruction Set Computer. A computer in which the processor's instruction set is limited to constant-length instructions that can usually be executed in a single clock cycle.

RJ11   A six-conductor modular jack that is typically wired for four conductors (i.e., four wires). It is the most common telephone jack in the world, used for connecting telephones, modems and fax machines to the female RJ22 jack on the wall or the floor.

Route The path that network traffic takes from its source to its destination. Also, a possible path from a given host to another host or destination.

RPC See *Remote Procedure Call.*

Router A device that is used to interconnect networks and intelligently route data traffic based upon the transmission protocol employed. A router is preferred in TCP/IP internetworks because of its ability to support the complex networks in which the protocol is typically employed. Individual LANs or groups of LANs can be treated as a logical subnetwork by a router within a larger, more complex network. Routers are devices that terminate data-link or logical-link protocols, making it possible for routers to match protocols from LAN to WAN.

RS232C Established by the Electronics Industries Association (EIA) in 1969, RS232C is a standard defining the electrical signaling and cable connection characteristics of a serial port, the most common type of communications circuit used today. DTE (Data Terminal Equipment) and DCE (Data Communications Equipment) classes of equipment are defined. Most PCs have DTE ports. The connection is typically a 25-pin D shell with a male plug on the DTE end. The DCE end is a female plug. IBM abbreviated the plug to a 9-pin D shell with the introduction of the PC AT in 1984. An RS232C connection includes several independent circuits sharing the same cable.

RS/6000 RISC System/6000. IBM workstation systems employing the Power RISC chips, typically used for computer-aided design activities.

RSA The public key cryptography algorithm used by Lotus Notes, RSA is considered to be the strongest security technology for digital data transmission available. It was developed by Rivest, Shamir, and Adleman, whose initials form the acronym RSA.

RTF Rich Text Format. A standard for encoding text and graphics developed by Microsoft.

QMF Query Management Facility. A data query utility that is part of IBM DB/2 database systems.

SAP (1) Service Access Point. An address in a network where service is provided. An SSAP, or source SAP, is the source address of a service request. A DSAP, or destination SAP, is the destination address of a service request. These addresses are typically network-unique numbers placed in data frames to ensure successful delivery of information. (2) Also, the initials of the SAP program, Systems Applications and Products in Data Processing, an industry-leading transactional system for business operations. SAP R/2 includes applications for the mainframe environment. SAP R/3 includes applications for open client/server systems.

Script A list of commands that invoke various software functions on a server or client system.

SCSI Small Computer Systems Interface. An industry-standard high-speed interface typically used for hard disk storage device attachments to PC or workstation systems.

Security Management SM. One of the five standard network management functions, SM facilities provide for the protection of the network resources. SM includes authorization facilities, access controls, encryption, authentication, maintenance, and examination of security logs.

Segment A LAN's physical elements, a term typically used when the LAN is part of a complex network. Sometimes the term "LAN segment" is used.

Server A system on a network that provides services to a requesting system, or client.

Server agent A program that runs on the Domino server, either triggered or scheduled, to perform various tasks associated with a Domino database. Server agents can be written in either LotusScript or Java. They are part of the design element, so they can be replicated and have all of the Domino/Notes security features.

Server farm An area reserved for a large number of server systems that has a raised floor (to avoid wiring clutter), enhanced cooling, uninterruptible power, and centralized console-based management.

Server task A program run on a server (e.g., Domino) that performs core functions such as HTTP data serving, replication, routing, and indexing.

Servlet A servlet is a service component that is a mini Java application that is designed to run within a Web server. A servlet dynamically generates information for display on a Web page.

Session The data stream between two programs over a network. A session between two programs typically involves assignment of resources (e.g., memory, disk storage) by the associated operating systems supporting the programs. These resources are assigned by the communicating computer systems until the session is explicitly terminated.

Shared media A term used to describe typical multidrop LANs (e.g., Ethernet or token-ring) in which the connected PCs or workstations share the bandwidth of the media.

SHTTP Secure HyperText Transport Protocol. A transaction protocol for the Internet that creates secure channels at the application layer, SHTTP secures documents that compose the transaction. Not widely implemented but potentially more secure than SSL.

SGML Standard Generalized Markup Language. An industry-standard document tagging language used to create formatted documents when interpreted by a document compiler.

SIDF System-Independent Data Format. A media format standard for data backup that is part of the SMS standard. See *SMS*.

Single-mode fiber Optical fibers used for long-distance transmissions.

SLIP Serial Line Interface Protocol. A protocol for IP data transmission over serial lines (RFC 1055), such as telephone circuits or RS232 cables interconnecting two systems. SLIP is now being replaced by PPP. See *PPP*.

Smalltalk An object-oriented language developed in the early 1970s by Xerox at its Palo Alto Research Center (PARC).

SmartIcons The term used to describe application-specific icons in Lotus Development applications, which are smart because they simplify or automate tasks within an application when selected. SmartIcons can be created by users, depending upon the application, to create a more customized environment.

S/MIME Secure MIME. An e-mail security technology for encrypting and digitally signing e-mail messages. S/MIME is an IETF-proposed standard. It builds security on top of the industry standard MIME protocol and a set of Public Key Cryptographic Standards (PKCS).

SMP Symmetric MultiProcessing. A computer architecture in which tasks are distributed among two or more processors.

SMS Storage Management Services. A set of standards for data backup, including application programming interfaces and data formats, created by an industry consortium led by Novell Corporation.

SMTP The Simple Mail Transport Protocol, which utilizes TCP/IP, is a widely used e-mail protocol developed for the Internet. (RFCs 821, 822).

SNA IBM's mainframe-based Systems Network Architecture.

SNMP Simple Network Management Protocol. Issued in August 1988, SNMP includes a minimal but powerful set of facilities for monitoring and controlling network elements using a simple Structure of Management Information (SMI), MIB, and the protocol.

SNMPv1 The common acronym for SNMP after SNMPv2 was produced.

SNMPv2 SNMP Version 2. Proposed in December 1992, SNMPv2 includes security enhancements, interoperability with SNMPv1 products, and RMON (Remote Monitoring) concepts to support management of a hierarchy of networks.

Socket A service interface to the Internet; a process opens a socket, identifies the network service required, binds the socket to a destination, and then transmits/receives data.

SOM Systems Object Model. A rich, language-neutral technology for building, packaging, and manipulating objects that can be used easily by both object-oriented programming languages and procedural languages.

SONET Synchronous Optical NETwork. A standard for high-speed- -51.84-Mbps (OC1) to 2.488-Gbps (OC48)--data transmission over a fiber-optic network being used for telephone networks today and planned to be the platform technology for ATM data transmission services over a WAN.

Source program The high-level language text form of a computer program (e.g., C or FORTRAN source). Also called source code.

SPAM Unwanted, unpleasant e-mail.

SPX Novell's Sequential Packet eXchange network protocol.

SQL Structured Query Language. A standard computer language that is used to describe requests for information from a relational database.

SSL Secure Sockets Layer. A channel-based security protocol, developed by Netscape Communications, that secures the channel along which an Internet transaction is taking place.

Subnet A set of networking nodes wherein each node can communicate directly to every other (e.g., a LAN). A set of subnets form a network (e.g., a routed internet of LANs).

Subnet address   The subnet portion of an IP address. In a subnetted network, the host portion of an IP address is split into a subnet portion and a host portion using an address (subnet) mask.

Subnetwork   A collection of OSI end systems and intermediate systems under the control of a single administrative domain and utilizing a single network access protocol. Examples: private X.25 networks, a collection of bridged LANs.

SVGA   Super VGA. A de facto industry video graphics standard offering up to 1024 by 768 resolution and up to 256 simultaneously displayed colors.

Switch   From a network perspective, a computer-controlled device that can switch digital network bandwidth from one destination to another on demand.

Switched Ethernet   A digital switch that connects network segments together while supporting the Ethernet protocol.

Switched media   A term used to describe networking environments in which all the bandwidth is delivered from digital switches over the media to receiving systems (e.g., ATM).

Switched network   A network providing switched communication service; that is, the network is shared among many users, any of whom may establish communication between desired points when required.

System architecture   The principles of design used for a system.

SystemView   IBM's network management system based on System/390 systems as primary hosts.

T1   A digital data transmission service that can transport up to 1.544 Mbps. Digital communication is full-duplex. The bit stream can be viewed as 24 channels of 64 Kbps that are multiplexed on the aggregate 1.544-Mbps stream.

T3   A digital data transmission service that can transport up to 44.746 Mbps, incorporating 28 T1 circuits.

TCP   Transmission Control Protocol. A transport-level protocol for connection-oriented data transmission, TCP is the major transport protocol in the Internet suite of protocols providing reliable, connection-oriented, full-duplex streams. TCP uses IP for delivery.

TCP/IP   The set of applications and transport protocols that use IP to transmit data over a network. TCP/IP was developed by the Department of Defense to provide telecommunications for internetworking.

Telnet   The virtual terminal protocol in the Internet suite of protocols, Telnet allows users of one host to log into a remote host and interact as normal terminal users of that host.

Template   In terms of Lotus Notes, a template contains the design of a Domino database from which other instances, or replicas, can be created.

Terminal emulator   Software that allows a PC or workstation to emulate (appear as) a dependent display terminal to a host computer system.

Text editor   A simple text and word processing application typically used by computer programmers to create and edit their source programs.

Thick Ethernet (10base5)   Ethernet physical medium (wiring) in which a doubly shielded, 50-ohm coaxial cable is used.

Thin Ethernet (10base2)   Ethernet wiring in which a single-shielded, 50-ohm coaxial cable is used.

Thread   A single flow of control within a process, where a process is an application program with one or more concurrently executing threads. A thread is to a process as a task is to a multitasking program.

TIFF   Tagged Image File Format. TIFF provides a way of storing and exchanging digitized graphic data. The current specification supports black and white data, halftones or dithered data, and grayscale data.

Total Quality Management   TQM. An approach to managing a business in which business processes and team organizations are focused on a constant cycle of quality and cost improvements leading to improved profitability.

Twisted-pair Ethernet (10BaseT)   Ethernet wiring in which an unshielded pair of entwined wires is used.

Token-ring   A LAN protocol that uses token passing for media access control and connects systems on a cable ring. A master card on the token ring initiates a free token. When a LAN adapter with data to send (source) receives this free token, it replaces the token with its data and sends it to the next LAN adapter on the ring for relay. When the target LAN adapter of the data receives it, an acknowledgment is sent back to the source, which then initiates a new free token.

Transaction   A data transfer or information request between applications that has the properties of Atomicity, Consistency, Isolation, and Durability, or ACID.

Transport layer   A network service that typically provides end-to-end communication between two systems on a network while hiding details of the underlying data transmission.

Trunk   A communication line between two switching systems.

Tunneling   Tunneling refers to encapsulation of protocol A within protocol B, such that A treats B as though it were a data-link layer. Tunneling is used to get data between administrative domains that use a protocol that is not supported by the internetwork.

Twisted pair   A wiring system used to connect telephones to telephone panels or to connect LANs. A pair of insulated wires are twisted together to avoid noise pickup, forming a single cable.

UDP   User Datagram Protocol. A transport protocol in the Internet suite of protocols, UDP, like TCP, uses IP for delivery; however, unlike TCP, UDP provides for exchange of datagrams without acknowledgments or guaranteed delivery.

UNIX   The operating system originally designed by AT&T and enhanced by the University of California at Berkeley and others. Because it was powerful and essentially available for free, it became very popular at universities. Many vendors made their own versions of UNIX available--for example, IBM's AIX, based on OSF/1. The UNIX trademark and definition has since come under the control of X/Open, which will issue a unifying specification.

Upload   A term used to describe the transmission of a file from a PC to a mainframe or from a client to a server. See *Download*.

UPS   Uninterruptible Power Supply. A device that is used to provide temporary backup power to a computer system.

URL   Universal Resource Locator. A uniform method of specifying where different documents, network resources, and media reside on the Internet. Also called Uniform Resource Locator.

UTP   Unshielded Twisted-Pair cable used for LAN cabling.

V.22bis   The designation of the 2400-bps (bits per second) modem standard.

V.32   The designation of the 9600-bps (bits per second) modem standard.

V.32bis   The designation of the 14,400-bps (bits per second) modem standard.

V.34   The designation of the 28,800-bps (bits per second) modem standard. See V.FAST.

V.42   The designation of the error control standard for modems.

V.42.bis   The designation of the data compression standard for modems.

V.FAST   Prerelease name of the V.34 modem standard.

VBScript   A software scripting language derived from Visual Basic, Microsoft's application development language, which is very similar to JavaScript.

VGA   Vector Graphics Array. A standard for PC graphics, introduced by IBM with the PS/2 family in 1987, VGA provides for 640 by 480 pixels and up to 256 simultaneous colors.

VIM   Vendor Independent Messaging. A cross-platform messaging API for building message-enabled applications, VIM is supported by a number of companies including IBM, Apple, Lotus, Borland, and Novell.

Virtual circuit   A network service that provides connection-oriented service regardless of the underlying network structure. See *Connection-oriented.*

Virus   A program that replicates itself on computer systems by incorporating itself into other programs that are shared among computer systems.

Visualization   Applications that replace numerical tables and low-resolution graphics with images of high information content that enable users to see complex information and relationships quickly and easily.

VM   IBM's Virtual Machine operating system for mainframe computers.

VRML   Virtual Reality Markup Language. A specification for defining 3D environments on the World Wide Web in a platform-independent, document-centered ASCII language. In addition to geometric objects, light sources, object materials, and special effects can be defined.

Wabi   Windows application binary interface. A product written by Sun Microsystems to let applications written for Microsoft's Windows run unmodified on UNIX systems.

WAIS   Wide Area Information Service. A document-database server that allows the indexing of huge quantities of information and then making those indexes searchable across networks, such as the Internet.

WAN Wide Area Network. A long-distance network for the efficient transfer of voice, data, and/or video between local, metropolitan, campus, and site networks. WANs typically use lower transfer rates (64 Kbps) or high-speed services such as T1, which operates at 1.544 Mbps. WANs also typically use common-carrier services (communications services available to the general public) or private networking through satellite and microwave facilities.

Waterfall model A method of software development in which each development phase cascades into the next. The typical phases from start to finish are requirements definition, specification, design, coding, testing, installation, and maintenance.

Web page A file stored on a Web server containing HTML commands.

Wide Area Network See *WAN*.

Wiring Hub See *Hub*.

Workflow application An application that facilitates the flow of work among users on a network.

Workstation client An engineering workstation, such as an RS/6000 system, or a PC used to do design or development activities.

World Wide Web A network of servers that use HTTP to link documents across the Internet. The World Wide Web, or WWW, connects gopher, FTP, and WAIS servers, making them transparent to the end user.

WWW See *World Wide Web*.

WYSIWYG What You See Is What You Get. A term used to describe a feature of some graphic applications that render text or graphics images such that the appearance on the display precisely matches a hardcopy image.

X.25 ITUT standard for data transmission over a public data network. It was designed originally for connection of terminals to host computers. X.25 transports packets from point to point (via virtual circuits) over a WAN.

X.400 ITUT standard for message-handling services. To conform to X.400, client e-mail applications maintain their user interfaces but would change the file format of each e-mail message produced to conform to the X.400 standard. Correspondingly, they would each accept the X.400 format for incoming e-mail messages. The X.400 server would then handle the messages from any number of unique e-mail applications transparently.

X.500 ITUT standard that defines a file organization and interface to distributed directory data for network users and resources.

XGA eXtended Graphics Array. A video graphics standard introduced by IBM in 1990 offering up to 1024 by 768 resolution with up to 65,000 simultaneous colors.

XML Extensible Markup Language. XML is a meta-markup language that provides a format for describing structured data. This facilitates more precise declarations of content and more meaningful search results across multiple platforms on the Web. XML is a subset of SGML that is optimized for delivery over the Web; it is defined by the World Wide Web Consortium (W3C), ensuring that structured data will be uniform and independent of applications or vendors. XML will enable a new generation of Web-based data viewing and manipulation applications. It is primarily intended to meet the requirements of large-scale Web content providers for industry-specific markup, vendor-neutral data exchange, media-independent publishing, one-on-one marketing, workflow management in collaborative authoring environments, and the processing of Web documents by intelligent clients. The language is designed for the quickest possible client-side processing consistent with its primary purpose as an electronic publishing and data interchange format.

X/Open A standards acceleration body, founded in 1984 by Bull, ICL, Olivetti, Nixdorf, and Siemens. IBM joined X/Open in 1988. X/Open does not normally define standards but chooses from existing standards. X/Open actively supports IEEE POSIX projects.

X Recommendations The ITUT documents that describe data communication network standards. Well-known ones include X.25 Packet Switching standard, X.400 Message Handling System, and X.500 Directory Services.

XSL XML Stylesheet Language. XSL is a language for expressing stylesheets. It consists of two parts: (1) a language for transforming XML documents, and (2) an XML vocabulary for specifying formatting semantics. Given a class of structured documents or data files in XML, designers use an XSL stylesheet to express their intentions about how that structured content should be presented, that is, how the source content should be styled, laid out, and paginated onto some presentation medium such as a window in a Web browser or a set of physical pages in a book, report, pamphlet, or memo.

Xstation A dependent display terminal client that uses XWindows application support across a client/server network.

XWindows A network GUI, developed at MIT, that gives users "windows" into applications and processes not located on their system. A vehicle for distributed applications among users of heterogeneous networks.

Appendix C

References

Alwang, Greg, "Instant Groupware," *PC Magazine,* no. 3, vol. 17, February 10, 1998, pp. 175-186.

Anonymous, "Customers Rate Lotus, Microsoft, and Netscape in New Independent Satisfaction Study of Web Server Software," *Business Wire,* March 12, 1998a.

Anonymous, "Domino's, Danka, Philips Deploy IBM & Lotus Web Products," *Newsbytes,* November 24, 1997a.

Anonymous, "Growth Spurt Forecast for Knowledge Management," *Globe & Mail,* August 27, 1999, p. R5.

Anonymous, Groupware Has Power to Give Companies a Competitive Edge, but Most Organizations Aren't Plugging into Its Potential, *World News Today,* September 18, 1996.

Anonymous, "IBM/Lotus Development Corp. Internet Groupware System Lets People Share Information Effectively Using Internet and Intranets," *Industry Week,* December 15, 1997b, p. 41.

Anonymous, Lotus Leads in Groupware, Computer Reseller News, [CRN,] September 16, 1996.

Anonymous, "The Netscape Intranet Vision and Product Roadmap" *http://home.netscape.com/comprod/at_work/white_paper/ intranet/vision.html.*

Anonymous, "Netscape, Lotus Web-Site Servers Chosen," *Internet Week,* February 16, 1998b.

Anonymous, "Network Computers: IBM Bullish on Network Computers for 1998; Customers Cite Fast Performance, Easy Administration, Low Costs," EDGE: Work-Group Computing Report, January 5, 1998c.

Boar, B. H., *Implementing Client/Server Computing: A Strategic Perspective.* McGraw-Hill, Inc., New York, 1993.

Bernard, Ryan, *The Corporate Intranet,* John Wiley & Sons, Inc., 1996.

Brooks, Peter L., "The Sweet Smell of Access," *WebMaster,* March/April 1996, pp. 28-31.

Cunningham, Mike, "Why Build An Intranet?", *e-Business Advisor,* no. 8, vol. 17, September, 1999, p. 18.

Derfler, F. J., and Freed, L., *How Networks Work.* Ziff-Davis Press, Emeryville, CA, 1993.

David Drucker, "No Lotus Notes Killer," *Internetweek,* October 8, 1999.

Degnan, Christa, "Feedback On New Exchange Is Mixed," *PC Week,* October 4, 1999, p. 17.

Eckel, George, *Intranet Working.* New Riders, 1996.

Gartner Consulting, "Workgroup and Intranet Computing: Cost of Ownership Study, Management Summary," San Jose, CA, December 1997.

Halfhill, Tom R., "Inside the Web PC," *Byte,* March 1996, pp. 44-56.

Hayes, G., and Macleish, K., "Group(Where)," *Computerworld,* no. 47, vol. 31, November 24, 1997, p. 87.

IBM, *Image Plus - High Performance Transaction System,* GC31-2706-0, 1990.

Jacobsen, O., and Lynch, D., "A Glossary of Networking Terms," RFC 1208, March 1991.

Krantz, A. S., *Real World Client/Server.* Maximum Press, Gulf Breeze, FL, 1995.

Lamb, J. P., and Lew, P. W., *Lotus Notes & Domino 5 Scalable Network Design.* McGraw-Hill, Inc., New York, 1999.

LaPlante, A., "`Instant' Intranets," *Computerworld,* December 22, 1997, p. S1.

Mahon, Andrew, "Lotus, IBM, and Knowledge Management," Lotus Development Corporation, February 23, 1998.

Malamud, C., *Analyzing Sun Networks*. Van Nostrand Reinhold, New York, 1992a.

Malamud, C., *Stacks: Interoperability in Today's Computer Networks*. Prentice-Hall, Englewood Cliffs, NJ, 1992b.

Marshak, David S., "The Future of Lotus Notes--Will the Domino Theory Prevail?" Workgroup Computing Report, Seybold Group, no. 10, vol. 19, October 1996.

McFadden, C., "Client/Server Training," Client/Server Computing: Managing the Open Enterprise, CD-ROM, Faulkner Information Services, April 1994.

Meleis, Hanafy, *Toward the Information Network*, Computer, October, 1996.

Mullen, S. and Holden, R., *Enterprise Considerations in R4 Application Development*, Lotusphere 96 Proceedings, January 1996.

Neilsen, S. O., et al., "Lotus Notes and Domino R5.0 Security Instrastructure Revealed," IBM Corporation, 1999.

Rist, O., "Groupware is Still a Schizophrenic Enigma," *InternetWeek*, January 19, 1998, p. 42.

Roberts, B., "Web-Based Groupware Lags Even as Market Is Growing," *WebWeek*, January 5, 1998, *http://www.webweek. com/ 1998/01/05/software/19980105 lags.html*.

Schneider, J., Shouldering the Burden of Support, *PC Week*, Novermber 15, 1993, p. 123.

Semilof, M., Expert Discusses Multimcdia Implementations on Networks, *Communications Week*, September 1993, pp. 23-24.

Stallings, W., Working with a Net, *WebMaster*, November/December 1995, pp. 22-26.

Tapscott, D., and Caston A., *Paradigm Shift*. McGraw-Hill, Inc., New York, 1993.

Vaskevitch, D., *Client/Server Strategies—A Survival Guide for Corporate Reengineers*. IDG Books, San Mateo, CA, 1993.

Williamson, Mickey, *Getting a Grip on Groupware*, CIO, March 1, 1996.

Yourdon, Edward. Java, the Web, and Software Development, IEEE Computer, August 1996.

Index

@DBLookup, 148
@functions. *See* formula language
@URLOpen function, 158
@UserRoles function, 157

A
Access Control Lists. *See* ACLs
access models, knowledge
    management, 122
ACID (atomicity, currency,
    isolation, durability), 153
ACLs (Access Control Lists)
    Domino Administrator, 77
    Domino applications
      (data bases) and, 46, 163
    Domino server, 86
    naming, 77
action bar buttons, 156–157, 159
administration. *See* Domino
    Administrator
ADSM (Tivoli Storage
    Manager/TSM), 185
Agent Manager, 85
agents
    Domino software programs, 145
    LotusScript, 157, 158
American Standard Code for
    Information Interchange
    (ASCII), 5
anonymous users, 86
anti-spam feature of Domino
    server, 55–56
API backup, 61–62
applets (Java), 145, 157, 158

Application Development Team,
    173, 174, 175
Application Review Board,
    166–167
applications. *See also* Domino
    applications (databases);
    Domino Designer;
    Intranet applications;
    Intranet rollout; Lotus
    Notes client; requirements;
    Web applications
    back-end applications,
      139–140
    broadcast applications, 138
    browser-based applications, 24
    business graphics applications,
      102, 105–106
    business unit applications,
      134, 135, 136
    calendaring and scheduling,
      100, 101, 105, 108
    combination applications,
      140–142
    comparing and selecting,
      96–97, 102–106,
      107–127
    complete applications,
      137–139
    development domains, 67, 68
    directory applications, 100,
      101, 105
    discussion applications, 138
    e-mail applications, 99, 100,
      101, 103, 106, 107

Reader Feedback Sheet

Your comments and suggestions are very important in shaping future publications. Please email us at *moreinfo@maxpress.com* or photocopy this page, jot down your thoughts, and fax it to (850) 934-9981 or mail it to:

Maximum Press

Attn: Jim Hoskins

605 Silverthorn Road

Gulf Breeze, FL 32561

_____

_____

_____

_____

_____

_____

_____

_____

_____

_____

_____

_____

_____

_____

_____

_____

_____

101Ways to Promote
Your Web Site
by Susan Sweeney, C.A.
288 pages
$29.95
ISBN: 1-885068-37-9

Marketing
With E-Mail
by Shannon Kinnard
320 pages
$24.95
ISBN: 1-885068-40-9

Business-to-Business
Internet Marketing,
Second Edition
by Barry Silverstein
528 pages
$29.95
ISBN: 1-885068-37-8

Marketing on
the Internet,
Fourth Edition
by Jan Zimmerman
480 pages
$34.95
ISBN: 1-885068-36-0

Building Intranets
with Lotus Notes &
Domino, 5.0,
Third Edition
by Steve Krantz
320 pages
$32.95
ISBN: 1-885068-41-7

Exploring IBM
Personal
Computers,
Tenth Edition
by Jim Hoskins
and Bill Wilson
384 pages
$34.95
ISBN: 1-885068-25-5

To purchase a Maximum Press book, visit your local bookstore
or call 1-800-989-6733 (US) or 1-850-934-4583 (International)
or visit our Web site: *www.maxpress.com*

*Exploring IBM
RS/6000 Computers,
Ninrh Edition*
by Jim Hoskins
and Doug Davies
444 pages
$39.95
ISBN: 1-885068-27-1

*Exploring IBM
AS/400 Computers,
Ninth Edition*
by Jim Hoskins and
Roger Dimmick
576 pages
$39.95
ISBN: 1-885068-34-4

*Exploring IBM
S/390 Computers,
Sixth Edition*
by Jim Hoskins
and George Coleman
472 pages
$39.95
ISBN: 1-885068-30-1

*Exploring IBM
Network Stations*
by Eddie Ho,
Dana Lloyd, and
Stephanos Heracleous
223 pages
$39.95
ISBN: 1-885068-32-8

*Exploring IBM
Technology, Products
& Services,
Second Edition*
edited by Jim Hoskins
240 pages
$54.95
ISBN: 1-885068-31-X

To purchase a Maximum Press book, visit your local bookstore
or call 1-800-989-6733 (US/Canada) or 1-850-934-4583 (International)
or visit our Web site: *www.maxpress.com*